# Agrarian Land Law in the Western World

Essays about agrarian land policy and regulation in twelve countries of the western world

# AGRARIAN LAND LAW IN THE WESTERN WORLD

**Essays about agrarian land policy and regulation in twelve countries of the western world**

*Edited by*

Margaret Rosso Grossman and Wim Brussaard

C·A·B International

C·A·B International
Wallingford
Oxon OX10 8DE
UK

Tel: Wallingford (0491) 32111
Telex: 847964 (COMAGG G)
Telecom Gold/Dialcom: 84: CAU001
Fax: (0491) 33508



A catalogue record for this book is available from the British Library.

ISBN 0 85198 727 3

Typeset by Leaper & Gard Ltd, Bristol, England
Printed and bound in the UK by Redwood Press Ltd, Melksham

# CONTENTS

# Contributors

**Torgeir Austenå** is Professor of Law at the Agricultural University of Norway. He received his JD in 1962 and his JSD in 1974 from the University of Oslo. He joined the Agricultural University in 1965 as Assistant Professor and became Professor in 1978. He specializes in the law of real property and civil procedure.

**Ben Boer** is Corrs Chambers Westgarth Professor of Environmental Law, Faculty of Law, the University of Sydney, New South Wales, Australia. Until 1992 he was Associate Professor of Law, Environmental Law Center, Macquarie University, Sydney, New South Wales, Australia. He earned LLB, BA, and LLM degrees at the University of Melbourne. He works in the areas of natural and cultural heritage law, law relating to indigenous people, environmental and social impact assessment, and the emerging jurisprudence of sustainable development. He is a member of the World Conservation Union (IUCN) Environmental Law Commission and has worked on an environmental legislation project in Nepal in conjunction with IUCN. He is co-convenor of the Centre of International Environment Law for the Australasian and Pacific Region.

**Wim Brussaard** is Professor of Agrarian Law at Wageningen Agricultural University, the Netherlands, where he lectures on Agrarian, Environmental and Physical Planning Law. He received his Masters Degree in Dutch Law from the University of Leyden in 1965. From 1965 to 1981, he was a member of the Law Department of the National Physical Planning Agency in The Hague. He has published in Dutch, German, and American law journals.

**Cynthia Button** is a student in the College of Law at the University of Saskatchewan, Canada. She has studied in Tanzania, East Africa and in the College of Arts and Sciences at the University of Saskatchewan. She plans to practise corporate and commercial law in Saskatoon, Saskatchewan.

**Carl F. Dombek** is Executive Director, The Law Society of Saskatchewan, Regina, Saskatchewan, Canada. He was previously Director of Legal Services for the Ontario Ministry of Agriculture and Food. He received his BA from Brock University, Ontario, and his law degree from Dalhousie University Law School, Halifax, Nova Scotia. He practised law in Toronto and Kingston, Ontario, and worked on a Masters of Law at Queen's University, Kingston, Ontario. He has written and lectured extensively.

**Rudi Gotzen** is Secretary of the Board of Directors, Belgian Farmers' Association, Louvain, Belgium. He is legal counsel of the Belgian Secretary of State for Agriculture and European Affairs, Brussels; Research Assistant at the Law Faculty, University of Louvain (K.U. Leuven); and a Director of the Belgian Agricultural Law Association. He received his education at Onze-Lieve-Vrouwe College, Antwerp (1970), Facultés Universitaires Notre-Dame de la Paix, Namur (Candidate in Law, 1972, with distinction), and University of Louvain (Master in Law, 1975, with high distinction; *Agrégé* in Law, 1977). His books and legal articles focus mainly on the subject of agricultural law.

**Margaret Rosso Grossman** is Professor of Agricultural Law, Department of Agricultural Economics, University of Illinois at Urbana-Champaign (UIUC), USA. She received her JD *summa cum laude* in 1969 from the UIUC College of Law; her educational background also includes a BMus (1969, UIUC), AM (1970, Stanford Univeristy), and PhD (musicology, 1977, UIUC). She has published numerous articles in the area of agricultural law in American, Dutch and Italian law reviews. In 1986–7, she held a Fulbright research fellowship under the Western European Regional Research Program. She has frequently been a visiting professor in the Department of Agrarian Law, Wageningen Agricultural University, the Netherlands. She was 1990–1 President of the American Agricultural Law Association.

**Ian Hannam** is Executive Officer (Catchment Protection), Department of Conservation and Land Management, Soil Conservation Service, New South Wales, Australia. His education in New South Wales includes a Diploma in Agriculture from Wagga Agricultural College; Bachelor of Arts and Master of Letters, University of New England. He is currently completing the PhD at Macquarie University. He has been employed for 20 years with the Soil Conservation Service in New South Wales, with experience in soil conservation and land management. He has published extensively in the areas of field soil erosion processes and their management, land resource planning and classification systems, sustainable land use, and protected land legislation.

**Louis Lorvellec** became Professor of Law, University of Nantes, France, in 1981. He received the Masters (1967) and *Docteur D'Etat* (1972) in Law from the University of Rennes and in 1973 became *Professeur agrégé de droit privé.* He has been Professor of Law and Dean of the Law School, University of Pau. He was Visiting Scholar at the Agricultural Law Center, University of Arkansas at Fayetteville, USA in 1989–90. He is a member of the board of editors of the *Revue de droite rural* and Vice-president of the International Association of Agricultural Law Teachers.

**Paola Porru** is professor *associato* of Agrarian Comparative Law and holds the chair of *Diritto Agrario Pubblico* at the *Dipartimento Economico Estimativo Agrario e Forestale, Facoltà di Agraria,* University of Florence. She received the *laurea* in Law at the University La Sapienza in Rome and specialized in Agrarian Comparative Law in the Institute of Comparative Law, University of Florence. Since 1987, she has been the Italian delegate within the *Comité Européen de Droit Rural,* and she is a member of the *Istituto di Diritto Agrario Internazionale e Comparato* in Florence. She has published extensively in the field of agricultural law.

**Christopher P. Rodgers**, LLM (Cantab), LLB (Wales), is Reader in Law and Director of the Centre for Law in Rural Areas, at the University of Wales, Aberystwyth. He is also an assistant delegate general, for the Comité Européen de Droit Rural (CEDR). He read law at the University College of Wales and Sidney Sussex College, Cambridge, where he was an Evan Lewis-Thomas Law Scholar. He graduated with first class honours from Cambridge (LLM, 1978). He is a Solicitor of the Supreme Court (admitted 1981). His books are *Agricultural Law* (1991) and *Housing – the New Law; A Guide to the Housing Act 1988* (1989); he is contributing author on agriculture to *Halsbury's Laws of England* (4th edn, 1990). He is regular contributor to legal journals in the United Kingdom on the subjects of agricultural and landlord–tenant law.

**David Round** is Lecturer in Law at the University of Canterbury in Christchurch, New Zealand, where he teaches Environmental Law and Jurisprudence. A native of New Zealand, he has for many years been deeply involved in the conservation movement.

**Michele Slatter** is Senior Lecturer in Law at the University of Canterbury in Christchurch, New Zealand. She graduated from Durham and London Universities, and from 1980 to 1987 lectured in the Law School at the University of East Anglia, Norwich. She wrote and lectured extensively in agricultural law for the legal profession and the Agricultural Training Board. She maintains an active interest in both English and New Zealand agricultural law.

**Francis Snyder** is Professor of European Law in the University of London (University College) and at the European University Institute, Florence. He is also Visiting Professor at the College of Europe, Bruges. He holds a BA from Yale University, was a Fulbright Scholar at the *Institut d'Etudes Politiques de Paris*, received a JD from Harvard Law School, and obtained a *Certificat de Droit et d'Economie des Pays d'Afrique* and a *Doctorat de Specialite (3eme Cycle)* from the *Universite de Paris I (Pantheon-Sorbonne).* In 1988 he was awarded the title of *Officier dans l'Ordre des Palmes Academiques.* He has published extensively on European Community law, the law of the Common Agricultural Policy, and the European Community's external relations. His current research concerns European Community institutions, European economic law, and European Community law in its social, political, and economic context.

**Menno van der Velde** is lecturer in European Community Law in the Department of Agrarian Law at Wageningen Agricultural University. He studied law, international relations and geology at the University of Amsterdam, where he received his Masters Degree in Dutch Law in 1981. From 1975 to 1976 he was a research assistant in the Department of Law of the University of Amsterdam; from 1975 to 1981 he taught law at the University's Department of Economics. From 1981 until 1984, he was lecturer in Geology and Society at the Department of Mathematics and Sciences of the University of Amsterdam. Since 1984 he has been working in Wageningen. His publications deal with landscape law, environmental law, and European Community law.

**Wolfgang Winkler** is Lecturer in Agricultural Law at the Faculty of Agriculture, University of Göttingen, Germany. Born at Remscheid in 1937, he studied law at the Universities of Marburg, Innsbruck, and Munich. He received a Doctorate from the Faculty of Law, University of Munich. Since 1965, he has been a researcher at the Institute of Agricultural Law at the University of Göttingen, particularly in the field of comparative agricultural law. He has published numerous books and articles in several languages in the field of agricultural law.

**Helge Wulff** has been Professor of Law at The Royal Veterinary and Agricultural University of Denmark since 1973. He received an LLM degree from the University of Copenhagen in 1953, and was employed in the Ministry of Agriculture of Denmark (1953–73) and in the Danish Forestry Service (1969–73). He served as chairman of a Government Commission on ownership of farms (1978–9), and as Visiting Professor in Administrative Law at the University Center of Aalborg, Denmark (1976), in Public Law at the University of Montpellier I, France (1985), and in Agricultural and Environmental Law in the Department of Agricultural Economics, University of Illinois at Urbana-Champaign (1988). He has written numerous books and articles on Agricultural, Forestry, and Environmental law.

# INTRODUCTION

Agrarian land forms an important component of the world's land surface, and in many nations, agricultural, forestry, and other rural uses occupy a majority of the land area. This agrarian land provides the basic resource for cultivating the food and fibre products essential for humankind. But in addition, agrarian land is valued for its open space, for its contribution to the natural environment, and for its conservation, landscape, and aesthetic values.

In many nations today, land in the countryside is increasingly subject to pressures and claims from competing uses; besides agriculture, these include urban development, transportation, recreation, forestry, landscape and nature conservation. The same land may be claimed as the appropriate site for more than one of these (often conflicting) uses. For example, often the most productive farmland is also best-suited for development. Pasture land may harbour important habitat for valuable species of wildlife. Improved transportation systems may claim areas of land traditionally used for farming. These and other competing claims on agrarian land may be assigned different values, depending on the nation and the type of conflict.

Furthermore, land-use conflicts are not the only issues that involve agrarian land. In some countries the geographical structure of rural areas and the improvement of that structure have long been an important focus of attention. Increasingly, the state of the rural environment is a significant issue. Though agrarian land is to some extent the victim of pollution from non-agricultural activities, the harmful effects of agricultural land use on water, air and natural elements (e.g. wetlands) are receiving enhanced scrutiny in many nations. The relationship between landowner and farmer, too, has been the focus of attention in a number of countries. And, as the chapters that follow will indicate, other agrarian land issues, sometimes unique to a specific nation, are significant.

Different nations demonstrate considerable diversity in the proportion of land that is agrarian, the value assigned to the land, and the preferred uses for that land. A number of political, social, and geographic factors influence a nation's approach to agrarian land and the issues it raises. In countries where rural land is relatively scarce, non-agricultural uses may be strongly discouraged or even prohibited; in nations with an abundance of agricultural land, fewer land-use restrictions may apply. In some nations, landowners enjoy a great deal of freedom in their use of farmland; in others, the public good takes precedence, and individual rights may be severely limited. In these nations, the right to own or to farm agrarian land may be subject to government approval. Landowner–tenant relationships may be highly regulated, and numerous governmental and quasi-governmental agencies may play a role in decision-making about agrarian land.

Law plays an important role in the allocation and use of agrarian land. Reflecting and implementing government policy, law can ensure that the individual landowner retains freedom in land-use decision-making, or it can impose serious restrictions on the landowner's freedom. Each nation has a more-or-less unique government and legal system that helps to determine the nature of the law and policy that govern agrarian land. Regardless of differences between countries, however, certain of the rural land issues mentioned above, especially pressures for development and concerns related to the natural environment, are now evident in many nations. Each nation's regulatory responses to these issues develop in the context of its own legal system. Nonetheless, the nature of the law and regulations that result, and the country's experience with the law and regulations, may well be relevant to other nations that struggle with the same issues.

A number of considerations governed the choice of countries to be included in this volume. Within the limits of 'western' and a reasonable number of chapters, some variety was desirable. Thus, countries both within and outside the European Community have been included; a chapter on relevant European Community law provides an overview of relevant EC law and policy. Non-European nations, too, have been included. The twelve countries represent different types of governmental organization and administrative structure. Their legal systems also vary; some of the countries have legal systems rooted in civil law; others, in common law. Both large countries with broad expanses of agrarian land and small countries with limited amounts of rural land are represented, as are mountainous countries with difficult farming conditions and countries with more ideal farmland. To some extent, choices have also been influenced by the availability of authors and space. As in other books of this type, other selections could have been substituted. It is hoped, however, that the chapters included here represent the intended variety of legal approaches to the numerous issues concerning agrarian land.

In the context of this book, agrarian land law has been defined rather broadly to ensure that each author could discuss the most unique and interesting aspects of his or her nation's law. At a minimum, agrarian land law includes the laws and regulations concerning the use of rural land, particularly in the context of physical planning law for rural areas. Other legal programmes intended to prevent the conversion of agricultural land to non-agricultural uses are also relevant, as are restrictions on subdivision or agglomeration of rural land. Agrarian land law also includes the regulation of land consolidation or land reallocation, where those mechanisms are applicable.

In addition to these rather obvious components of agrarian land law, however, other laws and regulations affect agrarian land, often significantly. Soil protection laws, for example, may be important for keeping agricultural land productive; these include laws focused on soil productivity, prevention of erosion, and protection of land from other environmental damage (for example, water or land pollution). Laws and regulations authorizing setaside or diversification of agricultural land use also form part of the picture. Land-management provisions – for example, those affecting forestry and nature conservation – often have a direct impact on agrarian land. In some instances, provisions that regulate the landlord–tenant relationship also affect the use of agricultural land significantly. Furthermore, other issues, such as the law of water use or law regulating public access to farmland, may also form an important part of the total picture of agrarian land law.

Within these broad parameters (and a rather strict space limitation), each author was encouraged to focus on the laws and regulations most relevant to agrarian land law in the author's nation, and particularly on those legal programmes unique to that country. In the framework of their choice, authors were asked to identify special government policies for rural land, as well as relevant agrarian land legislation, particularly laws to protect and preserve farmland, keep it in farm use, and resolve conflicting uses and claims on agrarian land. Operation of government policy, connections between planning law and development, application of environmental laws on rural land, and jurisdiction of special agricultural courts were also suggested subjects. Authors had the opportunity to evaluate the effectiveness of their country's agrarian land legislation.

The breadth of these guidelines and the diversity of agrarian land law in the different countries have resulted in a variety of approaches. The reader will discover, among other concepts, laws that leave little land-use choice to landowners, policies that seem to favour development of land over agricultural use, and regulatory systems that have been implemented poorly, if at all. Some authors have chosen to analyse a limited number of important legal schemes in detail, while others have discussed a broader selection of laws. To some extent, this choice has been influenced, too, by the governmental–administrative structure of the author's country. That is, when agrarian land issues are regulated on a national basis, it is possible to provide a more detailed description of the regulatory system. In federally organized nations, in which states have significant regulatory responsibility, a comprehensive description of each state's system is impossible, and representative choices must be made.

The final chapter of this book offers some comparisons and conclusions about a number of the agrarian land law issues discussed in the national chapters.

Taken together, the chapters included here present (in the words of the French author) a 'freeze frame from the movie of agricultural law'. They paint a picture of agrarian land law taken from a 'movie' that changes constantly as land-use issues develop, and laws and regulations are enacted to resolve these issues.

December 1991

Margaret Rosso Grossman
*Urbana, Illinois, USA*
Wim Brussaard
*Wageningen, The Netherlands*

# 1

# Agrarian Land Law in the European Community

Menno van der Velde and Francis Snyder

## I. Introduction

Agriculture is the chief land user in Europe: more than half of the total European Community area is agricultural land (Eurostat, 1990)[1]. By adding forests, rough pastures and marshes used for extensive grazing, Meeus *et al.* (1988, p. 15) set the share of land used by agriculture even higher: to 95% of the total territory.

Agriculture is the chief policy domain in the European Community (hereafter EC)[2]: about three-quarters of the total EC legislative production is directly related to the regulation of agriculture. By adding those authoritative decisions that sustain the EC's institutional structure, and are thus indirectly relevant for agriculture, the claim of agriculture on the EC agenda is even greater.

These proportions are commensurate with the place of agriculture in the EC budget. For some time the proportion of EC expenditure that is devoted to agriculture has exceeded 60% of the total annual budget. Currently it amounts to 58%.[3]

The share of agriculture in the employed civilian working population in the EC as a whole is, however, currently only 7% (Commission, 1991d). It varies from 2.2% in the United Kingdom to 27% in Greece. The proportion of the total population employed in agriculture has declined markedly since the foundation of the Community. Even taking into account any increase in employment in related sectors, such as foodstuffs or the environment, the trend is clear. If this trend is compared with the relatively fixed proportion of the budget that agriculture constitutes, it is apparent that agricultural spending represents potentially (and does so in fact) a significant political issue. Indeed, many of the recent changes in the EC's agricultural policy are a response, more or less direct, to this issue.

It would be easy to assume that the important role occupied by agriculture on the EC agenda is reflected by direct legal powers of the EC and its institutions[4] in relation to agricultural land. Such an assumption, however, would be misleading and indeed incorrect. The EC Treaty states expressly in article 222 that it shall in no way prejudice the rules in Member States governing the system of property ownership. Moreover, even within this wide framework, the EC has little direct control of land. Nor does it have a physical planning policy or a land consolidation programme. Legal powers regarding the ownership of agricultural land, together with these related instruments, are within the domain of the Member States.

Nevertheless, the EC's common agricultural policy confers broad regulatory powers on the EC institutions (Snyder, 1985, 1990a). Within the scope of this policy, and to some extent as a politically unavoidable consequence of its effects, the EC has taken numerous measures which have had a direct effect on the use of agricultural land. For example, it has forbidden the use of land for vineyards or hops. Dairy farming is restricted to those parcels where dairy farming existed in 1983, or to which it has been transferred in accordance with EC regulations since then. These and other restrictions are based ultimately on the EC Treaty and are enshrined in EC regulations.

These wide-ranging – if apparently indirect – powers of the EC over land use are potentially available for all agricultural production that comes within the realm of the common agricultural policy. In this way, one of the main policy fields of the EC in terms of policy formulation, budget expenditure, regulation and litigation, has a great indirect, and increasing direct, relevance for land use.

To explain this relevance of EC law for land use, we will first describe the law that implements the common agricultural policy. This body of law can be divided into the law relating to market management and the law relating to structural policies. Both have seen an increase in direct regulation of land use, which culminated in the setaside, extensification and conversion programmes under the recent structural policy regulation.

After this condensed description of the law relating to the common agricultural policy, we describe the EC law concerning the rights of entry into farming: the rights of property, land tenure and establishment as a farmer.

The continued attempts at renewal of EC policies have taken two directions, which for our purposes are closely related. On the one hand, the EC has sought to make agriculture simply part of a more broadly defined policy of rural development or environmental management. On the other hand, it has attempted to expand its policy domains and legal competence, thus diminishing the relative importance of agriculture. In the final part of this chapter we consider relevant aspects of these attempts to widen the scope of EC law, emphasizing in particular their relevance for the EC's powers with regard to land use.

## II. The Common Agricultural Policy

### A. Agriculture in the EC Treaty

In a few broad strokes the Treaty establishing the European Community assigns to agriculture its central place in West European integration. The activities of the European Community must include the adoption of a common policy in the sphere of agriculture (EC Treaty, article 3(d)). Agriculture ranks among the foundations of the Community. The common market shall extend to agriculture and trade in agricultural products. The operation and development of the common market for agricultural products must be accompanied by the establishment of a common agricultural policy (EC Treaty, article 38).

The Treaty does not define the concepts 'agriculture' or 'agricultural holding'. However, 'agricultural products' are defined as the products of the soil, of stockfarming and of fisheries and products of first-stage processing directly related to these products (EC Treaty, article 38(1)). These products are listed in Annex II to the Treaty.

The objectives of the common agricultural policy are stated in the EC Treaty, article 39(1):

**1.** to increase agricultural productivity by promoting technical progress and by ensuring the rational development of agricultural production and the optimum utilization of the factors of production, in particular labour;
**2.** thus to ensure a fair standard of living for the agricultural community, in particular by increasing the individual earnings of persons engaged in agriculture;
**3.** to stabilize markets;
**4.** to assure the availability of supplies;
**5.** to ensure that supplies reach consumers at reasonable prices.

The Treaty specifies three factors that must be taken into account in working out the common agricultural policy (article 39(2)):

**1.** the particular nature of agricultural activity, which results from the social structure of agriculture and from structural and natural disparities between the various agricultural regions;
**2.** the need to effect the appropriate adjustments by degrees; and
**3.** the fact that in the Member States agriculture constitutes a sector closely linked with the economy as a whole.

As the objectives of the common agricultural policy are disparate and potentially conflicting, they may not all be simultaneously and fully attained. Consequently, the Community institutions may give any one of them temporary priority in light of economic factors or conditions. In doing so, however, they may not discriminate between producers or consumers within the Community (EC Treaty, article 40(3), para. 2). They must also, where necessary, take account, in favour of farmers, of the principle of Community preference.

The EC Treaty provides two pillars to support the common agricultural policy: market management and structural policy. Of these two pillars, market management attracted the main attention of the founding fathers. Structural policy remained largely the Member States' affair. In the more than 30 years of its existence, the market management pillar dwarfed the structural pillar, resulting in an obvious imbalance. The reasons for this imbalance were both economic and political, as Member States were reluctant to concede the EC real powers concerning structural policy.

Eventually, however, both the market management and structural policy pillars were modified. One reason was the accession to the EC in 1973 of the United Kingdom (together with Denmark and Ireland), then of Greece in 1980, and finally of Spain and Portugal in 1986. With a very small percentage of the population engaged directly in agriculture, the United Kingdom opposed the allocation of such a large proportion of the EC budget to the agricultural sector. The three Mediterranean countries have very different agricultural structures from those of the northern European countries and tended to benefit more from structural policy. Another, more important reason was the problem of chronic over-production. Efforts to resolve this problem were taken only gradually and reluctantly. As a result, the restructuring of the common agricultural policy – its instruments, policy mix and expenditure – has taken a very long time (Snyder, 1990b).

## B. Market management

Article 40, paragraph 2 of the EC Treaty states that a common organization of agricultural markets must be established. This article leaves three options as to the type of regulatory scheme. In practice, however, Community-wide market organizations for nineteen particular products, or groups of related products, have been set up, covering the majority of temperate zone agricultural products[5]. Thus not all agricultural production is directly protected by a common market organization. However, a side-effect of the existing market organizations is that land that might otherwise be used for unprotected production is tied to protected agricultural production. Hence the effects of the common agricultural policy extend outside the immediate range of the products covered by the various regulations.

The common market organizations may include all measures required to attain the objectives of the common agricultural policy. The Treaty mentions in particular the regulation of prices, aids for the production and marketing of the various products, storage and carry-over arrangements and common machinery for stabilizing imports or exports. The common market organizations are limited to the pursuit of the objectives of the common agricultural policy (EC Treaty, article 40(3)).

The common organizations of markets establish and regulate prices for agricultural products, and control import and export trade in these products. The details of each common market organization differ according to the importance and characteristics of each product group. The main structure of the common market organizations centres on intervention buying (van der Velde, 1992), the imposition of levies on imports, and the subsidization of exports. Here we are concerned only with the first, because it has the most direct relevance for land use.

The aim of intervention buying is to stabilize the markets in agricultural products. Where the intervention system applies, a guaranteed minimum price is set for the relevant agricultural products. Originally, the Community had a legal obligation to purchase every quantity of Community-produced products offered to it at that guaranteed intervention price. This price, and other prices for the regulation of import and export, are set by political agreement in the decision-making authority of the European Community: the Council deciding on a proposal of the Commission. Agricultural price decisions are in fact taken by the 'Agricultural Council', consisting of the EC Member States' agricultural ministers. This yearly agreement is then written into the law of the EC by the formulation of a plethora of regulations.

At the beginning of the common agricultural policy the European Community was not self-sufficient for the entire range of temperate zone agricultural products. Community preference, that is the protection of EC grown crops and the exclusion of the same products grown outside the EC, combined with other aspects of the common agricultural policy and technological innovation to cause a sharp increase in self-sufficiency.

However, from the very start of the common agricultural policy, surplus production has been endemic in some product sectors. This was shown clearly in 1958 in the first General Report on the Activities of the Community (Commission, 1958). In a few decades the self-sufficiency rate of the Community grew rapidly into a chronic excess of production over demand in an increasingly wider range of products.

The architects of the market management system intended the prices fixed by decision-making in the Commission and Council tandem to be set at a level that would give a modern rationally operated family farm a profitable margin. The price would not be so high as to keep inefficient obsolete farms in production. For these obsolete farms the second pillar, the structural policy, was to improve production circumstances by speeding up the introduction of modern farming standards throughout the EC. As a result of such structural changes, these farmers could then derive an adequate income from the market management schemes.

However, the year-by-year decision-making process repeatedly resulted in prices that were higher than the Commission found wise. Driven by national concerns, the Council pushed the pedals of the tandem decision-making machine harder than the Commission, leaving it no choice but to step out or go along. The Commission went along.

In time the Community budget could no longer support limitless intervention buying with the attendant stock-piling of products that had to be dumped on the world market, exported as food aid or given away through various schemes. The common organization of the agricultural markets had to move into the direction of putting quantitative restrictions on the obligation of the Community to buy home-grown products, as well as of measures controlling total production. In this way land use restrictions were woven into the largest pillar of common agricultural policy, the market management schemes.

Various mechanisms were devised to limit expenditure. A guarantee threshold set the quantities for intervention buying beforehand. If this threshold was surpassed by actual production, the guaranteed prices would be lowered by a given formula in the following year. The guarantee threshold remains the main mechanism for the common organization of the market in cereals (Regulation 2727/75, article 3a, as amended[6]).

In the common organization of the market in milk and milk products, the Community went further by combining intervention buying with a prefixed amount of production eligible for support. In 1984 production quotas were set for this product group (Regulation 804/68, article 5c). The quota was tied to the holding, which in most Member States is interpreted as being tied to the land (van der Velde, 1991, 1992). Hence the use of land for dairy farming is directly regulated by the market management system of the Community. In order to be able to deliver milk to the market, a dairy farmer has to have land with milk quotas. The Member States are to register these quotas and the land to which they belong. Transfer of dairy quota to other parcels of land must be effected by the Member States. By giving up dairy quota farmers can obtain compensation for cessation of production. Member States can exclude from these cessation schemes those areas where erosion abatement, and especially the prevention of desertification, gets preference (Regulation 1637/91).

Earlier, surplus production in the common organization of the market in wine led the EC to place the new planting and replanting of vines under Community control. In principle, all new planting of vines is prohibited until 31 August 1996 (Regulation 822/87, article 6(1), 1st para.), with the exception of new planting in respect of areas intended for the production of quality wines the production of which is recognized as being far below demand. This general prohibition is, however, subject to some important exceptions. Among these exceptions are areas intended for new plantings carried out under measures for the consolidation of holdings or measures concerning compulsory purchase in the public interest adopted under national legislation.

Any natural or legal person or group of persons intending to carry out new planting must apply in writing for authorization to the competent bodies appointed by the Member States. The replanting of vines in plots previously under vines but from which they have been grubbed is only permissible where a natural or legal person or group of persons either has a replanting right under Community law or has acquired such a right on the basis of prior national law.

The European Court of Justice's case law on restrictions on the use of farmland may be illustrated by Case 44/79 *Liselotte Hauer* v *Land Rheinland-Pfalz* (1979) ECR 3727 (1980) 3 CMLR 42[7]. The main action concerned a challenge to an administrative decision refusing to authorize the planting of vines. Interpreting Community law, the European Court held the restriction on use of land by prohibition on planting of new vines under Council Regulation 1162/76 to be justified by the objectives of general interest, in particular the reduction of agricultural surpluses, pursued by the Community in application of the common agricultural policy. It gave special emphasis to the temporary nature of the prohibition and concluded that the prohibition did not infringe the plaintiff's right to property.

## C. Structural policies

The smaller pillar of the common agricultural policy, structural policy, became in time the locus for more efforts to curb production by regulating land use.

The common agricultural policy envisaged by the EC Treaty takes account of structural diversity in terms of natural conditions, farm size, production methods, the age and education of farmers, and economic and social differences (EC Treaty articles 39(2)(a) and 41).

In 1968 the Commission set up a framework for a substantive structural policy (Commission, 1968). One of the salient features of this framework, known as the Mansholt Plan after the then EC Commissioner for Agriculture, was to take at least five million hectares of EC agricultural land out of production on a permanent basis between 1970 and 1980. The Council did not adopt this major feature of the plan, but other elements were adopted by resolution in 1971 (O.J. C 52/1). The usual form for Community action was to be joint programmes between the Community and the Member States to which the Community would make a financial contribution, generally of 25%.

The resolution was subsequently implemented by several directives. In 1972 the Council issued the three basic structural policy directives: Directive 72/159 concerning the modernization of agricultural undertakings, Directive 72/160 on the promotion of cessation of farming and incentives for the use of arable land for improvement of the agricultural structure, and Directive 72/161 on socio-economic information and the training of persons employed in agriculture.

The original system proved to be little used by the Member States (Druesne, 1986, pp. 318–19). In response, the Council replaced the structural policy directives by Regulation 797/85 on the improvement of the efficiency of farming structures, which regrouped the system and strengthened it. In 1987, the Council amended this basic structural policy regulation by Regulation 1760/87 to introduce conversion and extensification of production.

Both regulations, and their subsequent amendments, were replaced in 1991 by Regulation 2328/91 (O.J. L 218/1). Its first article states as its aims: to introduce a common measure to help restore equilibrium between production and market capacity; to contribute to the improvement of the efficiency of farms by developing and reorganizing their structures; to maintain a viable agricultural community, including mountain and hill areas and less-favoured areas; to contribute to the protection of the environment and the lasting conservation of the natural resources of agriculture.

Member States were required by the original Directive 72/160 to introduce measures to encourage the cessation of farming and the reallocation of the resulting agricultural area for the purposes of structural improvement. Although the directive has been replaced by Regulation 797/85, the latter did not reproduce a specific Community scheme for the cessation of farming and land reallocation. This issue has been taken up by Regulation 1096/88 to encourage the cessation of farming.

The modernization directive 72/159 was carried over into title IV of Regulation 2328/91, the support for investments in agricultural holdings to make them more profitable and to improve living conditions and production circumstances. To be eligible for this support farmers must meet certain criteria (article 5): farming must be their main occupation; they must have adequate occupational skill and competence; they must keep proper accounts; they must draw up an approved development plan which when accomplished will produce a level of earned income comparable with that received for non-agricultural work in the region in question; and the level of earned income prior to the planned development either must be less than the modernization objective or the plan proposed does not provide for an income in excess of 120% of that objective.

Farmers whose applications are accepted and whose plans are approved are eligible for a range of incentives (articles 6 and 7). Among these are interest rate subsidies on investments made for necessary improvements and aid for investments in the adaptation of the holding for the purposes of reducing production costs, saving energy, and protecting and improving the environment.

Aid is however prohibited for certain situations relating to products for which no normal market outlets can be found. Limits are set on the amount of financial assistance that may be provided, with the exception of aid for the construction of farm buildings, for the transfer of farm buildings when justified in the public interest and for land improvements, and investments to protect and improve the environment (article 12).

### 1. Setaside of agricultural land

In 1988, the basic structural policy regulation was amended by Regulation 1094/88 to incorporate a setaside scheme for arable land to be implemented by the Member States. Regulation 2328/91, Title I, has the two-fold object of rendering the land that is set aside more fertile and reducing the pressure of surplus crops on the Community agricultural market.

Member States have an obligation to introduce an aid scheme designed to encourage the setaside of agricultural land. Aid for setaside may be granted for all arable land, irrespective of the crops grown, provided that the land has in fact been cultivated for a reference period to be determined by the Member States. Land growing crops not covered by a common market organization is excluded from the scheme. The agricultural land withdrawn from production must represent at least 20% of the arable land on the farm concerned.

The regulation defines withdrawal from cultivation: the land must be left fallow for a period of at least 5 years, with the possibility of termination after 3 years. Crop rotation is possible. Alternatively the land may be afforested or used for non-agricultural purposes.

The relevance of setaside for agricultural land use is underlined by the provision that Member States have to take the necessary measures to keep the land in good agricultural condition. They can make the necessary provisions for managing the land so that the environment and natural resources are protected (article 2(3)).

Member States determine the amount of aid to be paid per hectare of land setaside, subject to a minimum set by the Community of 100 ECU[8] and maximum of 606 ECU per year (article 2(5)). In exceptional cases the Commission can set a higher maximum amount of 700 ECU per hectare per year.

The setaside scheme has been amended to insert the opportunity for Member States to introduce an aid scheme for the use of arable land to grow products that are not to be used for human or animal consumption (article 2(4)). To be eligible for this aid, farmers have to set aside at least 30% of their arable land. In the case of cereals to be used for non-food goals, the maximum acreage is 50% of the holding.

### *2. Extensification of production*

Member States have to introduce an aid scheme to promote extensification of the production of surplus product. For this purpose surplus products are defined as products for which there are consistently, at Community level, no normal unsubsidized outlets (article 3(1)).

Extensification is defined as a reduction of at least 20%, for a period of at least five years, in the output of the product concerned without any increase in other surplus production capacity (article 3(2)).

Member States determine the conditions for granting aid, the amount of aid, the reference period for the product concerned and the proof to be given by the beneficiary for the purposes of verifying that production has in fact been reduced.

### *3. Conversion of production*

Article 4 of Regulation 2328/91 contains the obligation for Member States to introduce an aid scheme to encourage the conversion of production towards non-surplus products. The Council has to adopt a list of products towards which production may be converted and has to lay down the conditions and procedures for the granting of the aid.

### *4. Farming in less-favoured areas*

Areas in the Member States that suffer from permanent natural handicaps present special problems for agriculture. They are typically dependent on agriculture, but their economic viability is threatened by a tendency towards depopulation and a decline in agricultural activity. In 1975 the Council issued Directive 75/268 supporting schemes designed to deal with the needs of such less-favoured areas. This directive has been partly incorporated into Regulation 2328/91. The remaining provisions of the original 1975 directive are necessary to understand the system. The principal aim of both measures is to maintain reasonable incomes for those farming in certain disadvantaged areas.

Regulation 2328/91, article 17, authorizes Member States to introduce a special system of aids to encourage farming and to increase farm incomes in those areas to which Directive 75/268 applies, taking into account the situation and development objectives of each region. Under Directive 75/268 Member States were to notify the Commission of the areas to which they proposed to apply this scheme. To qualify as a less favoured farming area in the Community, areas nominated by the Member States had to possess certain characteristics. For the purposes of the directive, less-favoured farming areas, in principle, included mountain areas in which farming is necessary to protect the countryside, particularly against erosion, or to meet leisure needs, and other areas in which the maintenance of a minimum population or the conservation of the countryside are not assured (Directive 75/268, article 3(1)). Such areas had to have adequate access roads, be supplied with electricity and drinking water and, in tourist or recreation areas, with sewage disposal. For mountain areas to qualify they had to comprise local government districts, or parts of them in which the possibilities for using the land were subject to considerable limitation together with an appreciable increase in the cost of working it (article 3(3)). Such characteristics had to be due either:

**1.** to altitude and consequentially difficult climatic and growing conditions; or
**2.** at lower altitudes to the predominant presence of slopes too steep for mechanical cultivation or requiring expensive special equipment; or
**3.** to a combination of both these factors.

Areas in danger of depopulation, or in which countryside conservation was necessary, qualified as less-favoured farming areas, if they were made up of homogeneous farming areas that exhibited the following three characteristics:

**1.** infertile land, unsuitable for cultivation except at excessive cost;
**2.** low productivity with results appreciably lower than the mean in the general economic situation in agriculture; and
**3.** a low or dwindling population predominantly dependent on agriculture, where acceleration of population decrease would threaten the viability and continued habitation of the area (article 3(4)).

The Council drew up and adopted (under EC Treaty article 43(2)) the Community list of less-favoured farming areas that may benefit from the aids granted under the directive.

Regulation 2328/91 adopts the Community list of less-favoured farming areas laid down by the Council under the 1975 directive. In such areas Member States may grant an annual compensatory allowance to assist farming activities. The allowance is to be fixed with reference to the nature of the permanent natural handicap as defined by the earlier directive. Assistance may only be granted to farmers with at least 3 ha of cultivated area. This requirement is lowered to 2 ha for Spain, Portugal, Greece, the French overseas departments, the Mezzogiorno area, and the islands of Italy.

A farmer must undertake to pursue a farming activity that will increase the farm income for at least 5 years. This undertaking will not be enforced if the farmer ceases farming in the area concerned or receives a retirement pension, and in cases of force majeur (article 18). Member States may introduce additional conditions for the grant of assistance. They may set additional conditions to make farming methods consistent with the requirements of environmental protection and landscape maintenance (article 18(3)).

The amount of allowance paid to a particular farmer will be fixed with reference to the severity of the permanent natural handicap and the number and type of livestock and the particular agricultural product to be marketed (article 19). Aid may be granted towards joint investment schemes for fodder production and to improve and equip pasture that is jointly farmed, to joint investments in water-points in mountain areas, and to the provision of minor roads for immediate access to pastures and in the provision of shelters for herds (article 20). If economically justifiable, aid may be granted in addition to small-scale irrigation works provided that they are compatible with protection of the environment. Upper limits are set on expenditure eligible for Community assistance: collective investments shall receive no more than 100.293 ECU, investments in pastures no more than 501.4 ECU per hectare, and irrigation schemes no more than 5000 ECU.

### *5. Environmentally sensitive areas*

Earlier national measures such as the management agreement system in the Netherlands, and the United Kingdom scheme for Environmentally Sensitive Areas, gave rise in 1987 to the introduction on the EC level of aid in areas sensitive as regards protection of the environment and of natural resources and as regards preservation of the landscape and the countryside.

Title VII of Regulation 2328/91 enables Member States to start a specific aid scheme for farmers who undertake to introduce or maintain, for at least 5 years, farming practices compatible with the requirements of the environment and of natural resources or with the requirements of the maintenance of the landscape and of the countryside. The maximum aid consists of an annual premium of 150.4 ECU per hectare covered by the farmer's undertaking. The aid scheme serves the dual purpose of adapting agricultural production to market needs, and contributing to the introduction of the farming practices mentioned before. The aid is to compensate the farmer for the income losses resulting from this introduction. Member States determine the environmentally sensitive areas and define the required production practices.

### *6. Afforestation on agricultural holdings*

Member States may grant aid to farmers for the afforestation of their agricultural land. This aid may be combined with the aid schemes for setaside or cessation of production (article 25). To farmers whose chief occupation is farming, aid may be granted for investments in certain types of woodland improvements and for forest roads. The aid may cover the cost of adapting agricultural machinery for forestry work. Member States receive compensation for their expenses from EC funds up to certain maximum amounts, for instance up to 1824 ECU per hectare afforestation. Member States may grant an annual premium of 150.4 ECU per hectare for a period of no more than 20 years to those farmers who do not already receive a cessation allowance (article 26).

## III. Access to Farm Land

Access to farm land is potentially affected by the provisions of the Treaty of Rome concerning the free movement of workers and the freedom of establishment. Article 48 EC provides that the free movement of workers shall entail the abolition of any discrimination based on nationality between workers of the Member States as regards employment, remuneration and other conditions of work or employment. Article 52 EC provides for the abolition of the restrictions on the freedom of establishment of nationals of Member States. According to the second paragraph of this article, freedom of establishment includes the right to take up and pursue activities as self-employed persons and to set up and manage undertakings, in particular companies or firms, under the conditions laid down by the host member state for its own nationals. Both articles 48 and 52 have been held by the European Court of Justice to create rights that individuals can rely upon against the state in their national courts.

### *1. As farmer*

The definition of 'agricultural producer' in Community law has been considered by the European Court in several cases. In Case 139/77 *Denkavit Futtermittel GmbH* v. *Finanzamt Warendorf* (1978) ECR 1317, it was held that the concept of 'agricultural producer' was not precisely defined in the Treaty. It was to be defined *ad hoc* in relation to each particular agricultural rule or set of rules derived from the Treaty. Any national legislative definition was permissible and not discriminatory so long as it was based on objective distinctions and compatible with the purposes of the applicable EC regulations and the Treaty. Similarly, in Case 36/79 *Denkavit Futtermittel GmbH* v. *Finanzamt Warendorf* (1979) ECR 3439, German legislation giving priority to agricultural producers who worked the soil, as against feed lots, was held not to be discriminatory within the meaning of article 40(3) EC.

A number of directives affect the ownership of farmland as a farmer. The farm manager Directive 63/261 provides for the right of an agricultural worker for at least 2 years to switch to independent farming. By its terms a special permit for aliens is still allowable but it must be granted as of right. Directive 63/262 provides for the right to pursue agricultural activities on agricultural holdings that have been abandoned or left uncultivated for at least 2 years. No special permit is required. Directive 67/530 provides that farmers of at least 2 years' standing are entitled to transfer from one holding to another.

The French Court de Cassation held in *Von Kempis* v. *Geldof* (1976) 2 CMLR 152 that, by virtue of Article 52 EC, the need to obtain an administrative permit to farm must be abolished.

Directive 67/531 provides for the abolition of discriminatory restrictions on the application of the law on agricultural leases. Directive 63/261 concerns the right to take on lease any property.

### *2. As landowner*

Article 222 of the EC Treaty, stating that it shall in no way prejudice the rules in Member States governing the system of property ownership, was in question in Case 339/82 *Commission* v. *Ireland.* Section 45 of the Irish Land Act forbade aliens to acquire non-urban land without the prior consent of Land Commission. The case was settled out of court.

Article 54(3)(e) EC provides that the Council and the Commission shall carry out their duties to achieve the freedom of establishment, *inter alia* by enabling a national of one member state to acquire and use land and buildings situated in the territory of another Member State, insofar as this does not conflict with the principles laid down in article 39(2) concerning the common agricultural policy. Directives 63/261 and 63/282 concern the right to acquire, occupy or exploit any property.

Directive 67/530, article 3(2) requires Denmark to abolish the Danish rule that persons not resident in Denmark and companies and firms not registered there, wishing to acquire immoveable property obtain prior authorization from the Ministry. In Case 182/83 *Robert Fearon & Co. Ltd.* v. *Irish Land Commission* (1984) ECR 3677, (1985) 2 CMLR 340 the European Court of Justice held permissible, so long as there was no discrimination, the expropriation of Irish farmland owned through an Irish company by five United Kingdom nationals, none of whom lived within 3 miles of the land.

## IV. A Broader Policy Domain

In addition to existing market management and structural policy, the Community has special programmes to broaden the scope of its activities. To mention but a few: a programme for intensifying collective irrigation projects in the Italian Mezzogiorno (Regulation 1362/78); a common action for afforestation in certain Mediterranean areas of the Community (Regulation 269/79); a special programme to stimulate the development of agriculture in certain problem areas of Western Ireland (Regulation 1820/80); and a special programme for the development of agriculture in Portugal (Regulation 3828/85). Mediterranean programmes and integrated development programmes have increasingly taken up an important position on the EC agenda (Commission, 1990b and 1991c, paras 408–10). The purposes of these programmes are, among others, to increase the quality of the soil, to combat erosion by afforestation and to stimulate land consolidation. The Commission has also adopted Community Support Frameworks (CSFs) for poorer regions in seven Member States (Commission, 1990a, point 1.3.145). Taken as a result of reforms to the structural funds by Regulation 2052/88, these programmes are based on the specific needs and development potential of local areas. They are drawn up by the Commission together with national, regional and local authorities.

The internal market programme, embedded in the Single European Act to amend the European Communities' Treaties, added to the EC Treaty new titles concerning economic and social cohesion (Title V, articles 130a–130e) and the environment (Title VII, articles 130r–130t). Each of these new titles affects agriculture.

The strengthening of the economic and social cohesion of the Community aims particularly at reducing disparities between the various regions and the backwardness of the least-favoured regions. In order to achieve this goal, the various structural policies are co-ordinated by Regulation 2052/88 to establish a partnership between the Community and the Member States in the integrated development of backward regions. The structural policies under Regulation 2328/91 are to be co-ordinated into a programme of rural development, the so-called objective 5(b). Commission Decision 89/426 (O.J. L 198) lists the rural areas eligible for funding under objective 5(b).

The environmental programme of the EC has led to an increased emphasis on the need to integrate environmental concerns with the Community's agricultural policy (EC Treaty, article 130r(2)). The Environmental Impact Assessment Directive 85/337, article 4(3), provides that projects of certain listed classes shall be made subject to an environmental impact assessment where Member States consider that their characteristics so require. With regard to agriculture, these classes include:

**1.** projects for the restructuring of rural land holdings;
**2.** projects for the use of uncultivated land or semi-natural areas for intensive agricultural purposes;
**3.** water-management projects for agriculture;
**4.** initial afforestation where this may lead to adverse ecological changes

and land reclamation for the purposes of conversion to another type of land-use.

In addition, a European Environmental Agency has been established by Regulation 1210/90 to monitor and provide information on environmental protection measures. For the immediate future its role is to be primarily the collection and evaluation of environmental data and the drafting of expert reports in order to help the Community to monitor the application of its legislation. The Council has also enacted Directive 90/313 on freedom of access to environmental information. It is designed to require public authorities to make information relating to the environment available to any natural or legal person on request and without having to prove an interest. These reforms are likely to have a great effect on land use in the EC in the future.

## V. Impending Changes in the Common Agricultural Policy

Confirming the reorientation of the common agricultural policy since the adoption of the Single European Act, Mr Ray MacSharry, the EC Commissioner for Agriculture, recently proposed guidelines for reforming the common agricultural policy. His 'Reflections Paper' (Commission, 1991a), approved by the Commission on 31 January 1991 and currently being debated by the EC Council, was a response to the continuing growth in surplus production, the failure of the common agricultural policy to increase farm incomes, environmental problems due partly to intensive agriculture, and the escalation of the financial burden on the Community. Mr MacSharry identified the policy's base failing as the fact that price support is linked directly to the quantity produced, thus creating a permanent incentive to greater production and further intensification. His proposed solution, one means of integrating agriculture into the internal market, is essentially a policy of social regulation.

Mr MacSharry proposed to control production by the implementation of substantial cuts in price support, together with a significant redistribution of support, for example by means of income aids on a full, partial but degressive, or conditional basis. In his view, this combination of economic instruments represents a return to the correct application of the basic principles of the common agricultural policy; however, it requires a redistribution of support (Commission, 1991a, p. 12). It will be targeted mainly towards smaller farms, leaving the larger, usually more efficient farms to rely mainly on the market. As summarized in the Commission's 'Press Notice,' dated 1 February 1991, (Commission, 1991b, point 1.2.131), '[t]he basic objectives of the reform are to reorientate the common agricultural policy socially and economically so as to enable a sufficient number of family farms to remain on the land and thereby preserve the natural environment and contribute to rural development'.

Two aspects of the 'Reflections Paper', in particular, raise very significant legal issues. The first is the proposal's overtly 'social' or redistributive aim seeking to protect the larger number of small farmers, numerically the vast majority in the Community, while leaving the larger, more competitive farmers to fend for themselves. This aim raises, though of course it does not necessarily violate, the basic principle of non-discrimination among producers, as stated in article 40(3) EC. Secondly, the Commission proposal attempts to re-interpret the objectives of the common agricultural policy, as stated in article 39 EC. It involves a much greater emphasis on structural policy, and indeed an attempt to insert into the common agricultural policy aims properly so-called, as stated in article 39(1), the list of factors to be taken into account in making agricultural policy, which are given in article 39(2) EC, and usually viewed as distinct (see this chapter, section IIA). It is therefore noteworthy that the European Court of Justice has also recently taken a broader view of the objectives of the common agricultural policy[9].

## Acknowledgement

We wish to thank Nathalie Habbar for excellent research assistance and Emir Lawless of the European University Institute's library for invaluable help with EC databases.

## Notes

1. Eurostat, *Agriculture Statistical Yearbook 1990*, p. 7 gives 225 830 000 ha for total EC 12 as of 1988, of which 128 507 000 ha is used by agriculture, 53 776 000 ha is wooded area, 39 777 000 ha is other area and 3 570 000 ha is water.
2. Here we are concerned only with the European Economic Community (EEC), not the European Coal and Steel Community (ECSC) or the European Atomic Energy Community (Euratom). The three Communities are legally distinct, each being based on a separate treaty, but they share the same institutions. The EEC is the most general in scope. By virtue of its founding treaty, the 1957 Treaty of Rome, it includes the common agricultural policy. Conventionally, the three communities are known together as EC. The 1992 Treaty on European Union article G renames the EEC as European Community. We will use the abbreviation EC throughout.
3. The total 1990 budget of 49 milliard ECU showed 26.5 milliard ECU for the

Agricultural Guarantee Fund and 2.1 milliard ECU for Agricultural Structures. Source: Office (1991, p. 62). See note 8 for significance and value of the ECU.

4. There are four EC institutions: an Assembly, a Council, a Commission and a Court of Justice. The Assembly calls itself the European Parliament, but has in the main only the powers of advice. The Council consists of the representatives of the Member States, and is the central power both as legislator and executive. The Commission is the independent executive, supervising the Member States, participating in legislation with the exclusive right of initiative, and exercising the powers conferred on it by the Council. The Court of Justice ensures the observance of the law by adjudicating cases brought before it by the institutions, Member States and, with some restrictions, private citizens. National judges can, and in some circumstances must, ask the Court's advice on the interpretation of the directly effective EC law.
5. The exceptions are alcohol, honey, potatoes, wood, and wool.
6. EC regulations are published in the *Official Journal of the European Communities* (O.J.). They are frequently changed, without making a complete new version available. Readers are refered to the *Repertory of Community Legislation*, published with the *Official Journal*, to ascertain the latest collection of the original version and subsequent changes.
7. The case-law of the Court of Justice is collected in the *Reports of Cases before the Court*, usually abbreviated as ECR. The *Common Market Law Reports* (CMLR) is another source.
8. The European Currency Unit (ECU) is the weighted basket of the currencies of all the Member States, calculated daily. The ECU evolved from an accounting unit into a parallel currency. In 1990 the average value of 1 ECU was 0.71 UK pound or 1.26 US dollar.
9. See Case C-331/88 *Regina* v. *Minister of Agriculture, Fisheries and Food ex parte Federation Europeenne de la Santé Animale (FEDESA)* (1991) 1 CMLR 507; and Case 131/87 Re Trade in Animal Glands: *EC Commission* v. *EC Council* (1991) 1 CMLR 780.

## References and Further Reading

Clout, H. (1984) *A Rural Policy for the EEC?* Methuen, London and New York.

Commission (1958) *Eerste Algemeen Verslag over de Werkzaamheden van de Gemeenschap.*

Commission (1968) *Memorandum on the Reform of Agriculture in the EEC. Commission Document COM (68) 1000.*

Commission (1990a) *European Communities Bulletin*, 6.

Commission (1990b) *European Communities Bulletin Special Report*, 4/90.

Commission (1991a) *Communication of the Commission to the Council on the Development and Future of the CAP (Reflections Paper)*, COM (91) 100.

Commission (1991b) *European Communities Bulletin*, 1/2.

Commission (1991c) *24th General Report on the Activities of the European Communities 1990.*

Commission (1991d) *Report on the Agricultural Situation in the Community 1990.*

Druesne, G. (1986) *Droit matériel et politiques de la Communauté Européene.* Presses Universitaires de France, Paris.

Eurostat (1990) *Agriculture Statistical Yearbook* 1990.

Harris, S., Swinbank, A. and Wilkinson, G. (1983) *The Food and Farm Policies of the European Community.* Wiley, Chichester.

Hill, B.E. (1984) *The Common Agricultural Policy: Past, Present and Future.* Methuen, London and New York.

Kapteyn, P.J.G. and VerLoren van Themaat, P. (1989) *Introduction to the Law of the European Communities after the Coming into Force of the Single European Act.* Kluwer, Deventer.

Meeus, J.H.A., Ploeg, J.D. van der, and Wijermans, M.P. (1988) *Changing Agricultural Landscapes in Europe: Continuity, Detoriation or Rupture?* International Federation of Landscape Architects Conference 1988, Rotterdam.

Office (1991) *Vade-mecum budgetaire de la Communauté, Troisième edition, Situation 1990.* Office des publications officielles des Communautés Européennes, Luxembourg.

Snyder, F.G. (1985) *Law of the Common Agricultural Policy.* Sweet & Maxwell, London. Translated: *Droit de la Politique Agricole Commune* (Economica, Paris, 1987); *Diritto agrario della Comunita europea* (Giuffre, Milano, 1990).

Snyder, F.G. (1990a) *The Common Agricultural Policy of the European Economic Community,* reprinted from 1(2) *Halsbury's Laws of England,* 4th edition reissue. Butterworth, London.

Snyder, F. (1990b) The special legal status of agriculture: Assumptions and contradictions in economic law. In: Snyder, F., *New Directions in European Community Law.* Weidenfeld & Nicolson, London, pp. 100–46.

Velde, M. van der (1991) Cow tourism: an analysis of quantitative management of milk production and law in the European Community. In: *Living Law in the Low Countries, Special Issue of the Dutch and Belgian Law and Society Journal Recht der Werkelijkheid.* VUGA, 's-Gravenhage, pp. 57–69.

Velde, M. van der (1992) Under the rule of law: The quest for legality in the implementation of the European Community's common agricultural policy. In: F. von Benda-Beckmann and M. van der Velde (eds), *Law as a Resource in Agrarian Struggles.* Agricultural University Wageningen, Wageningen, pp. 295–314.

# 2

# AGRARIAN LAND LAW IN BELGIUM

Rudi Gotzen

## I. Agrarian Land Legislation in Belgium

The Belgium legislation concerning agrarian land is already old, though there has been an important extension in the post-war years. There are four types of land laws in Belgium. The first group of laws tends to regulate the use of rural land to avoid conflicts. Here we can quote the rural code of 7 October 1886, the forest code of 19 December 1854 (in Flanders largely replaced by a Flemish decree of 13 June 1990), and the legislation concerning physical planning for rural areas (law of 29 March 1962; in Wallonia codified in the 'Code wallon de l'aménagement du territoire et de l'urbanisme' of 14 May 1984).

The second group of laws concerns land reallocation (law of 22 July 1970; in Flanders completed by the law of 11 August 1978).

Thirdly, the law of 4 November 1969, as amended by the law of 7 November 1988, concerning farm leases contains important principles affecting the use of agrarian land.

Finally, regulations tending to protect and maintain the natural environment also affect the use of agrarian land. These are either Belgian laws or decrees issued by the local governments in Flanders or Wallonia (law of 7 August 1931 concerning the protection of monuments and landscapes, largely replaced by a decree of 3 March 1976 in Flanders and a decree of 17 July 1987 in the French speaking part of Belgium; law of 12 July 1973 concerning the protection of nature, completed in Wallonia by a decree of 11 April 1984) or European Directives (setaside programmes, enacted in Belgium by a regulation of the Secretary of State for Agriculture of 23 July 1990).

Since 1980 and certainly since 1988, Belgium has been a federal state, divided between Flanders, Wallonia, and the capital Brussels. These regions have their own legislative and executive power in the matters fixed by the constitution. Concerning agriculture, attention must be focused on Flanders and Wallonia. These regions are fully entitled to regulate such important matters as physical planning, forestry, land reallocation, protection of nature, environmental problems, and protection of monuments and landscapes. Flanders and Wallonia are entitled to issue their own legislation, these 'regional' laws being called decrees. National authorities cannot overrule decrees, as long as they remain within the constitutional limits of the powers given to the regions.

In certain more cultural matters such as education and tourism, Belgium is divided in two parts, the Dutch speaking people (Flanders and the Dutch speaking inhabitants of Brussels) and the French speaking people (the French speaking inhabitants of Brussels and Wallonia) with the same right to issue decrees. Until 1988 the protection of monuments and landscapes was such a cultural matter, but now it is a regional matter, considering the link with the legislation concerning physical planning.

Finally, the national authorities (national Government and Parliament) are still responsible for the full area of agriculture as well as towards Europe, particularly in matters where Member States of the European Community can issue their own rules.

## II. Description of the Agrarian Land Law

### A. The use of rural land

#### *1. Rural and forest codes*

The most ancient laws directly regulating the use of land in the country are the rural code of 7 October 1886 and the forest code of 19 December 1854 (in Flanders largely replaced by a Flemish decree of 13 June 1990). In the Belgian tradition there has always been a clear distinction between farming and forests.

The rural code regulates the relations between neighbours concerning the settling of boundaries between the estates and the discharge of waters used for irrigation or coming from wetlands. The rural code also establishes the right of all owners to close their estates. The enclosures can be put at the boundaries of the estate, or may have to be put at a certain distance (ditches, quickset hedges). Trees may not be planted at a distance of less than 2 m from the border of the estate. In the zones indicated by the country-planning acts for agricultural activities, no timber trees can be planted at a distance of less than 6 m; a licence issued by the local authorities is also required.

The forest code of 19 December 1854 (completed in Wallonia by a decree of 16 September 1985 and in Flanders largely replaced by a decree of 13 June 1990) regulates the management of (mostly public) woods. In the generally accepted legal tradition of a clear distinction between forest and agricultural land, the Flemish decree of 13 June 1990 states in article 3, section 3 that the forestry rules do not apply to fruit trees, nurseries, Christmas trees, gardens and temporary plantations on agricultural land in accordance with the European setaside programmes.

### *2. Country planning*

Modern town and country planning was organized in Belgium by the law of 29 March 1962. In Flanders the law of 1962 was completed by a decree of 28 June 1984; in Wallonia the whole legislation concerning physical planning is codified in the 'Code wallon de l'aménagement du territoire et de l'urbanisme' of 14 May 1984. From the viewpoint of agrarian land law, these statutes are extremely important for the preservation of the agricultural acreage.

The entire surface of Belgium has been fixed in plans with binding legal consequences. Each area of Belgium – Flanders, Wallonia and the city of Brussels – is entitled to legislate in the matter of physical planning. The practical working base is laid down in sector plans, covering large areas. There are twenty-five plans in Flanders, twenty-two in Wallonia and one plan for Brussels. The plans contain a graphic view of the existing activities in the area, based on aerial photographs. This existing situation is translated in zones for agriculture, woods, nature, industry, housing, and other uses. The exact delimitation of the zones is based on the planning policy of the public authorities. Specific areas for agriculture are indicated on the plans. These agricultural zones are intended for any agricultural activity in a broad sense. Only buildings belonging to farms are allowed. Forestry zones may be used only for the planting of forests; no buildings are allowed, except small hunting or fishing lodges.

The sector-plans are legally binding for the citizens as well as for the public authorities of cities and municipalities. These local authorities have the right to issue more detailed local plans.

## B. Land reallocation

Since 1949 Belgium legislation has contained statutes concerning land reallocation. Actually the basic statute is the law of 22 July 1970, modified for Flanders by the law of 11 August 1978. Until now land reallocation has affected 250 000 ha. For a total survey of the regulations concerning land reallocation, we must also include the law of 12 July 1976 concerning specific regulations for land reallocation in accordance with large-scale public development works, and the law of 10 January 1978 concerning land reallocation asked for by the concerned farmers.

The law of 22 July 1970 is the basic text. In the context of this chapter, comments concern this general statute. Land reallocation improves the working conditions for farmers by reallocating parcels of land in order to form larger farms, with land concentrated in the neighbourhood of the farm buildings and with better access. This reallocation can be completed by development works such as new roads, water and electricity supply, drainage, irrigation, improvement of brooks and rivers. In Flanders, where rural areas are more and more affected by urban and industrial development, land reallocation can also be used for more general aims of land preservation, including the preservation of the beauty of a landscape and the conservation of natural sites. Actual land reallocation has therefore not only an economic goal, the improvement of agricultural structures, but also a wider aim, namely a general arrangement of rural areas to keep or to redress the balance between economic and ecologic activities.

The decision to organize a land reallocation is made by the ministers who are responsible for agriculture and town and country planning in the local governments of Flanders or Wallonia. This decision can be made on the initiative of the local governments or on the initiative of at least twenty persons, landowners or tenants, who are interested in the operation.

At first a provisional perimeter is marked out, and all the relevant facts concerning the affected parcels are listed. Public notice of this provisional plan is given, and during a thirty-day comment period, all remarks and protests must be made. Afterwards the responsible government makes the final decision and marks out the perimeter of the land reallocation.

For every land reallocation, a specific commission of seven members in Wallonia and eleven members in Flanders is nominated. This commission is the operating agent in charge of the whole reallocation and is entitled to make all the necessary decisions. The various commissions are assisted by a specialized public administration (in Flanders, the Flemish Land Company and in Wallonia, the Walloon Office for Rural Development) that prepares and carries out all the decisions concerning land reallocation.

The committee makes a list of all land affected by the reallocation, with a detailed valuation considering the agricultural value, including the specific characteristics of every piece of land. A list of owners and of tenants is also made. Public notice of these elements is given, and a thirty-day comment period follows. Afterwards the commission makes the final lists. Every interested person can contest the results and bring the problem to court.

The next step consists in the planning of new works such as roads, sluices, brooks, and canals. These plans are submitted to the advice of all the concerned local authorities. Afterwards the plan is transferred to the responsible government for final decision. Once the decision is made, the committee can start with the execution of the planned works.

The final step is the reallocation of all the land to the owners and the tenants in such a way that each receives again an estate of the same agricultural value as before. Financial compensation is possible for loss of value that could affect certain owners or tenants. From the legal viewpoint, land reallocation transfers the ownership of the old parcels to the new reallocated pieces of land. The same rule applies to tenancies; the rights of a tenant are transferred to new parcels. Article 30, however, gives the right to the commission to change the situations in order to restrict the number of landlords for every tenant. In such a case, landlords can get a new tenant. Practical problems, such as the length of the tenancy, the price, and financial compensation for works and improvements executed by the tenant, are solved by the commission with an agreement between parties. If necessary the problem goes to court for judgement.

The final reallocation of all the concerned land is written down in a detailed survey of all the new parcels, with notice given to the public and a thirty-day period for remarks and protests. Afterwards the commission makes the final list. Again, this list can be contested; the judge can correct the financial compensations, but the reallocation made by the commission is final and cannot be changed.

In order to make land reallocation easier, the Flemish Land Company (in Flanders) or the Walloon Office for Rural Development (in Wallonia) can acquire in preference to other candidates any piece of land offered for sale within the areas destined to be reallocated. The Minister responsible for land reallocation lists all the areas in the country where land reallocation is necessary; this official list is published by way of a regulation and regularly adapted. This specific right of pre-emption can be used when a piece of land is offered for sale, except when the buyers are family members or persons who are already joint owners. The actual tenant, however, has a preferential right to pre-empt according to the law of 4 November 1969 concerning farm leases. The vendor must follow the same procedure for the tenant and for the land company, giving notice of the offer by way of a registered letter or a document served by a court official (*huissier*). The land purchased by the Land Company (or in Wallonia, the Office for Rural Development) can be used by each specific commission in order to obtain a more equitable land reallocation.

### C. Agricultural holdings

The Belgian legislation concerning agricultural holdings is the most important agricultural law. Nearly two-thirds of the total agricultural acreage of 1 370 000 ha is used by tenant farmers; in many cases the agricultural holdings form the most important element of the farm. This explains why, more than in many other countries, tenant farmers need security of tenure to encourage them to improve the land and to follow the necessary expansion of capital equipment. Some statutory protection was introduced in 1929, but this first law was strengthened and improved in 1951. A totally new statute was introduced in 1969. The law of 4 November 1969 is still the basic statute concerning agricultural holdings. An improvement of the text was necessary, however, both to strengthen the rights of the tenant and to increase the return for the landlord, considered as an investor. After 9 years of discussion the Belgian parliament finally introduced a new statute of 7 November 1988, significantly amending the basic law of 1969.

The law of 4 November 1969, as completed by the law of 7 November 1988, offers important security of tenure for agricultural holdings. According to article 1, the law applies to every contract of tenancy concerning land that is used mainly as a farm. The key concept in this definition is the word 'farm,' meaning in the context of the law of 1969 a real agricultural business where crops and cattle are mainly raised for sale. The law on agricultural holdings does not concern forests.

The law of 1969 confers security of tenure by clearly stating that every farm lease is made for a period of at least 9 years. As long as no notice to quit is served, new periodic tenancies of 9 years follow the first period. A notice to quit an agricultural holding can only operate effectively in the circumstances accepted by the law in articles 6, 7, 8, and 8bis. The most important ground on which a notice may be served is the intended agricultural business by the landlord himself.

The farmer has also the right, in preference to other candidates, to acquire all the land within his tenancy. This specific right of pre-emption applies unless the buyers are close relatives or persons who are already joint owners. The right of pre-emption is also annulled when the sale concerns building plots or purchases made by public authorities for public purposes.

For agrarian land law, the most important articles regulate the freedom of husbandry. The rights of tenant are guaranteed by articles 24, 25, 26, 27 and 28, discussed below.

### *1. Freedom of husbandry*

Article 24 states clearly that all contractual stipulations limiting the freedom of husbandry are void. Tenants are free to use their agricultural holdings in the way they think best. This rule of freedom includes grassland as well as arable land; meadows may be changed to arable land and *vice versa.* Every normal agricultural method can be used, without interference from the landlord. As long as tenants run a farm in the sense of article 1, namely a real agricultural business where crops and cattle are raised mainly for sale, they enjoy complete freedom of husbandry. This applies even to accessory commercial activities such as the direct sale of commodities to consumers. A global transformation of the farm into a business or a commercial activity, such as dairies, restaurants, or riding-schools, is strictly forbidden (article 29). A second limitation on the freedom of husbandry is imposed by the obligation to work as a good farmer; lazy tenants, depreciating the value of the estate, can have their leases forfeited by the judge because of bad husbandry.

Freedom of husbandry allows the tenant to choose a very intensive manner of farming or a rather extensive way of working, with little use of pesticides and fertilizers. So, without any problem, tenants can play a role in a setaside programme or a public programme to preserve natural conditions in certain areas, as long as they remain busy in a farm in the sense of article 1. Other activities, such as forestry or just 'green-keeping' without an economic aim (i.e. preserving the natural aspect of a landscape without getting an economic benefit), cannot be carried out without the clear consent of the landlord.

Article 24 also guarantees the right of the tenant to dispose freely of all the produced commodities. Contractual limitations imposed to sell cattle or crops to certain partners or firms are void. The freedom of the tenant includes the right to store the produced commodities at the most convenient place.

Some contractual limitations are possible, however, according to the text of the second and the third paragraphs of article 24. Provisions in the lease to require the return of the land at the end of the period in an equivalent agricultural state as at the start are valid. It is clear that the tenant's duty is fulfilled when the land is returned in a comparable agricultural state; there is no need to restore the original situation of pastures and fields. The freedom of husbandry is indeed a prevailing right, allowing the tenant to change pastures in fields and *vice versa,* following the evolution and the needs of every agricultural season and the changing elements of the farm business such as the amount and the species of cattle.

Buildings and plantings which are of no further use can be removed when they become a nuisance for the farming business. The written consent of the landlord is necessary. If the landlord refuses, the tenant can go to court which can authorize the removal and specify the conditions, including financial compensation for the landlord. Hedges, bushes, trees and roads specifically mentioned in the lease can never be removed without the written consent of the landlord; in this case, the tenant has clearly agreed to maintain these elements of the holding.

### *2. Buildings and constructions*

According to article 25, tenants are entitled to erect all the buildings and constructions that are necessary for their farming business. The landlord's consent is not needed, though this consent has consequences for the amount of compensation to be paid at the end of the lease. The rule of article 25 applies to new buildings as well as to all kinds of constructions and improvements of existing buildings, roads, bridges and fences. This right exists as long as the tenure goes on, but ends when a notice to quit has been served.

The right of construction is guaranteed on two conditions. First, the buildings and constructions must be used for a farm, in the sense of article 1. Buildings for non-agricultural use can be constructed only with the clear consent of the landlord. Secondly, the buildings and constructions have to be useful for the agricultural holding by improving the working or living conditions. The improvement or the erection of dwellings for the people on the farm is also possible.

As long as the tenancy goes on, the tenant is considered to be the owner of the buildings and constructions. The tenant has to pay all the taxes and must keep all these constructions in repair.

On termination of the tenancy the farmer has the choice between taking the structures away or requesting the landlord to pay for these items. According to article 25, section 2, tenants can freely remove, at any time in the course of the lease, buildings and structures they have constructed, except when authorization has been given by the landlord or the court, in which case the same authorization is necessary. The right of removal cannot be used for constructions integrated into existing structures and therefore having lost the character of an independent item. The tenant must in any case restore the original situation, in order to avoid any loss of value of the land.

The farmer might prefer to request the landlord to pay the value of the remaining structures at the end of the lease. When tenants have the landlord's written authorization, they are entitled to a sum equivalent to the added value for the land, calculated at the end of the lease. The law also fixes a minimum price to be paid, namely the total cost paid by the tenant, insofar as these costs are not amortized (at amortizement of 4% per year). The landlord's authorization can be replaced by authorization of the court, which can be granted after a detailed examination of the proposed works, based on the opinion of an official agricultural engineer from the Belgian ministry of agriculture. The farmer's rights to compensation are in that case identical to those when a written consent of the landlord exists. When tenants have used their article 25 rights without asking for authorization, they are fully in their rights, but the compensation they can receive on termination of their tenancy will be limited to a maximum of 3 year's rent for all the land rented from the same landlord.

Because tenants can build important structures, landowners should be aware of these situations, especially when land is sold. To avoid bad suprises article 26, section 3 states clearly that landlords who sell their land have the duty of declaring all the structures and constructions erected by the tenant. In this way the buyer gets relevant information about the ownership of the buildings and the possible compensation to be paid at the end of the tenancy. All the concerned parties (landlord, tenant and purchaser) can also, if they wish, make a deal whereby the tenant receives a certain sum and relinquishes rights to remove the concerned structures.

### *3. The right to plant trees*

Because forestry and agriculture are clearly separate activities both in this legislation and in the laws concerning physical planning, clear rules are necessary concerning the right to plant trees. Article 28 forbids the landlord to plant new trees on the agricultural holding. There are only three exceptions to the general prohibition. Fruit trees can always be replaced by new ones. The same possibility exists for timber trees, but only on grassland. Finally, trees that are necessary for the conservation of the estate, such as trees protecting buildings and fields against winds and rains, can always be replaced or even newly planted.

Tenants are subject to the same prohibition as the landlord. On their own initiative, they can only replace trees (fruit trees or timber trees) or plant trees that are necessary for the conservation of the estate (replacements or new plantings). Every planting of new trees of any kind, however, is possible with the written consent of the landlord; this consent is indispensable and can never be replaced by any other procedure. Concerning new plantings of fruit trees, article 28 gives the tenant the right to carry out new plantings of at least half an hectare, joining an existing stand or a public road, and only in those areas where fruit growing is a usual agricultural business. The tenant also needs a permit from of the Ministry of Agriculture; the permit is granted when the fruit planting corresponds with an economically and technically sound way of running a farm in the fruit-growing areas.

On termination of the tenancy, the farmer is entitled to compensation for any added value because of the plantings. The added value is calculated at the end of the lease for all trees younger than 18 years. All plantings, even timber trees, are considered to be fully amortized after 18 years. When the tenancy ends on the initiative of the farmer, the compensation is limited to a maximum of 5 year's rent for all the land rented from the same landlord. Finally, article 28 entitles the landlord to ask for compensation also in case of a loss of value caused by any planting.

## D. Protection of nature and landscapes

### *1. Protection of landscapes*

The freedom to organize the economic agricultural activity can be affected by regulations tending to protect nature or to maintain the existing conditions of classified areas. Until now the most important legislation in this area is the law of 7 August 1931 concerning the protection of monuments and landscapes. In Flanders this law is completed by a decree of 3 March 1976 and in the French speaking part of Belgium by a decree of 17 July 1987. This legislation allows public authorities to protect monuments and rural areas by classifying the buildings or the landscapes. In such a case, limits can be put on the owners' rights to use their property freely. These restrictions, insofar as they cause damage to the owner's or the tenant's rights, can be counterbalanced by financial compensation to be paid by the public authorities concerned.

As far as agriculture is concerned, the law states clearly that the farmer's freedom concerning plantings and crops cannot be restricted (article 6 of the law of 7 August 1931 and article 18, section 2 of the decree of 17 July 1987). This means that in the management of the farm the choice of plantings and crops remains free. Public authorities cannot impose or forbid the production of certain commodities. Insofar as the destination of the land is not changed and within the limits of a normal farm, the freedom of the farmer is guaranteed (Court of Appeal of Antwerp, 26 April 1990, *Rechtskundig Weekblad* 1990–1, 367). This does not mean that the farmer could change the external aspects of the classified landscapes, for instance by cutting trees that are expressly protected.

The practical consequences of a decision to protect a landscape are still burdensome for every farm. Article 18, section 2 of the decree of 17 July 1987 states clearly for the French speaking part of Belgium that hedges, bushes, alleys, and forests, as well as wetlands and places of special interest for the fauna and the flora, can be protected.

### *2. Protection of nature*

The law of 12 July 1973 designed to protect nature allows the creation of natural parks and nature reserves. In these areas natural evolutions can take place. Every interference by human activities can be forbidden.

General measures to protect animals and plants can be taken in certain areas or countrywide. Article 1 of the law, however, indicates expressly that the law of 1973 does not have the purpose of regulating the way of running a farm or a forestry estate. Only wild animals and plants can be protected.

## *3. Setaside programmes*

The implementation of the European Community's regulations to restrict the production of cereal crops on arable land (Council Regulation 1094/88 and Commission Regulation 1272/88) is a competence of the Belgian Secretary of State for Agriculture. The Regulations have been implemented by an order of the Secretary of State for Agriculture issued on 20 October 1988 as modified by an order of 23 July 1990. The preparation of these ministerial orders included consultation with the local governments of Flanders and Wallonia responsible for forestry and environmental problems.

The ministerial orders provide for payment of aid to farmers who undertake to setaside areas of land producing arable crops for a period of 5 years. Individual persons, as well as holdings that have chosen the form of a company, can apply on condition that the holding is managed by a full-time professional farmer. Setaside land must be left fallow either for the whole period or in the form of arable rotation; in the latter case different parcels of land can be setaside each year as part of an arable process. Setaside land can also be converted to woodland or used for non-agricultural purposes. In addition, the farmer can apply for an extensive way of grazing.

Applications for setaside schemes are accepted only for areas of land really used in the holding and declared as such in the annual official census of agricultural holdings. The withdrawn areas of land may be composed only of parcels of at least one hectare and in total must constitute at least 20% of the area of land on the holding used for producing arable crops on 15 May 1987 and on 15 May of the year of the application.

Fallowed setaside land must be kept in good agronomic condition by maintaining an appropriate vegetation that is not meant to be harvested but used as an organic fertilizer. Existing trees, hedges, and watercourses must be kept in good condition.

Land in agricultural areas, as designated by the laws on physical planning, can be converted to woodland when the conditions of article 35bis, section 5 of the rural code are respected (i.e. plantings need a permit from the local authorities and can only be done at a distance of 6 m from the neighbouring parcels). In addition, only certain species of trees can be planted and a complementary permit from the Flemish or Walloon Government (responsible for physical planning) is required.

Land used for non-agricultural purposes cannot be transformed in a permanent way; applicants commit themselves not to undertake any activity requiring a permit as imposed by the legislation concerning physical planning.

The choice for an extensive way of grazing implies the duty to maintain a permanent meadow with very limited artificial or chemical additions and with a restricted number of cattle per hectare.

Setaside payments are yearly payments. The rates, depending upon the nature of the soil, are between 8000 and 20 000 Belgian francs. (From 1 July 1991 the rates will increase for new demands to 10 000 and 25 000 Belgian francs.) These amounts are reduced when the choice is made for extensive grazing or for non-agricultural use.

To avoid unjustified notices to quit given to tenants, the ministerial order clearly states according to article 9 of Regulation 1272/88 that the areas of land that are chosen by the applicant must have been used by the applicant since 15 May of the year preceding the year of the application. In this way a landowner cannot apply for a setaside payment concerning land used by a tenant, because a notice to quit can only be effective after a period of 2 or 3 years.

Landowners as well as tenants are eligible for aid. Tenants wishing to convert farmland to woodland or to use the land for non-agricultural purposes must obtain the consent of the landowner. Tenants wishing to fallow setaside land or to use extensive grazing must declare that they enjoy sufficient security of tenure to take on the requested 5-year commitment.

Setaside obligations are tied to the land. When the land is sold or leased, the commitment follows the land except by forced sales or expropriation. By succession on death, legal successors are bound by the original commitment to setaside land. When the successors of a tenant have their lease terminated by the landlord, they are no longer bound by the commitment for the land affected by the notice to quit. Obligations and payments cease without an obligation to repay any setaside payments already received. The person who takes over the right to farm the concerned land, however, can freely commit to go on with the setaside scheme for the remaining period.

The setaside regulations are a good test-case for the specific aspects of tenant farming. Although only limited areas of land have been brought in a setaside scheme (444 ha in the years 1988–90 with 45 applicants), the legal principles are important and could be used as precedent. The basic principle of the law of 4 November 1969 is specific protection for tenants running a real farming business (article 1). As long as this condition is fulfilled, tenants are free to organize the farm business as they like (article 24). According to these rules, the ministerial order of 20 October 1988 clearly states that tenants wishing to practise afforestation or to use the holding for non-agricultural purposes (including tourist facilities, caravan and camping sites, riding schools and livery stables, and game and natural reserves) need the consent of the landowner to be eligible for aid. When the applicant wishes to fallow setaside land or to use extensive grazing, he must only declare that he enjoys sufficient security of tenure. In case of rotational fallow (one of the oldest ways of farming) or extensive grazing, no problem occurs. In both cases there clearly is a farming business including the concerned setaside land. The Belgian Court of Cassation has already held in a ruling of 23 October 1981 that, even when the tenant has only a few cows per hectare, the law of 4 November 1969 still applies (*Pasicrisie*, 1982, p. 275). In another case, the Court of Appeal of Liege has held in a decision of 15 December 1983 that a limited stock of sheep still can be a real farming business and thus protected as a farm lease (*Revue de notariat belge*, 1987, vol. 87). When the tenant applies for permanent fallow, however, the situation is less clear. The ministerial order of 20 October 1988 requires only the tenants' statement that they enjoy sufficient security of tenure. It seems wise for a prudent tenant to ask the consent of the landlord; though this consent is not required to receive the setaside grant, it may avoid possible discussions later on. According to article 29 of the law of 4 November 1969, it is the duty of the tenant to keep all the rented land in use within a farming business. The exact decision about whether permanent fallow is part of normal agricultural activity can only be made by the courts. Until now there are no legal precedents. The detailed rules of the ministerial order of 20 October 1988 impose significant agricultural duties to maintain the production capacities of the concerned land that still gives a sufficient income to the farmer by way of the setaside payments. One might therefore conclude that permanent fallow, being only a temporary situation (5 years), falls within the normal farming business.

## III. Evaluation of the Belgian Agrarian Land Legislation

### A. Freedom in organizing the farm business

Agrarian land legislation in Belgium basically allows farmers to organize the agricultural business following economic needs and technical evolutions. Belgian legislation organizes the country by way of physical planning to avoid conflicts between different aims and activities concerning land, such as housing, industry, services, public facilities, recreational structures, roads, railways and watercourses. Within the areas meant for agriculture, farmers enjoy great freedom in organizing their business. This basic political option is clearly granted, not only to owners but also to tenant farmers. The rules of the law of 4 November 1969 concerning farm leases, articles 24 to 28, are fundamental; freedom of husbandry is a basic right in the tenancy legislation.

### B. Levels of government

The Belgian Ministry of Agriculture has always organized an economic policy towards development of agricultural activities. The legislation has been respectful of and close to the Common Agricultural Policy. Also today agriculture is still under national authority, with a well-organized national Ministry directed by a Secretary of State. Additionally, however, since 1980 Belgium has become a federal State with significant authority for the regional governments of Flanders, Brussels and Wallonia. More specifically for agrarian land law, the regional governments have important powers because they govern physical planning, land reallocation, forestry legislation, protection of nature and landscapes, and the whole environmental legislation.

In the actual situation one can say that policy-making for rural land has become much more complicated and demands co-operative action between various levels of government (the European Commission and Council, the national government, the regional governments).

Legal disputes are decided by the ordinary courts (judge of the peace, tribunal, Court of Appeal and Court of Cassation) or the supreme administrative court (Council of State). Belgium has no specific courts to decide issues connected with agriculture or with agrarian land.

## C. Evaluation of the agrarian land legislation

Until now the Belgian agrarian land legislation has been very effective in achieving its goals. Agriculture has been able to develop and to follow the technical and economical evolutions of agriculture in Europe. The total area of agricultural land (1 369 380 ha of a total of 3 051 871 ha or 44.9% of the country) and the number of holdings (91 874) indicate the vitality of the sector, though Belgium, certainly in Flanders and in the neighbourhood of Brussels, has become a highly industrialized country with a high population density.

New problems, mostly concerning water and ground pollution, are emerging. Until now there have been no environmental laws directly regulating the use of agrarian land. Environmental policy relies more on levies and indirect incentives.

In the future, however, new aspects of the European socio-structural policy concerning environmental protection and preservation of the countryside could impose more direct regulations concerning the use of agrarian land.

Also for the future, it is clear that governmental policies for rural land will have to be co-ordinated between the different levels of government to maintain the fundamental freedom for every farmer to organize the farm business in the most effective way. 'Green-keeping' (i.e. preserving the natural aspect of a landscape in a rural area without getting an economic benefit) and direct payments are certainly not the most effective way to preserve a good working agriculture.

### D. Special care for tenant farmers

Considering the importance of tenant farming in Belgium where two-thirds of the total area of agricultural land is used by tenants, the Belgian legislation will always preserve special attention for the rights of the tenant farmers, based on the freedom of husbandry as mentioned in articles 24 to 28 of the law of 4 November 1969.

Specific legal problems exist when the farm is run by a tenant, and it is often difficult to determine the exact rights of the tenant and the landowner. The new European socio-structural policy, with pre-pension schemes, setaside programmes and more extensive ways of production, could raise legal problems in the relationship between tenant and landlord. The landlord–tenant system has worked well during periods of expanding production. It does, however, face an important challenge when European and national policies are beginning to favour less intensive production practices and lower production of the staple products of agriculture. New regulations concerning agrarian land law should take in account the basic principles of a sound relationship between landlord and tenant, i.e. an equitable return to both landlord and tenant, guaranteed security of tenure and freedom of husbandry for the farmer, and a sufficient incentive for a reasonable and prudent landlord to maintain the willingness to lease the land again.

## Further Reading

Beguin, E. and Raucent, L. (eds) (1989) *Droit rural. Réformes.* Academia-Bruylant, Louvain-la-Neuve and Brussels.

Boes, M. (1986) *Monuments et sites.* In: *Répertoire notarial,* Vol. XV, Livre XIX, Larcier, Brussels.

Eeckloo, R. and Gotzen, R. (1990) *Pacht en Voorkoop,* 2nd edn. Belgische Boerenbond, Louvain.

Gotzen, R. and Herbots, J. (eds) (1989) *De nieuwe pachtwet.* Kluwer, Antwerp.

Haumont, F. (1988) *Urbanisme,* In *Répertoire notarial,* Vol. XIV, Larcier, Brussels.

Heyerick, M. (1987) *Ruilverkaveling van landeigendommen.* Kluwer, Antwerp.

Raucent, L. (ed.) (1988) *Droit rural. Bilan et perspectives.* Academia-Bruylant, Louvain-la-Neuve and Brussels.

Renier, V. (1973) *Le droit de l'agriculture.* Vander, Brussels and Louvain.

# 3

# AGRARIAN LAND LAW IN DENMARK

Helge Wulff

## I. Introduction

### A. The origin of agrarian land law

The origin of modern agrarian land law in Denmark is above all a radical land reform that was carried through in the 18th and 19th centuries. It comprised laws on land consolidation, land tenure and the ownership of land, as well as limitations of the size of farms and the preservation of the existing family farms. In the course of time the land law increased in volume; in the 19th century a forestry act and water legislation came into being. In the 20th century comprehensive legislation on land-use planning, conservation of nature, extraction of raw materials, water supply, and protection of the environment was added. Today agrarian land law in Denmark (as everywhere else) consists of a great number of detailed, complicated, and technical laws and regulations. Only the most important will be mentioned in this chapter.

The following information on Danish agriculture and Danish law might help the reader to understand the Danish agrarian land law.

### B. Danish agriculture

Denmark covers only 43 000 square kilometres out of which 2 787 000 ha or 65% are agricultural land and 11.5% forests. Most agricultural land is under cereals and cash crops. The crop production is to a large extent used as feed for livestock production, which consists mainly of pork meat, milk and milk products, beef and veal. The agricultural production covers the needs of the domestic market and two-thirds is exported, which equals 25% of the total exports of the country. The importance of agriculture for the national economy means of course that, when introducing new restrictions on the use of farmland, the legislator must take into account the extent to which those restrictions affect agricultural production.

The agricultural area is managed by 81 500 farms whose average size is about 35 ha. Their number has fallen and their size has increased during the last decades. More than 94% of Danish Agricultural holdings are owner-occupied. In 1989 tenancy of whole farms comprised less than 2000 farms, representing about 2% of all holdings and 2.4% of the total agricultural area. However, in 1989 about 19% of the total agricultural area was rented. That is due to the fact that most Danish farms today consist of a holding owned by a farmer who has rented adjoining land.

Many farms have turned into specialized enterprises: animal operations or farms with crop production only. They are highly mechanized and have increased the total agricultural production of the country. However, everything has its price. Modern agriculture has left its marks on the countryside: drainage has made lakes, watercourses, and wetlands disappear. The cultivation of heath and sandy areas has caused the disappearance of valuable landscape elements. The use of fertilizer and pesticides, and problems with disposal of manure have caused pollution of watercourses, groundwater, and coastal areas.

In the last 50 years the agricultural area has declined due to urban development, road making, and afforestation. It is also threatened by urban sprawl, see sections IIIA. and IV.

## C. The legal system

Danish law belongs to the Scandinavian family of law. It is neither common law nor civil law. There is no comprehensive code such as the French *Code Civil* or the German *Bürgerliches Gesetzbuch.* Danish law is closely related to the law in Norway, Sweden, Finland and Iceland. In many fields the Scandinavian countries have succeeded in creating a uniform system of law. However, this is not the case with respect to agrarian land law, which is very different in the five countries due to differences in geography, agriculture, etc.

Denmark has a written Constitution of 1953 which among other things lays down who are the principal authorities in Denmark: the Queen, the Parliament (*Folketinget*), the courts and local government. The Queen exercises her powers through ministers who are responsible to the *Folketing*, which is elected by the people. The legislative powers are vested by the Constitution in the Queen and the *Folketing.*

According to article 73 of the Constitution, no person is obliged to cede his property unless it is for the common good and upon receiving full compensation. The article governs not only the total transfer of an area to public authorities but also to some extent limitations on land use, i.e.

conservation easements (see section IID).

A citizen who feels that a statute violates article 73 can bring the matter into court. That has happened in a few cases where the statute did not give the citizens the compensation they felt entitled to according to the article. In the field of agrarian land law, the landowners have never had success. Courts decisions seem to show that article 73 of the constitution does not apply to land-use regulation unless it practically deprives the landowner of almost all use of his property.

# II. The Agrarian Land Law

## A. The planning act

In Denmark, land use is first of all regulated by the planning legislation, now The Planning Act of 1991 (Lov nr. 388 af 6.6.1991). That is also true of farmland.

### *1. Plans*

In each county, the county council draws up a regional plan that contains guidelines for a division of the county into areas of different uses: urban areas, areas for summer residences, recreational areas, nature reserves, areas reserved for the extraction of raw materials, and also areas reserved for agriculture and afforestation (which to a large extent will take place on private farmland).

Each municipal council draws up a 'municipal plan', which divides the municipality into areas of different uses according to the guidelines of the regional plan.

The regional and municipal plans have been elaborated on the basis of a 'sector planning' concerning, e.g. the protection of the landscape, the use and allocation of water resources, the extraction of raw materials, and the protection and use of farmland.

The regional and municipal plans do not place all farmland into the areas reserved for agriculture. The plans place a large part of Danish farmland in recreational areas or in areas that must be protected because of their scenic beauties. Here the farmers are protected against e.g. 'urban sprawl' but not against conservation easements, and they must tolerate camping sites and holiday centres in the neighbourhood. In the areas reserved for agricultural purposes, the interests of farming dominate.

Within the framework of regional and municipal plans, the municipal councils may – and sometimes shall – draw up 'local plans' for the creation of a new residential area, an industrial plant, or a public institution. The individual landowners and the local farmers' unions may give their opinion of the plan if they think that it interferes with the interests of farmers.

Local plans have a binding effect on landowners. The function of the regional plans and the municipal plans is to serve as guidelines for the drawing-up of local plans, the development schemes of local government and above all for the discretionary decisions that are made in pursuance of a great number of statutes mentioned below.

Finally it should be mentioned that the Planning Act authorizes the Minister for the Environment to issue 'national planning directives', which can be general instructions on future planning in a special field. However, most directives are concerned with very precise problems, for example the future location of an airfield, a power station, or a new pipeline network. Directives order the local authorities not to permit any change in the use of the area that would make it more difficult to construct the airfield or the power station, if it some day is decided to do so.

### *2. Zoning*

The purpose of zoning is to prevent 'urban sprawl' and to ensure that landowners obey the regional and municipal plans.

The statute divides the whole country into urban zones, summer house areas, and rural zones. Urban zones and summer house areas are laid out by means of local plans according to the regional and the municipal plan. In these two zones future residential areas, industrial areas and areas for summer residences are located.

The rural zones, on the other hand, are kept free from this sort of development. In the rural zones it is necessary to obtain the county council's – in some cases the municipal council's – permission to develop and build and to alter the use of existing buildings and land without buildings. This rule does not apply if the proposed building or the land is intended to be used for agricultural purposes.

## B. The legislation on farm structures

### *1. The Agricultural Holdings Act* (Lovbkg. nr. 504 af 17.7.1989)

This statute regulates the management and the size of farms, tenancy, and the acquisition and ownership of farms.

The statute applies to agricultural holdings. In the 1920s (and sometimes later) most farms, market gardens, and plant nurseries were registered as 'agricultural holdings' in the 'Cadastre' and 'Land registry'. A few large horticultural enterprises are not registered and not governed by the statute.

Agricultural holdings and their lands must be used for agriculture, horticulture, and forestry. If the yield of the land is too feeble to make farming worthwhile, the farmer must at least not use the land for other purposes. The person who actually manages an agricultural holding, whether it is the owner him- or herself, a tenant, or a manager, must live permanently on the holding.

Originally each agricultural holding was to be worked as a separate enterprise, independently of other farms. The farmer could only to a very limited extent rent his neighbour's land or increase his holding permanently by purchasing adjoining land. The law was very strict on this point, because most registered agricultural holdings were family farms, and it was the aim of the law to preserve the family farm in Danish agriculture and avoid the creation of too large agricultural enterprises.

However, the technical and economical development in agriculture in the last decades have made most registered holdings too small for survival. So the present statute allows the farmer within certain limits to farm several holdings together as one enterprise. He can also obtain permission to increase his agricultural holding permanently by purchasing adjoining land. The limit is 125 ha unless the farmer can prove that he needs more land for the disposal of manure from his animals.

Subdivision of agricultural holdings may not be carried out without a licence from the land authorities. This ensures that the holdings are not split up into small enterprises, for example in case of succession.

As stated above in section IB, tenancy of whole farms is rare in Denmark. Therefore, it is not surprising that the Danish legislator has never felt the need of protecting the tenants (who are sometimes farmers of large estates). The statute only requires a written contract specifying the rent and the term of the lease. It does not regulate the rent, which is solely determined by the market price. Nor does the statute give the tenant a right of pre-emption of the holding or a right of renewal at the end of the term. On the other hand the owner has no right to change the rent, unless it is allowed for in the contract.

There are few limitations on the right to rent a whole farm. However, the term of the lease must not exceed 30 years. Tenants must live on the holding whether they personally manage the farm or not. They must not own or rent land from more than five agricultural holdings.

As a general rule only individuals may acquire agricultural holdings in the rural zones. Persons who acquire an agricultural holding in these zones must live on the farm permanently for 8 years whether they actually manage the farm or not. If the area of the holding exceeds 30 ha, they must also have a training in agriculture and they must not farm out any part of the land.

Persons who wish to acquire an agricultural holding need a special licence from the land authorities if they already own a holding and the new holding is above 30 ha. However, they have a right to obtain that licence, if they can prove that they need more land for the disposal of the manure from their animals or if there are not any neighbours who wish to buy the holding for that purpose. A licence is also required and seldom granted if a farmer wishes to acquire a third holding.

The rules on the transfer of agricultural holdings by succession or between family members are less severe.

Legal entities (corporations, co-operatives, associations, etc.) are not allowed to acquire – or rent – agricultural holdings. The only exceptions are farm corporations in which a person, who meets the conditions of the statute to acquire the holding himself, possesses the majority of the votes in the corporation.

### 2. *EC law*

The Agricultural Holdings Act does not compel a farmer to cultivate marginal farmland, and he may also profit from the setaside scheme of the EC regulation nr. 1094/88 (cf. 1272/88) and from the programme concerning the management of environmentally sensitive areas, EC regulation nr. 797/85 and nr. 1760/87. Farmers can also benefit from the afforestation scheme of EC regulations nr. 797/85 and nr. 1609/89 (see section C). (The EC regulations are transformed into Danish law by Lovbkg. nr. 631 af 22.9.1989.)

### 3. *The land consolidation act* (Lovbkg. nr. 467 af 22.6.1990)

A special statute authorizes local land boards to carry through land consolidation schemes, but the need for land consolidation has always been limited in comparison to many other countries, so it will not be discussed here.

## C. The forestry legislation

About 20% of the Danish forest area consists of larger or smaller woods belonging to farms, so it seems natural to mention the land-use regulations concerning forests in this chapter. The Forestry Act (Lov nr. 383 af 7.6.1989) submits most forest land in Denmark to restrictions that oblige the owners to preserve their forests. The land must be used for forestry only and not turned into farmland, building sites, gravel pits, etc. The land must be covered with trees, which form or within a certain time span will form a close high forest. The choice of tree species is free from restriction. However, the forest authorities may issue licences to use forest land for other purposes than forestry.

It is part of the Danish Government policy and the common agricultural policy of the EC to promote the afforestation of private farmland. In the regional plans, special 'afforestation areas' are laid out. The plans can be implemented in two ways: either the Government Forestry Service or local authorities acquire the land from the farmers, or the farmers afforest their land themselves. The Forestry Service and the local authorities have the power to purchase the land from the farmers in the open market or (very rarely) acquire it by expropriation (Lov nr. 339 af 24.5.1989).

Farmers are of course not obliged to afforest their land even if it is stipulated in the regional plan, but they may obtain grants for the afforestation according to a special statute (Lovbkg. nr. 631 af 22.4.1989). This statute implements the Agricultural Structure Policy of the EC, which includes aids to the afforestation of farmland in the Member States in order to reduce agricultural production, EC regulations nr. 797/85 and nr. 1609/89. The areas that are afforested will be submitted to the restrictions of the Forestry Act.

Most private forests are open to the public in the daytime – by foot and only on the roads (according to the Nature Conservation Act).

## D. The Nature Conservation Act

The purposes of the statute (Lovbkg. nr. 530 af 10.10.1984) are to protect Danish landscapes and to give the public an opportunity to enjoy the Danish countryside. In Denmark the classical instrument of realizing these purposes is the conservation easement, which may forbid the owner to build houses, etc. exploit raw materials, drain the land, or even use pesticides if it might harm plants and animal life. A conservation easement can also give the public a right of access to an area.

The decision to submit land to a conservation easement* is made by a local board. The decision is a kind of expropriation that entitles the owner to compensation according to the provisions of the Constitution.

Nature reserves are created in accordance with the regional planning through conservation easements combined with a restrictive administration of the Planning Act, the Forestry Act, the Raw Materials Act, etc.

The provisions of the Nature Conservation Act also establish protective zones along beaches, watercourses, lakes and forests where the construction of buildings and the exploitation of raw material require a licence from the Nature Conservation authorities. Water streams, lakes and salt marshes are protected against dredging and filling, afforestation, etc. Beaches and uncultivated areas are to a certain extent open to the public.

These provisions of the Nature Conservation Act are not considered an expropriation, and the landowner is not entitled to any compensation.

---

*In this chapter the term 'easement' covers the concepts of easements and covenants of Anglo-American law.

## E. The Environmental Protection Act

The statute (Lov nr. 358 af 6.6.1991) protects soil and ground water against pollution by making it illegal to deposit liquids or solid substances on the ground, or to discharge these substances into the subsoil, if there is a risk of pollution. Substances likely to pollute water may not be discharged into watercourses, lakes or the sea. County councils and municipal councils may grant exemptions from these provisions.

Pursuant to the Environmental Protection Act, a special ministerial order (bkg. nr. 568 af 22.9.1988) has been drawn up. According to this order farmers may never apply more manure to their land than plant production requires. The quantity per hectare per year must not exceed the manure produced by 1.7–2.3 animal units, depending on the kind of animal production (1 animal unit equals one milk cow or three sows). Should the farm produce such large amounts of manure that the rules cannot be followed, the farmer must enter an agreement with another farmer in the neighbourhood who can dispose of the manure. There are special provisions on the application of liquid manure to fields without plant cover, and it is totally forbidden from harvest time until 1 November.

The order requires of farms with more than thirty animal units a certain storage capacity for animal manure, unless there exists a written agreement about storage on another property (9 months' storage capacity for farms with more than 120 animal units).

Another order prescribes plans for rotating crops on most farms and also plans stating a farmer's need for nitrogen and phosphorous fertilizer. Moreover, 65% of the land of a farm shall consist of green fields, i.e. be grassland or laid out in certain crops (winter barley, maize, beets, and outdoor vegetables).

Landowners must acquire a special licence from the municipal council if they wish to begin production of swine and poultry if the operation exceeds 250 animal units. If the operation is placed less than 50 m from a habitation or 100 m from an urban area, the licence is required even if the production does not exceed 15 animal units. Larger chicken farms and fur farms also require a permit. If the farmer complies with the conditions of the permit, he is during the first 8 years after the issue of the permit protected against the interference of environmental authorities.

## F. Other statutes

There are a number of other statutes that also regulate the use of farmland and these are discussed below.

The Raw Materials Act (Lov nr. 358 af 6.1.1991) makes the extraction of raw materials for profit illegal without a licence from the county council.

The licence is granted only in accordance with the regional plan.

According to the Hunting and Wildlife Act (Lovbkg. nr. 801 af 11.12.1987), wildlife reserves may be established. That is a kind of expropriation that entitles the landowners to compensation for the loss of their hunting rights.

The beds of watercourses and lakes belong to the riparian owners. According to the Watercourse Act (Lov nr. 302 af 9.6.1982) riparian owners have the right to drain their land and channel the drain water to the watercourse, but they must not in any way change the natural state of the stream. Farmers who are not riparian owners must not drain their land and lead the drain water to a stream on their neighbour's property. The statute contains detailed rules on drainage, and it obliges the riparian owners to maintain their streams to make sure that the natural flow of the water is not impeded by vegetation, refuse, etc. (Some watercourses are maintained by local government.)

In private law, only riparian owners have the right to use the water in watercourses and lakes for irrigation, and only a landowner has the right to use the groundwater for irrigation. However, the owners cannot make use of that right without a licence from the county council (the Water Supply Act, Lovbkg. nr. 337 af 4.7.1985). The council determines if the water is suitable as drinking water, for irrigation, etc. and also takes the need of other landowners for water into consideration.

## G. How are conflicting uses and claims on agrarian land resolved?

The conflicts between the various uses of agrarian land are solved in many different ways.

**1.** Motorways and important institutions are built according to statutes, which also decide where the motorway or institution should be placed. In this case, that conflict is solved by Parliament.

**2.** According to the Agricultural Holdings Act and the Forestry Act, most farms and forests must be preserved and the land must not be used for purposes other than agriculture and forestry. In this case, too, the conflict between various claims on the land is solved by Parliament. Exemptions from the provisions of the statutes may be granted by local land boards and the local forest inspectors. These exemptions are usually granted in accordance with the guidelines of regional and municipal plans.

**3.** Where the legislation does not solve the conflicts, regional and municipal plans must do so. When drawing up the plans, the authorities must weigh the different interests against each other. The regional and municipal plans are sometimes described as 'synthetic' plans whose purpose it is to solve conflicts between different claims on the land according to an overall view.

**4.** Evidently the regional and municipal plans are not detailed enough to solve every conflict of interest with respect to agrarian land. However, landowners who wish to use their land for a purpose other than farming must obtain a permit from the many authorities that deal with the legislation mentioned above. Each authority is free to refuse a permit if it feels that the landowner's project would be harmful to the interests the legislation tries to protect.

### H. Judge-made law

The use of agrarian land is to some extent also regulated by a judge-made law.

If landowners use their property in a way that interferes with their neighbours' enjoyment or use of their lands, the neighbours can bring an action against them. The court may order landowners to stop their activities or at least reduce the nuisance to a reasonable level. The court may also award the neighbours damages. The nuisance must be substantial and exceed what the neighbours are expected to tolerate – anywhere or considering the nature of the area. The cases in this field deal with very different problems including noise, odours and pollution from industries, large animal farms etc.

This case law regulating relations between neighbours has lost some of its importance. Modern environmental and planning legislation reduces the number of conflicts. When conflicts do occur, the neighbours usually prefer to avoid the slow and costly court proceedings. Instead they ask administrative authorities to apply environmental regulations.

If a landowner makes his neighbours suffer a direct financial loss, however, they can obtain damages only by bringing an action against him in court. The court will award them damages if it finds that the landowner has caused the loss intentionally or by negligence (the *culpa* rule). In the field of agrarian land use, this rule is often applied with respect to water pollution.

## III. Agrarian Land Law and Government Policy

### A. The aims of government policy

The aims of government policy on the use of agrarian land have changed and multiplied through the years. Since the land reform of the 18th and 19th centuries (see section IA), the aim of government policy with respect to farm structures has been to promote and preserve individual ownership, the owner-occupancy system, and a large number of family farms in Danish agriculture.

This policy has been modified during recent years. The preservation of the owner-occupancy system is still part of government policy, but the need for capital in agriculture has made it necessary to permit farm corporations to acquire and rent agricultural holdings, something which until recently was absolutely forbidden. The idea of preserving the family farm is not really government policy any longer, but the provisions of the Agricultural Holdings Act still hinder the creation of big agricultural enterprises through the purchase or renting of land (see section IIB1).

Last century it was also the aim to break up the old village system where the farmers of the village for centuries had cultivated their farmland in common. Authorities and farmers carried through a land consolidation, whose purpose was to gather the land of all farmers separately in one or a few plots near their buildings. Land consolidation may still be considered a – not very important – part of government policy (see section IIB3).

In the beginning of the 19th century, it became an important aim of government policy to preserve the forest area, which was rapidly declining. It is still government policy to preserve and enlarge the forest area, with emphasis on both the production value of the forests and the importance of the forests to the landscape and outdoor life.

Through the years the government has offered financial aid to improve productivity of the soil, especially by drainage, which has been very important to Danish agriculture. Financial aid has also been granted for irrigation, even for reclamation of land from lakes and coastal areas. The legislation in this field, however, has been repealed.

After the First World War, the protection of nature also became the aim of government policy, and the legislation in this field has been amended and developed until today. It has sometimes met with opposition from farmers. The preservation of landscapes and areas of scenic beauty is realized not only by means of the Nature Conservation Act but also by the Planning Act, the Forestry Act, and various other statutes.

In the middle of this century the danger of 'urban sprawl' became obvious. It became the aim of government policy to prevent a scattered and random building of dwellings, weekend cottages, industrial enterprises and other structures over all the open spaces, because experience from other countries has shown that for many reasons it is necessary to avoid an impractical and disorderly extension of urban areas. Otherwise the risks, among other things, are too many environmental conflicts between farms and new residential areas, an unnecessary destruction of landscapes and areas of scenic beauty, and too large a reduction of the agricultural area of the country. Therefore it is essential to regulate land use in the countryside. In Danish law the instruments are the Planning Act and the Forestry Act.

Little by little it became evident that the claims on farmland were many and that the agricultural area was rapidly becoming smaller (in 1938 it covered 76% of the total area of the country and in 1988 only 65%). In the 1970s it was considered necessary to give the preservation of valuable farmland a high priority. The means to realize that policy are the Agricultural Holdings Act, the planning legislation, and the Planning Act. It is probably still the official policy to protect valuable farmland even if it might seem a little out-of-date in a period when surplus production exists in many fields, the EC tries to reduce the agricultural area, and the harmful effect of modern intensive farming is becoming more and more evident. The crisis has also slowed the demand of urban and industrial areas for more land.

After the Second World War the demand for public access to the open country for recreational use became stronger. It is government policy that access to the open country shall be available for everybody – not only for those members of the public who can afford to acquire their own property in the countryside or to buy hunting rights, etc. Hence legislation provides public access to the beaches, forests and uncultivated land, as mentioned above.

Last but not least, government policy on the prevention of land and water pollution should be mentioned – especially that from modern specialized and mechanized farms (see section I). That pollution has been increasingly important in the last decade. The result has been the formation of land-use regulations which are mentioned in section IIE.

## B. Which authorities implement government policy?

### *1. Central administration*

At the central level most of the legislation mentioned above is the responsibility of the Ministry for the Environment. The Agricultural Holdings Act, land consolidation, and the implementation of the EC regulations are the responsibility of the Ministry of Agriculture.

The Ministries draw up bills, issue rules and regulations, issue guidelines to other authorities, and make decisions on complaints concerning the decisions of local authorities.

Some complaints about the decisions of the local authorities are decided by central boards of appeal whose chairpersons are lawyers (e.g. the Environmental Board of Appeal and the Nature Conservation Board of Appeal).

### *2. Local administration*

At the local level, the legislation was, until a few years ago, administered by a confusion of local boards and commissions. This was particularly true in the fields of regional planning, control of urban sprawl, drainage, irrigation, soil and water pollution, and nature conservation. Some of these authorities might almost be called local 'courts' because the chair was a judge who to some extent was obliged to obey certain rules of procedure that were not too different from the rules of court procedure.

Today, however, the local administration is managed by the county and municipal councils. Both the planning process and many decisions in individual cases include a weighing of many considerations – urban development, preservation of farmland, conservation interests, and a landowner's personal interests. This weighing of interests is considered to be of a 'political nature', which should be the responsibility of popularly elected political authorities: municipal and county councils.

There are still some independent boards and commissions left, for example the local nature conservation boards whose chairpersons are local judges and which make many decisions pursuant to the Nature Conservation Act. The reason these boards still exist is probably a fear that the municipal councils would not put as high a priority on nature conservation interests as on other interests they must consider.

Local boards also deal with decisions according to the Agricultural Holdings Act. The reason these boards exist seems to be a wish of the farmers' unions to be represented on the boards and in this way to influence the administration of the statute.

## C. Which means are used to implement government policy?

### *1. Legal instruments*

The most important legal instrument is of course the statute. To a large extent, however, modern statutes leave a good part of the regulation of the citizen's conduct to administrative authorities and limit themselves to marking out the framework for the activities of the administration. This means that the Ministers for the Environment and Agriculture can issue rules of law by ministerial orders (*bekendtgørelser*) which are legally binding for the citizens. The rules have to be changed frequently. Therefore, it is desirable not to be bound by the laborious legislative procedure.

County and municipal councils can work out plans for land use, etc. as has been described in the previous sections.

When the law forbids a certain activity, for instance the construction of buildings in a rural zone, the county councils and municipalities have far-reaching powers to grant the necessary exemptions, licences and permits, and to dictate the terms that are deemed necessary in each individual case. When dealing with applications for exemptions, licences and permits, the authorities most often adhere to circulars and guidelines issued by the ministries. By reading these, the applicants will be able to see what considerations form the basis for the authorities' decisions.

Finally, the authorities are in many cases entitled to place certain obligations on the citizens in the form of concrete orders. Examples are conservation decisions and land expropriations.

One last legal means of control within the environmental legislation should be mentioned: agreements. The environmental authorities can make management agreements with a farmer about the tending and care of an area submitted to a conservation easement or the management of environmentally sensitive areas. They can also buy areas in the free market with a view to planting forests and establishing recreational areas. However, in Danish law land-use regulations are more important than agreements and purchase of land.

### *2. Other instruments*

Financial aids are also used to implement government policy; these include, for example, aids to afforestation and the setaside of marginal farmland. It is also contemplated to levy duties on the sale of fertilizer in order to limit pollution.

## IV. Evaluation of the Agrarian Land Law

On the whole the legislation on regional and municipal planning, including the provisions of local plans, has been successful. Municipal plans and local plans, introduced in 1977, have found their place in Danish land-use law. The regional plans have been criticized for being behind their time. Especially the regional and sector plans have resulted in a vast number of immensely complicated rules, regulations, guidelines and background material which have been difficult for local government to handle and for landowners and their legal advisers to deal with. This tends to reduce the efficacy of the planning legislation. The government tries to simplify rules and procedures.

The planning legislation, the Agricultural Holdings Act and other laws seem to have succeeded in controlling urban sprawl and in preventing too much valuable farmland from being converted into building sites and other non-agricultural uses.

The control of the use of land has in fact been so strict that the planning legislation has been criticized for ‘stifling’ the rural areas. Therefore it is tempting to make an effort to induce small factories and people from urban areas to move into the countryside to revive local commerce and heighten ‘the quality of life’ in the rural districts. This may be a good idea, but it certainly also means that the administration of the statute might become too slack. It is difficult to find the point of balance.

The Agricultural Holdings Act is usually considered to function well. However, the statute has been revised so often over the years in accordance with the technical and economical development in agriculture that one may well wonder whether it really determines the farm structure of the future or at thc utmost delays development a little.

The protection of forests has been very effective and has helped to bring the forests through the 1960s and 1970s when the building activity was intense and when there might have been good money in building bungalows, weekend cottages, hotels, social institutions, and office buildings in forest areas. Today the planning legislation, which did not exist at the time, might offer almost as much protection. Until recently the forestry legislation has not been able to stop some farmers from neglecting the management of their forests to some extent. Under the new Forestry Act of 1989 the forest authorities will in different ways try to advise the owners how to deal with their forests. As the choice of tree species is unrestricted, the forestry legislation has not been able to prevent a reduction of deciduous forests (and especially of our national tree, the beech) in favour of coniferous trees, which often are more profitable. The government now tries by means of financial aid to enlarge the deciduous forest area.

The Nature Conservation Act seems by and large to have functioned well, but the protection of wetlands against drainage, dredging and filling and against pollution, which has been strengthened over the years, still needs improving. The government now proposes new land-use restrictions on farmland in order to save small watercourses and lakes. According to the proposed provisions, farmers must not cultivate land a certain distance from water courses and lakes. A detail perhaps, but this proposal has met with a violent opposition from the farmers.

The provisions of the statute on public access to beaches, forests, and uncultivated land do not seem to satisfy the needs of the urban population, and the government contemplates opening most roads and paths in the countryside to the public.

The government has just finished the implementation of the EC regulations on the setaside scheme, afforestation, and environmentally sensitive areas. So it is too early to evaluate the success of the EC programmes in Denmark.

Agricultural water pollution has not abated fast enough. The provisions discussed in section IIE do not seem sufficient. So new measures are being discussed and will probably be applied in 1991–2. The problem is very difficult to solve, because the farming world reacts violently to any new regulations, the economic conditions of farmers are difficult, and it is against the trends of this decade to introduce too severe restrictions on free enterprise.

Even if the Danish agrarian land legislation to some extent seems to be satisfactory, it has not solved the important problem of agricultural pollution. Besides, the land legislation is only a tool in the hands of the municipal and county councils, which make the plans and daily decisions, and of the Ministries, which influence local administration by means of guidelines. The success of the agrarian land legislation depends on the authorities whose duty it is to uphold it.

In the beginning of the 1990s, unemployment, taxes and a falling supply of social services will be a problem in many parts of the country. It still remains to be seen whether the political authorities in localities affected by the crisis have the will to respect their own planning and to protect farmland with areas of scenic beauty, forests and valuable landscapes from the construction of industrial plants, hotels and summer residences.

## Further Reading

Andersen, B. and Christiansen, O. (1988) *Kommuneplanloven, 3. udgave.* (The Municipal Planning Act). Jurist- og Økonomforbundets Forlag, Copenhagen.

Basse, E.M. (1987) *Erhvervsmiljøret.* (Environmental Business Law). Gad, Copenhagen.

Bjerring, J. and Møller, G. (1987) *Miljøbeskyttelsesloven.* (The Environmental Protection Act). Jurist- og Økonomforbundets Forlag, Copenhagen.

Ginnerup-Nielsen, M., Jørgensen, Chr., Kjær, J. and Wulff, H. (1984) *Landbrugsloven.* (Commentaries to the Agricultural Holdings Act), Supplement 1987. Gad, Copenhagen.

Herslund, B., Holmboe, E. and Brix, B. (1979) *Råstofloven.* (The Raw Materials Act). Juristforbundets Forlag, Copenhagen.

Illum, K. (1976) *Dansk Tingsret (3. omarb. udgave v. V. Carstensen).* (Danish Law of Property). Juristforbundets Forlag, Copenhagen.

*Karnovs Lovsamling.* (The Karnov Annotated Statutes) (1990). Karnov, Copenhagen.

Nielsen, V., Brix, B., Koesler, V. and Ploughmann, O. (1973) *Naturfredningsloven, almindelig fremstilling og kommentar.* (The Nature Conservation Act, common version and comments). Gad, Copenhagen.

Nørby Jensen, P. and Wulff, H. (1981) *Hvad må min nabo?* (The Law on Relations between Neighbours). Gad, Copenhagen.

Revsbæk, K. (1986) *Planer og forvaltningsret.* (Planning and Administrative Law). Gad, Copenhagen.

von Eyben, W.E. (1977–8) *Dansk Miljøret 1–5.* (Danish Environmental Law, Vols 1–5). Akademisk Forlag, Copenhagen.

von Eyben, W.E., Abitz, E.A., Andersen, B. *et al.* (1986) *Miljørettens Grundbog.* (Fundamental Environmental Law). Akademisk Forlag, Copenhagen.

Wulff, H. (1970) *Skovloven.* (The Forestry Legislation). Ministry of Agriculture, Copenhagen.

Wulff, H. (1979) *Landboret.* (Agrarian Land Law). DSR Forlag/Royal Veterinary and Agricultural University, Copenhagen.

# 4

# AGRARIAN LAW IN FRANCE

Louis Lorvellec

A traveller flying over France sees a quilt made of rather small plots, planted fence row to fence row, green spots of forests, and some high mountains. Everywhere, small villages and medium-sized towns are connected by a spider's-web network of roads. This first image of France reflects our traditional landscape, but with closer scrutiny this image becomes tarnished. Farms without farmers, villages with closed and crumbling houses, big tracts of land laying fallow, surface and underground waters polluted by effluents of modern stock farms or by fertilizers: the threat of disaster fuels a new agrarian law and haunts agricultural lawyers.

For a long time in France, agrarian law could be defined as the body of laws and regulations concerning rights on land when land was considered the only principal asset. For the self-sufficient, non-commercial agriculture of the 19th and early 20th centuries, agrarian law, agricultural law and rural law could be commingled[1]. In the mid-20th century, the necessity of distinguishing agrarian law and agricultural law first arose because farmers had to enter into a greater variety of contracts. Legal liens in the agricultural area related to assets other than land, because land was not the only important asset that the modern farmer needed. Agrarian law became only a part of agricultural law, which was considered as the law on farming. In the mid-1970s the French became concerned about the physical environment. Increasingly, land was considered a natural resource, not only for agricultural production but also for recreational activities. French agrarian law became not only part of agricultural law but also part of land planning law (*droit de l'aménagement*). Together agricultural law and land planning law frame an overall body called rural law (*droit rural*).

At the end of the 20th century, French agrarian law reflects the physical environment of France and a long history of changing political and economic balances. These include the balance between the traditional right of property and the collective economic as well as ecological interest on one hand, and the balance between freedom of trade and enterprise and the increasing role of the centralized French state or EC authorities on the other hand.

Our purpose in this chapter is to summarize French agrarian law. This chapter, however, can only be a freeze frame from the movie of agricultural law. So many questions arise about the future of agriculture or rural zones, and about the role of law in shaping this future, that drawing a single perspective is quite impossible.

The first section will describe the physical environment and historical background of French agrarian law. In the second section, an examination of modern rules will show that in spite of the lack of any priority for agricultural uses, some specific legal protections have been framed for fragile agricultural zones by administrative control of other activities such as forestry of development. More and more, co-ordination of different land uses is now promoted (agriculture/forest; agriculture/leisure; agriculture/building). The third section will describe the two major factors affecting agricultural land use:

**1.** the adoption of regulations with the aim of promoting the most economically efficient farming activity; and
**2.** environmental concerns that have fuelled new laws in the last two decades and changed the so-called 'productivist' trend of the French agrarian law of the 1960s.

## I. Geographical and Historical Background

French agrarian law reflects a specific physical environment. France enjoys a temperate climate with regular rains and mild winters, few large rivers or dangerous floods, relatively high mountains and vast plains. France apparently needs no special regulations to prevent massive erosions or special disasters like desertification or to protect very fragile soils. The average acreage of farms is rather low (20 ha in the 1960s, 28 ha in the late 1980s). Of all agricultural land 50% is operated by owners, 2% by sharecroppers, and the rest by tenants. The whole French agricultural territory has been cultivated for almost two centuries, except for certain forests.[2]

The historical background of French agrarian law is naturally based on the *Code Civil* of 1804. Regarding land law, the two pillars of the *Code Civil* were the absolute right of property and freedom of contract, which applied to many contracts involving land sales, leases, etc. In this period of 'triumphant individualism', the use of land seemed to depend on the owner's will, and was generally based on old methods of fertilization and soil conservation. But behind the *Code Civil*, several laws and regulations shaped a more sophisticated system of property than described by some scholars. For example, the individual right of property was seasonal in many regions. As soon as the crops were harvested, owners of livestock herds, as a collective group, were allowed to graze every field in the parish (*Code Civil*, article 648; C.R. articles 189–99). In the mountains, a collective right to graze was developed by a 'thicket of customs'[3] and even by old international agreements, such as those concluded between Spain and France. In the forests, either private or state-owned, similar rights existed (*Code Forestier*, articles L. 137–1 and L. 146–1).

In the *Code Civil* itself, the individualistic right of property was limited. Article 651 stated that 'the law provides obligations binding owners one to another, independently of any agreement'. Article 652 developed the very simple principle: 'some of these obligations are framed by the law on rural policy (*police rurale*)'. It was established by a decree of 1791 (Protot, 1989), in which the revolutionary legislature set many important principles about crop protection, rights and duties of shepherds, rural policemen and so on. Many articles were codified in the initial codification of 1955 as part of the second book of the *Code Rural*.

With the purpose of reconciling conflicting uses of neighbouring lands, the authors of the *Code Civil* framed an important body of legislation, including easements, servitudes such as rights of way for landlocked property owners, flooding privileges, etc.

In the 20th century, government regulation accelerated, fuelled by an attempt by the government and the law-makers to shape a new agriculture. Efficiency in land use was the first goal. With an incredible reliance on the power of law and regulations and a permanent distrust in the power of markets as well as of freedom of contract and wills, the French legislature framed a complicated law on agricultural land ownership and use.

Just after the First World War, to enhance the consolidation of land holdings, several laws created a redistribution procedure called *remembrement* (Atias and Linotte, 1980). This is discussed in more detail below. Instead of scattered pieces, landowners received regrouped tracts; new roads were built, and hedges were destroyed to create more efficient structures. Almost half of the French agricultural territory has been reshaped by this procedure. (New laws have been enacted: law of 9 March 1941, law of 11 July 1975, law of 31 December 1985; they are now codified, C.R. articles 1–58.) One of the causes of the initial fragmentation of holdings was the rule of equality in inheritance. In 1938, the French legislature enacted the first exception to this principle. When an 'agricultural unit of production' is to be divided, one of the heirs, already farming, can be chosen by a trial court as the only allottee of the farm (*décret-loi* of 17 June 1938, now *Code Civil*, article 832). In this system, called 'preferential allotment', the allottee must make a cash settlement to the other heirs. The question of efficient land use arises when multiple heirs apply for this preferential allotment; the court is to choose the best farmer among them.

During the Second World War and the period immediately following, the legislature framed the most important part of modern French agricultural law, the Landlord and Tenant Act of 1946, called *statut du fermage.* Previous laws of 15 July 1942 and 4 September 1943 were declared null and void as having been enacted by the ruling power of Marshall Pétain. Though frequently modified and now codified (C.R. article L. 411–1), this law is still in effect. This law is *impérative* (no freedom of contract). Every lease is for a minimum fixed period of 9 years, automatically renewable. The amount of rent is strictly limited. Owner-operated farming is broadly encouraged by a legal option for the tenant to purchase and a right to recovery of possession from the tenant by the landlord who plans to farm.

The next important step toward a new French agricultural law was the Agricultural Guidance Act of 1960 and the complementary Agricultural Guidance Act of 1962 (Law no. 60–808 of 5 August 1960; Law no. 62–933 of 8 August 1962). Farmers' unions, General de Gaulle's government and the legislators, while trying to reach the goal of income parity[4] and to increase the competitiveness of French agriculture, decided to create an economic holding pattern. This pattern established a legally ideal type of farm called 'family farming with personal liability'. Creating such holdings was the target of many structural regulations, premiums or subsidies for modernization and administrative control of farm-merging and, some years after, of settlement. By administrative controls or financial incentives, land use was in fact heavily regulated with the sole aim of increasing productivity, and not of protecting natural resources. This period is now called the age of 'triumphant productivism'.

This period ended in the late 1970s when several crises struck French and European agriculture. A demographic crisis developed with the increasing average age of farming family members and the desertion of important rural areas. Meanwhile a major ecological crisis appeared: the huge effort of modernization destroyed water, soil, and landscapes. In the 1980s the French legislature enacted many laws in an attempt to impose a more balanced model of rural development. Unlike the general rules of landownership written by the 'redactors' of the *Code Civil,* these new laws focused on the use and protection of agricultural land.

## II. Agriculture in Conflicting Land Uses

French agricultural law does not provide any general or special protection for crop or range land from irrevocable conversion to non-agricultural uses: the richest vineyard could be threatened by a property developer (Lorvellec, 1990a). Nevertheless, some specific regulations in the Urban Planning Code (*Code de l'urbanisme*), in the Forestry Code (*Code forestier*) and in a specific regulation enacted by the Mountain Act (*loi-*

*montagne*) of 1985 (Law no. 85–30 of 9 January 1985; Ourliac, 1985) protect farmland. This paradoxical defence of agriculture by 'non-agricultural' laws is a most important feature of French agrarian law and illustrates an obvious lack of comprehensive protection for agricultural land. This section describes this aspect of French agricultural law and traces two exceptions, a zoning system and a more complicated and integrated development system, which may provide for comprehensive protection.

## A. A paradoxical farmland preservation law

French agricultural law does not include measures for farmland preservation. On the contrary, most legislative efforts have occurred to facilitate the conversion of farmland to non-agricultural uses, primarily residential and industrial development. The decrease in farm incomes and the increasing gap between the value of crop land and urban land undermine efforts to develop a farmland preservation policy or regulation.[5] Agricultural law protects farmers, and a lucky farmer may sell plots to a developer! In France, better protection for farmland occurs indirectly through urban zoning policy, whose purpose is to avoid scattered residential development. The only farmland protection provided by agricultural law is some restriction on conversion of farmland to land laying fallow and in some cases to forest.

### *1. French agricultural law facilitates the conversion of farmland to urban uses*

By combining the words rural and urbanization, geographers and sociologists created the hybrid *rurbanization.* By allowing the conversion of farmland, French agricultural law makes this theoretical concept a reality. Three cases illustrate this trend. As mentioned before, the *statut du fermage* provides that every lease is for a fixed minimum period of 9 years. During this time, the landlord has a power of termination in case of specified acts of default, failure of the lessee to pay rent, and failure to farm in an acceptable manner. The landlord may bring an action against the lessee. A special agricultural land-tenure trial court (*tribunal paritaire des baux ruraux*) determines whether the failure to pay rent may be excused or whether the husbandry is bad enough for a statement of lease termination. Article L. 411–32 of the *Code Rural* provides an important exception to this judicially protected stability of tenants. At any time, the owner may give notice of termination if the leased land is to be converted to a 'non-agricultural use' and is located in a district where the non-agricultural use (dwelling, commercial, industrial) is permitted by a zoning ordinance or a specific administrative authorization. This exceptional power of termination is based on an economic balance: rents are very low because of government control, but the landlord is allowed to reap the capital profit from the farmland conversion.

The role of the 'SAFER' provides a second illustration[6] (Hudault, 1987, p. 538; Lorvellec, 1988, p. 25). The twenty-seven *Sociétés pour l'aménagement foncier et l'établissement rural* (Corporations for land planning and rural settlement) were created by the Agricultural Guidance Act of 1960 as non-profit public corporations controlled by the government and owned by farmers' unions, mutuals and other agricultural, or administrative entities. They may buy agricultural land, should it come on the market. Since 1962, they have used a legal option to purchase. They are to sell this land to beginning farmers or to sustainable family owned units; since enactment of a new law in January 1990, they may lease the land. The SAFER are very active and actually control the farmland market. Nevertheless, they cannot exercise their legal option to purchase farmland that will be converted to residential, industrial or commercial use (Law of 8 August 1962, article 7–IV–5).

The third case is that of the consolidation procedure (*remembrement*). Any farmland in 'the perimeter', which is the whole land involved in a consolidation procedure, may be 'redistributed' and allocated to any other owner. Article 20–4 of the *Code Rural* provides as an exception that the owner of a development site may conserve his right of property in his plot.

It should not be presumed that any developer can convert farmland to urban or industrial uses; whether conversion can be permitted is actually not provided by the French agricultural law. Special rules in the urban zoning law prevent scattered residential, industrial or commercial development and implement indirect farmland preservation measures.

## 2. Farmland preservation under urban zoning law

Urban zoning law is two-tiered (Jacquot, 1990). On one hand, 18 000 of the 36 000 French municipalities or *communes* have adopted a zoning map called POS (*Plan d'occupation des sols*). A kind of local farmers' Parliament, called *Chambres d'agriculture*, must be involved in the different phases of the drafting before the adoption of the map by the appropriate unit of local government. Usually, the territory is divided in urban districts ('U zones') and 'natural' districts ('N zones'): NA for future urbanization; NB with a 'frozen' already-scattered residential development; NC agricultural uses; ND environmentally sensitive areas. The NC zones are protected according to the agricultural value of land or quality of the underground resources (*Code de l'urbanisme*, article R. 123–18). In many cases, administrative courts invalidate zoning ordinances that do not respect this preservation of farmland. For example, the court may decide that a NA zone is too large and then invalidate the ordinance, but it may not rezone NC by itself. A new adoption of a different map by the local government is necessary. In these NC zones, only buildings necessary for the farm holding are permitted. In many cases, administrative courts, on judicial review of building permits, impose a strict interpretation of the term 'necessity'.

The other 18 000 municipalities, the smallest parishes or *communes* in France, have not adopted a zoning map. (Of communes with 1000 to 2000 citizens, 87% have a POS. This means that the majority of the French communes are very small.) Nevertheless, any building project must conform with national building regulations, some of which may not be circumvented even if there is zoning. A building permit certifies that a project meets those national requirements, the most important of which is called 'building limitation rule' (*Règle de constructibilité limitée*). Article L. 111–1–2 of the *Code de l'Urbanisme* states that any building project may be allowed only within the limits ('in the continuity') of existing villages, to avoid scattered residential development (Hocreitière, 1990). Farm premises and farmers' housing projects are permitted. This rule matches the effective requirements of the preservation of farmland, but it is not strictly enforced. In the last few decades, more extended plans have been formulated, to set long-term goals for land uses in an area wider than the tiny territory of the French communes. The aim is to promote rural development, and these plans are established apart from zoning ordinances (Acts, 1990).

The French zoning system provides indirectly for farmland preservation. This element of national urban policy, however, is not based on special concern about the consequences of agricultural land conversion. A more comprehensive and sophisticated development policy could protect more effectively against urban extension.

### 3. Protecting farmland from other non-urban uses

The absolute right of property in farmland may lead to the conversion of farmland to land laying fallow or forest. Whereas the pressure of high prices for building plots prevented French law-makers from framing limits on urban development, the low income given by wasteland or forest fuelled special rules on land uses, which set agriculture as a priority.

'Land laying fallow reallocation' is one of the most complicated procedure in French agricultural law. It is certainly the most ineffective. Theoretically, any person may make a claim for allocation of any 'laying fallow or inadequately cultivated land' (*terres incultes ou manifestement sous-exploitées*).[7] Articles 39 to 45 of the *Code Rural* provide special rules to protect landowners' rights during a first phase: landowners may agree to improve their methods of cultivation and submit a development plan to a special committee. Failing this, they are to accept the claimant as a tenant who will farm the land. The economic terms of the lease are established by a special agricultural land-tenure trial court.

Farmland can be threatened by forestry development. A special zoning ordinance may be issued by the *préfet* (public authority under the central government that administers each of the 94 French *départements*) in order 'to promote a better distribution of agricultural, forestry and recreational uses' (C.R. article 52–1). A zoning map defines special agricultural districts, in which any tree or timber plantation is prohibited. The offenders are not eligible for forestry tax relief programmes. Since 1987, department of agriculture officers have been allowed to destroy *ex officio* the illegal plantations. This preference for farmland over timberland is a general trend in French agricultural law. By the Landlord and Tenant Act, the landlord may give notice of termination of the lease to convert the leased farmland to a development project. No rule provides a similar right to a landlord wishing to convert farmland to forest. Furthermore, the *Cour de Cassation* ruled that a landlord had no right to recover possession to convert leased farmland to timberland[8]; under article L. 411–58 of the *Code Rural*, the landlord could recover possession of farmland to cultivate the land.

French agricultural law appears to rank land uses according to the short-term profit they offer the owner or tenant. The highest priority is urbanization, followed by agriculture, and then forests and fallow land. This cynical analysis is not strictly accurate; some laws protect sensitive or 'fragile' farmlands.

### B. Fragile farmland preservation

Soil erosion has not been a major concern for French agriculture. The destruction of hedges during the redistribution procedure (*remembrement*) and uncontrolled use of machinery by hill farmers could change our minds. The only significant soil erosion measures are regulations limiting timber-cuts on the most erodible montane soils (Chesné, 1990). Clear-cutting is allowed only as permitted by the *préfet* or the Agriculture Secretary (*Ministère de l'Agriculture*). Article L. 311–3 of the Forestry Code prohibits any clear-cut of a forest if necessary for soil conservation. Furthermore, the zoning ordinance may create 'damaged districts' (*zones dégradées*; C.R. article 52–2, 3°). Clear-cuts are prohibited and private landowners may be required to establish tree plantations, with the aim of protecting 'soil, cultivation and ecological stability' in accord with article 52–2–3 of the *Code Rural.*

Two special statutes go beyond soil conservation and provide a more general farmland preservation system. One has been enacted in the 'Mountains Act' of 9 January 1985 (Ourliac, 1985), the second in the 'Coastal Shore Act' (*loi-littoral*; Law no. 86–2 of 3 January 1986, article

L. 146–1 *Code de l'Urbanisme*). Both statutes are based on a wider conception of rural development and promote ecological as well as economic stability of rural and touristic areas. Whether this ideal of regulation based on ecological and economic harmonization will be effective is still an open question.

## C. The harmonization of different uses of land

Development programmes are a more recent aspect of government policy for rural land. Harmonization of economic, environmental, agricultural, recreational and residential development is the ideal or unattainable intended goal of the planning procedures. Nobody can adequately list all these procedures in France. So many acronyms, so many levels of government involved (national, regional, local), so many legal tools (laws, regulations, contracts, charters, plans) produce a crazy quilt of procedures (Acts, 1990).

Due to the necessity of selecting some examples in this mess, we will focus on the transformation of certain procedures concerning farmland uses into more complicated development procedures and on evolution of the law on leases in order to facilitate mixed uses of farmland.

### *1. Mixed farmland and urban development land reallocations*

Land development law (*droit de l'aménagement foncier*) has developed since 1941 with the purpose of improving farm working conditions and productivity. Since 1975, it 'conduces also to land planning of the communal territory according to the regulation of the urban planning schemes' (C.R. article 1, section 2). The law is now called the land and rural development law (*droit de l'aménagement foncier rural*).

Two procedures of land reallocation illustrate this trend. One is called 'farm and urban land redistribution' (*remembrement-aménagement*; C.R. articles 19–1 to 19–4; Lorvellec, 1990a, p. 50). In the territory demarcated by a plan (usually a *commune*), a procedure of land development is mixed with a procedure of urban planning. During the preparatory phase, an urban district is delimited. All owners of the commune receive a plot in this high-value zone and a parcel in the agricultural zone without regard to the location of their land before the reallocation. Each zone is shared according to the appraisal of the former ownership. The lack of subsidies for the expenses of housing development works undermined the few projects that were established in some tourist areas.

The second procedure is usually called 'Reallocation by article 10 of the law of 8 August 1962' or 'Public works land reallocation procedure' (Complementary Guidance Act of 8 August 1962, article 10, now codified in the Eminent Domain Code, *Code de l'expropriation*, article L. 23–1;

Jégouzo, 1982; Bon, 1981). Some important public works (highways, rail-tracks, airports, industrial plants, recreational centres, etc.) promote the conversion of much agricultural land. Developers, either public authorities or private corporations, bear the cost of the operations. For example, along a new highway or around a new airport, a zone is designed in which part of land is condemned. In this zone, a procedure of land consolidation is implemented, with the goal of distributing the burden of the farmland conversion among many landowners. Every owner endures a reduction of his ownership, and receives a part of the general compensation. Inconveniences and advantages of public works are shared. This procedure is commonly implemented. The mixed farmland and forestry land reallocation or consolidation procedure is not implemented (C.R. articles 52–3 and 52–4).

### 2. Evolution of leases of agricultural land

In the typical 'Landlord and Tenant Act' lease, mixed uses are prohibited to the detriment of both parties. Recently the legislature has allowed a mixture of agricultural and recreational uses.

In the mountains, the permanence of the tenant's right of possession prevented owners from allowing winter uses or building ski-facilities in leased pastures. As a consequence, leases, and not ski-lifts, disappeared in those areas (Cotton, 1972; Chesné and Martine, 1974). Article L. 481–1 of the *Code Rural* provides a special statute for the *contrats d'exploitation de terres à vocation pastorale* (pastureland leases). The areas in which such contracts may be used are now restricted by law to the mountains and to all 'regions where a sustainable pasturing activity or extensive agriculture is needed for environmental and soil protection as well as for the survival of a social life' (Law no. 72–12 of 3 January 1972, mod. Law no. 85–1496 of 31 December 1985, mod. Law no. 90–85 of 23 January 1990).

The purpose of these contracts is to establish rights of shared possession of the land between the tenant and the landlord, in order to achieve the dual objectives of farming by the tenant and recreational uses such as skiing, hunting or fishing, including the use of facilities operated by the landlord. In that case, the special statute dictates only a few terms of the contract.

The second example is more important. The improvement of farmers' income is frequently based on the extension of activities such as managing camp-grounds, bed-and-breakfast, 'farm-restaurant', or off-farm activities, such as farm-product canneries. Threats of lease termination prevented tenants from engaging in these activities. In recent years, the short-term sublease of premises and land for a vacation period or a recreational use (C.R. article L. 411–35) has been permitted by law. A more important reform under the Agricultural Adaptation Act of 1988 extended the general definition of agricultural activities to 'all activities carried on by a farmer as an extension of his own farming operation or production efforts or to all activities performed on his farm by the farmer' (Law no. 88–1202 of 30 December 1988, article 2). In many previous cases, the *Cour de Cassation* had held that the law implied a covenant on the part of the tenant to limit his activity on leased land to crop raising, which was considered the only agricultural activity. The reform of 1988 overruled this decision.

Legal concepts of agriculture as well as public policy of rural development promote the harmonization of different and simultaneous uses of rural land. The role of agriculture could be twofold in this scheme, both a source of income and a part of environmental management.

## III. Limitations Affecting Agricultural Land Use

In this section, we have to imagine a farmer on land legally dedicated to crop production. A very complicated agrarian law has been framed to prevent him from inefficient farming activity. On the other hand, new rules prevent him from doing environmental damage. Naturally, the harmonization of both aims will be the legal challenge of agricultural law in the next decade.

### A. Farmland productivity and the law

French agriculture is a part of a market-oriented economy. Nevertheless, no other professional activity is so heavily regulated. Since the Guidance Act of 1960, a governmental policy of 'productivism' increasingly fuelled controls and incentives for farmland uses and framed a new agricultural law, which can be compared with a school system based on awards and exclusion. Control of farmland use may be indirect; regulation of credit, development plans and production quotas influence the production decisions of young farmers or settlers. This section describes the effects of laws and regulations aimed directly at the enhancement of productivity. The structural policy is described in two aspects:

**1.** consolidation of holdings and procedures; and
**2.** 'structural administrative control' (*contrôle administratif des structures*).
Due to the lack of specificity of the French implementation of the European structural policies, the new setaside and extensification programmes are not traced in this chapter;[9] finally,
**3.** the tenancy law, insofar as related to agrarian land-use, is described.

### *1. Consolidation of holdings procedure*

As mentioned before, French farmland was divided into parcels too small for economic cultivation and too dispersed for rational and efficient operation. The use of machinery was inhibited in those small hedge-fenced plots. The procedure of consolidation was thus designed to ensure a more technologically efficient farming. This section focuses on the current legal system, ignoring the historical aspects of the legislation.

The objectives of any 'development system' are common: consolidating holdings, improving farm working conditions and productivity and, as already noted, contributing to the land planning of the territory of the *commune* according to the regulation of urban planning schemes. The general principles of the process are set by article 1 section 4 of the *Code Rural*:

> The land development procedures are executed, as a (national) government responsibility, by land development committees, according to the agricultural structural policy, to the forestry policy with regard to the environmental protection. The commissions have to enhance dialogue between all people concerned.

The balance between national government responsibility and local development committees is a typical scheme of modern French agricultural law. In this case, the state government bears almost the whole cost of land development, such as land surveyors' fees. A local land development committee (*commission communale d'aménagement foncier*) is created in each *commune* by the local representative of the central government (*préfet*) when 'he is informed by the local government, owners or farmers, of the necessity of a consolidation of holdings.' The committee is headed by a judge, a member of the local trial court. The members are the mayor, three farmers (either tenants or landlords), three owners (farmers or not), a person 'qualified in environmental problems', two public officers at the local Bureau of the State government for agriculture and one at the 'Tax Agency' (*administration fiscale*). In every *département* another committee (*commission départementale*) is incorporated, with power to review all decisions made by the local committees. Farmers, owners, public officers, mayors and a notary are members of this committee, the President of which is also a magistrate.

The first important advisory decision of the local committee is selecting the appropriate form of land development and drafting the territorial boundaries of the operation. After another advisory decision by the departmental committee, the local representative of the central government orders the procedure to be executed. After this decision is made, owners must avoid any action that could change the land value (C.R. articles 7 and 7–1), and must also inform the local committee of any conveyance of real property.

Selecting the appropriate form of land development can be difficult: French agricultural law provides seven different procedures from which the selection is to be made. Three of these are most important.

First, a consolidation by agreement is available. It is called 'exchanges of rural real estate' (*échanges d'immeubles ruraux*). Bilateral exchanges are voluntary. Multilateral exchanges are not necessarily voluntary. When an owner or a group representing less than a quarter of the land area and less than half of the number of owners objects to the project, arbitration by the departmental committee decides whether the multilateral exchange goes through (C.R. article 38–1). Only a group representing more than a quarter of the ground or half of the number can block the procedure. The costs of these exchanges may be borne by public subsidies.

Second, land redistribution (*réorganisation foncière*) has been framed by the law of December 1985 (Law no. 85–1496 of 31 December 1985, article 2; C.R. articles 9–18). According to article 9 of the *Code Rural*, the purpose of this procedure is 'the structural improvement of agricultural and forestry holdings through exchanges of parcels and reallocation of laying fallow or inadequately cultivated land'. Those mixed goals have probably not been understood, and this 'soft' procedure remains ineffective.

Third, the consolidation of holdings (*remembrement rural*) is the most effective way of land redistribution. Every year, about 300 000 ha are reallocated through this procedure; in total 13 million ha have been involved, out of the 22.6 million ha possible. The general legal aspects of this procedure are not very specific, compared with other similar European systems (Grossman and Brussaard, 1987–8). Many specific details are described in a longer paper (Atias and Linotte, 1980). All the owners are members of a public non-profit entity called *association syndicale*, the purpose of which is the achievement of works such as agricultural roads, destruction of hedges, drainage, etc. called 'connected works' (*travaux connexes*). The expenses are borne by the owners or tenants, whereas costs created by the reallocation itself are supported by the central government. Many people are critical of the impact of these connected works. For many reasons, environmental concerns were not the focus of the designers of the connected works projects who are members of the corps or rural engineers (Prieur, 1984, p. 916). Only in the last 15 years has the protection of the environment become one of the legal objectives of the consolidation.

Now a public inquiry called an 'impact inquiry' is mandatory before every procedure, to assess the consequences of the redistribution of land on the environment. Necessary connected works may be ordered. As European surpluses of agricultural commodities overwhelmed the markets, questions arose about the necessity of decreasing public expenditures for this type of procedure. The importance of increasing off-farm incomes of farmers by enhancing tourist activities seemed to be inconsistent with the destruction of traditional countryside landscapes, meandering creeks and old paths. The redistribution procedures must now accommodate the interests of both rural and agricultural development.

The four other procedures of common management of forest and farmland are generally ineffective.

### 2. Structural administrative control

France does not control agricultural land ownership, except through legal options to purchase given to the tenant and the SAFER. On the other hand, a complicated control of land use has been framed for 30 years. Enlargements (acquisition of any title to adjacent parcels by a farmer, owner, or tenant), break-ups of sustainable economic units, and settlements have to be permitted by a special administrative committee, whatever the farmer's title in land may be. This authorization is a legal condition for validity of any lease on land and is necessary for receipt of benefits from the agricultural social security system or any public subsidy.

Furthermore, any farmer or owner cultivating land in defiance of this law is subject to legal sanctions and fines. His land may be claimed and cultivated by another farmer to be selected by a trial court (C.R. article 188–7). Land sales are not controlled, but the operation of land by the buyer is controlled. For example, as a law professor, I may buy as many acres as I want without authorization, if I let the land to a tenant. If I want to operate a small part of the land that I bought, I need special authorization. If my neighbour's son, recently graduated from an agricultural school, wants to settle on this land, he needs no authorization. If he is already operating a farm and rents the land I bought, he might need authorization for this enlargement.

This kind of farming licence is based on an ideal type of holding that the Agricultural Guidance Act of 1960 defined as 'Family farm holding with personal liability'. Thus, a 'minimum settlement acreage' (*Surface minimale d'installation* or *S.M.I.*) was defined.[10] A national SMI was fixed by a 'National structural committee', members of which were farmers' unions, public officers, mayors and other local representatives, a notary and a lawyer. The President is a member of the *Conseil d'Etat*, the highest French administrative court. National coefficients or formulas are also fixed to adapt this acreage to 'industrial' feed lots. A 'department structural committee' fixes the local SMI. A reform enacted by law 90–85 of 23 January 1990 repealed a 'bracket-rule' and decided that 30% of the national SMI was the lowest local possible SMI and that no highest local SMI could be ordered by law. The national SMI is currently 25 ha. Local adaptations for specific crops are possible. For example, the SMI is 0.5 ha for greenhouse cultivated carnations in Nice and 250 ha for pastures in the Alps.

A local structural scheme (*schéma départemental directeur des struc-*

*tures*) fixes the priorities of agricultural development in a department. Detailed description of the system is beyond the scope of this chapter. A young, graduate, 'non-part-time' farmer may settle without authorization but needs authorization for any enlargement over two, three or four SMI (depending on the local scheme), or when he breaks up an existing holding into parts of less than two SMI.

This complicated system has been simplified by the reform of January 1990. Although strongly supported by the farmers' unions, it has been criticized for its lack of flexibility and, in many departments, its lack of respect for due-process rights. The control of enlargement will not disappear in the next years, insofar as it could support settlement enhancement policy. On the other hand, the concern about family farming will be balanced with the economic necessity of big units of extensively cultivated land.

### 3. Land uses in the relationship between tenant and landowner

The French Landlord and Tenant Act gives the tenant 'freedom of land use' (Chesné, 1985). No express covenant may limit this freedom. Nevertheless, the tenant's interest does not allow any change in the 'farming destination' of the land. Freedom of land use is expressed dramatically in article L. 411–28 of the *Code Rural*: 'The tenant may in widely separated parcels destroy hedges, fill unnecessary ditches and cut trees that create excessive division of land'.

On the other hand, before the law of 1 August 1984, the tenant was not allowed to change the original use of leased land, for example to convert a land devoted to crops to pastureland. However, since 1984, new article L. 411–29 of the *Code Rural* states that the tenant has to give his landlord a notice of projected conversion. If the owner disagrees, the special land-tenure trial court has to find whether the conversion wastes the real estate (*dégradation du fonds*). Even when authorized, the conversion is considered as an ameliorating waste.

A lease may be terminated in case of bad husbandry (article L. 411–53). No covenant can specify farming methods or general good husbandry, which is only a statutory concept. According to the *Code Rural*, the lease may be terminated before the term by a judgement, or not renewed if the landlord gives notice with the mention of alleged waste. The concept of bad husbandry is not equivalent to any injury to the real estate, but rather to any practice likely to reduce the working conditions and the income of farming on the leased land. Many cases have involved this issue (Moreau, 1980). For example, the *Cour de Cassation* ruled that a crop-share lease of a vineyard may be terminated when the farmer uses low-input methods, likely to reduce income from the leased land.[11] No case has determined the inverse question, whether 'productivist' methods may provoke the termination of lease, based on the threat to the environment.

## B. Environmental protection in land-use law

The topic of environmental protection has been a major concern in the past decade. In a recent tirade against farmers, the Minister of Environment accused them of permanent and unconscious wasting of water, air and land. Indignation was the public reaction of the farmers' unions, but off the record all the farmers acknowledged that the time has come for a real enforcement of law (Jégouzo, 1990).

In its first stage, environmental legislation used the binary and simplistic system of prohibition/allowance. Farmers' unions and law-makers struggled against any judicial control and regulation of agricultural nuisances and framed a right to farm statute. Under article 75, of the Agricultural Guidance Act of 1980, an agricultural activity shall not be considered a nuisance if the farming facility was established before the plaintiff bought or rented his house or land (law of 4 July 1980, article 75 codified article L. 122–16 of the *Code de l'Urbanisme*). However, this right to farm statute does not give any right to violate environmental laws or regulations. It simply limits the right of a non-farmer to sue a farmer neighbour for nuisance.

The separation between prohibition and allowance was also designed for specific activities. For example, uses of chemical pesticides and herbicides are regulated (Despax, 1980, p. 255; Prieur, 1984, p. 666), but the use of chemical fertilizers is not. The 'industrial feedlots' (*élevages industriels*), poultry and hog concentrations, are treated as 'classified facilities for the protection of environment' (*installations classées pour la protection de l'environnement*; Hélin, 1983; Lorvellec, 1981). For example, hog confinement facilities for more than 450 animals have to be authorized; facilities with 50–450 animals must be officially declared to the *préfet.* The authorization is given by the *préfet* after public inquiry and an impact survey, an advisory decision of the municipality board and of the Health Department committee (Jégouzo, 1983). The authorization is linked to a 'spreading out plan' for the effluents. An applicant must have legal access to sufficient real estate to spread out the effluents without any waste and excessive concentration of nitrates in the soil and groundwater. In addition, special protection for fresh water and the marine environment fuels other regulations (Le Moal, 1989) of several types of wastes.

This legislation never succeded. Conflicts arose during the last 2 years, with particular violence during the winter of 1989–90 in Britanny, which is now the primary agricultural region and consequently the most environmentally damaged region in France. But in this country, important disputes are not settled by courts. Political instead of judicial settlements transform the role of law into an unenforced statement of intent.

More has been accomplished with more complicated legislative schemes, based on a zoning policy and involving development goals and environmental protection, rather than a simplistic binary system of allowance/prohibition. 'Sensitive zones' regulated by the law of 16 July 1971, environmentally protected zones (ZEP) by the law of 31 December 1976, and more special regulations for national parks or for zones surrounding national parks are steps toward the enhancement of new methods of farming (Jégouzo, 1990). A general principle was set out in the Agricultural Guidance Act of 1980 (Law no. 80–502 of 4 July 1980, article 2–VI; Hélin and Jégouzo, 1980), which stated that the purpose of rural planning and management policy is 'the enhancement of the participation of farmers into the protection of environment'. But generally this law is oriented to pursuit of the traditional productivist policy.

More and more, legislative or regulatory instruments are set aside. Collective contracts (Comolet, 1989), as parts of the general conventions of planning binding on the central government and regions (*Contrats de plan Etat-régions*), provide that about FF1.14 billion or $0.2 billion will be expended in 5 years to fund incentives for rural development of sensitive zones and, particularly for farmers using new methods of cultivation, protecting the environment. The funds will supplement other European subsidies. Another hopeful sign is a new awareness of environmental concerns in the minds of young farmers. The problem is not framing new legislative tools, but encouraging collective and educational efforts to enforce the existing law and to create a new confidence in law in the French mentality.

## Conclusion

French agrarian law appears to be at a turning point and could become more efficient in the next decade. Increasingly local and integrated development policies could enhance contractual schemes of urban, agricultural, recreational, and other land-use planning. The most important loopholes in the existing legislation and regulations concern both soil protection and fertilizer use. Soil as a part of the ecosystem has first to be protected in the next decade, and so the general legal system of land use will probably be bifurcated. Some general laws will protect natural resources or backgrounds such as water, soil and air. Other laws will frame a sophisticated zoning and planning system, with an integrated protection of incomes and of environment. Farmers are called 'gardeners of the natural space'; this work of collective interest has to be supported, either by the consumers of agricultural commodities or by public subsidies.

The battles on the international markets of agricultural commodities threaten this future improvement. International agreements on both environmental and agricultural topics are necessary and perhaps possible.

## Acknowledgements

This chapter owes much to the supportive environment of the Arkansas Law School, where the author was a visiting scholar in 1989–90. The author is grateful to many people, most notably Martha Noble, Don Pedersen, Paul Schwartz and Ray Watson, for their helpful suggestions and corrections.

## Notes

1. The translation of *droit agraire* could be ambiguous. Some books are headed *droit agraire*: Dupeyron, Theron and Barbieri (1988); Megret (1970). The authors' aim is to study agricultural law. More books are headed *droit rural*: Hudault (1987); Lorvellec (1988). The French agricultural law review is also headed *Revue de droit rural* (published by Editions Techniques, Paris; first issue: 1971; ten issues a year). Since the codification in 1955, a large part of agricultural law is settled in the *Code Rural* (in this chapter mentioned as C.R. Thus, 'C.R. article L. 411–1' means 'article L. 411–1 of the *Code Rural*').
2. The French agricultural land surface is 35 million ha; the forest surface is 15 million ha. Three million ha of the 35 are now lying fallow, without any agricultural or urban use. The whole French territory is 55 million ha.
3. A new law was enacted in 1985 (Law no. 85–30, 9 January 1985, hereinafter 'Mountain Act of 1985'); Ourliac, 1985.
4. 'Parity' was set as the general goal of the agricultural policy by article 1 of the Guidance Act of 1960 ('parity of agriculture with the other economic sectors'). One of the most important aspects of this policy was 'the elimination of the causes of disparity affecting the income of farmers and farm labourers (compared) with the income of people working in other sectors of the economy, in order to raise the financial standing and the social status of the farming population to the level that other social and economic categories enjoy'. Under article 2, 'the purpose of the agricultural policy is to settle the income of farmers, farm labourers and farm managers as well as the agricultural capital yield at the same level as the other sectors of the economy'. Articles 3, 6–3°, 6–4° and 6–5° set methods of surveys of those different incomes and yields.
5. In a village of 2000 people in Britanny, the agricultural land's value is about 12 000 FF/ha or \$1000/acre and the 'urban' value is about FF60/m$^2$ or FF600 000/ha or \$50 000/acre.
6. Those non-profit joint-stock corporations (not associations) received subsidies

from the central government. There were 33, but mergers in the late 1980s reduced the number to 27. They have bought 1.5 million ha since 1960 and usually buy 15% of farmland coming on the market.

7. A reform of this procedure was passed by the Law no. 85–1496 of 23 December 1985, codified at C.R. articles 39 to 45. The average acreage of all reallocations of wasteland in France has been for years less than 3000 ha/year. The new European setaside programme and the extension of land laying fallow already indicate the need for updated legislation.
8. Cass. civ. 3° 10 January 1978, D. 1979, I.R. 397, note Chesné and Martine.
9. See in this book the chapter on European Community law (Chapter 1).
10. Law of 5 August 1960, article 7: 'Acreage of a holding operated by two man-work units, with a rational use of capital and technical skills, and providing a regular income for the manual workers, managers, land's and other fixed-asset owners'. Regular income is to be understood under the general goal of income parity.
11. Cass. civ. 3°, 20 May 1985, J.C.P. 1986, ed. not. p. 39, obs. Moreau.

## References


Acts (1990) of the Convention of the French Association du Droit de l'urbanisme, droit et urbanisme en milieu rural (Law and urban planning in rural areas). *Revue de droit rural*, pp. 1–89.

Atias, C. and Linotte, D. (1980) *Le remembrement rural.* Litec, Paris.

Bon, P. (1981) Expropriation en milieu rural et environnement. *Revue juridique de droit de l'environnement*, p. 241.

Chesné, G. (1985) La liberté économique du preneur. *Revue de droit rural* p. 263.

Chesné, G. (1990) La protection des terres contre l'érosion, contribution de droit forestier. (Acts of the International convention on 'Farmland and water protection, toward a right to food self-sufficiency'), Cairo, Egypt. *Bulletin du CEDEJ*, No. 26 (Pub: CEDEJ, 14 Gamayet el Nisr Street, Dokki, Cairo, Egypt; Dif: Lib. le point du jour, 58 rue Gay-Lussac 75005 Paris).

Chesné, G. and Martine, E.N. (1974) L'herbe et la neige. *Dalloz*, Chr., p. 139.

Comolet (1989) L'environnement sous contrat. *Revue Etudes Foncières*, 43, p. 5.

Cotton, G. (1972) Les conventions pluri-annuelles de paturage en montagne. *Revue de droit rural*, p. 425.

Despax, M. (1980) *Droit de l'environnement.* Litec, Paris.

Dupeyron, C., Theron, J.P. and Barbieri, J.J. (1987) *Droit agraire*, Economica, Paris.

Grossman, M.R. with Brussaard, W. (1987–88) The land shuffle: reallocation of agricultural land under the land development law in the Netherlands, *California Western International Law Journal*, 18, 209.

Hélin, J.C. (1983) Elevage industriel et protection du milieu. *Revue de droit rural*, p. 445.

Hélin, J.C. and Jégouzo, Y. (1980) Le volet aménagement rural de la Loi du 4 juillet 1980. *Revue de droit rural*, p. 488.

Hocreitière, P. (1990) La prise en compte de l'agriculture dans les procédures d'urbanisme. *Revue de droit rural,* p. 31.
Hudault, J. (1987) *Droit rural,* Dalloz, Paris.
Jacquot, H. (1990) L'évolution des techniques juridiques de l'urbanisme en milieu rural. *Revue de droit rural,* p. 17.
Jégouzo, Y. (1982) L'expropriation pour grands travaux et l'agriculture. *Revue de droit rural,* p. 354.
Jégouzo, Y. (1983) Protection du milieu, élevage industriel et droit de l'urbanisme. *Revue de droit rural,* p. 438.
Jégouzo, Y. (1990) Les instruments de protection de l'environnement rural: bilan et perspectives. *Revue de droit rural,* p. 77.
Le Moal, R. (1990) La protection des terres agricoles et de l'eau, les utilisations agricole de l'eau. In *Acts of the Cairo convention,* quoted in Chesné (1990).
Lorvellec, L. (1981) Elevages hors-sols et installations classées. *Revue juridique de droit de l'environnement,* p. 56.
Lorvellec, L. (1988) *Droit rural.* Masson, Paris.
Lorvellec, L. (1990a) La prise en compte du développement urbain dans les procédures d'aménagement rural. *Revue de droit rural,* p. 48.
Lorvellec, L. (1990b) Commentaire de la loi du 23 janvier 1990 relative à l'adaptation de l'exploitation agricole à son environnement économique et social (dispositions foncières). *Actualité Legislatives Dalloz,* Cahiers No. 20–1.
Megret, J. (1970) *Droit agraire,* P.U.F., Paris.
Moreau, J.P. (1980) *Les Baux ruraux.* Litec, Paris.
Ourliac, P. (1985) L'agriculture en zone de montagne. *Revue Française de droit administratif,* p. 472.
Prieur, M. (1984) *Droit de l'environnement.* Dalloz, Paris.
Protot, E. (1989) La formation du droit rural depuis la Révolution Française. *Revue de droit rural,* p. 473.

5

# THE LAW OF AGRICULTURAL LAND USE IN THE FEDERAL REPUBLIC OF GERMANY

Wolfgang Winkler

## I. Introduction

The predominant land uses in the Federal Republic of Germany are agriculture and forestry. In 1985 55.2% of the total area of the Federal Republic was devoted to agriculture, and 29.2% of the total area was used for forestry (*Statistisches Jahrbuch*, 1989, p. 74). With the growth and enlargement of developed areas, however, the amount of land devoted to agriculture has decreased. Between 1950 and 1977 more than 600 000 ha of agricultural lands were converted into developed areas (*Bodenschutzkonzeption*, 1985, p. 32). Agriculture and rural areas had been virtually identical until the end of the Second World War. Today rural areas are no longer exclusively characterized by farming but are moulded by manifold uses including housing, transport, recreation, and environmental conservation. Thus the regulation of agricultural land use presents several problems. First, it is necessary to avoid or resolve conflicts between different uses in rural areas. Second, agricultural soil as a production factor for plant and animal production is an object of regulation. A third problem is the maintenance and improvement of agricultural structure. Finally, the relationship between agricultural land use and environmental conservation has become increasingly important.

Until now regulations of the European Community have not been particularly important for agricultural land use. Rather, the main regulation is formed by the legislation of the Federal Republic supplemented by laws of the *Länder* according to the partition of the legislative powers between the Federal Republic and the *Länder*. Meanwhile most of the federal and EC Regulations, sometimes with slight modifications, apply also to the five new

*Länder* of East Germany*. Until now there are only few family farms in East Germany; most of the farms are either co-operative farms, partnerships or companies. A law of the former German Democratic Republic of 29 June 1990, which has remained in force after unification and has been amended by the Federal Act of 3 July 1991, aims at reorganizing the co-operative farms and adjusting farm structure to the new conditions.

The Federal Republic of Germany is composed of sixteen *Länder*; five are situated in the former German Democratic Republic. Legislative, administrative and judicial powers are partitioned between the Federal Republic and the states according to the Constitution. Four types of legislative powers must be distinguished:

**1.** matters of exclusive legislative authority of the Federal Republic (such as defence and few other matters);
**2.** matters subject to concurrent legislative powers of the Federal Republic and of the states. In these cases the states may enact laws as long as the Federal Republic does not use its legislative authority; Federal laws abrogate the analogous laws of the states;
**3.** matters of skeleton legislative powers of the Federal Republic (such as comprehensive land-use planning, law of the preservation of nature and landscape, law relating to water); in these matters the Federal Republic may issue only a framework legislation while the *Länder* are responsible for detailed legislation;
**4.** all matters that are not enumerated by the Constitution are subject to exclusive legislative authority of the *Länder* (such as the law of freshwater fishing).

Indeed the Federal Republic has used its legislative powers in an exhaustive manner; the legislation of the *Länder* is very limited.

On the other hand there are few Federal authorities. In general the Federal laws, too, are implemented by authorities of the states. There are generally four levels of public administration within a state (with the exception of the city states and of the small states):

**1.** government departments and a few other authorities on the level of the state;
**2.** districts (*Regierungsbezirke*);
**3.** counties (*Landkreise*);
**4.** local government.

The counties and the local authorities exercise the right of self-government; in particular, local authorities are responsible for comprehensive

---

*The figures in Chapter 1 refer only to the former territory of the Federal Republic, not including the territory of the former German Democratic Republic on account of the lack of comparability.

land-use planning in municipalities. At the same time, the counties and the local government may be entrusted with the implementation of Federal laws and the laws of the state concerned by commission of the authorities of the state.

## II. Conflicts Between Agricultural and Other Land Uses

The increasing and partly conflicting demands for land use have led to extensive land-use planning. A distinction may be made between the general land-use planning involving the co-ordination and control of demands for land use and special planning activities involving the arrangement of land use under certain points of view such as the improvement of agricultural structure, protection of nature and landscape, transport, water resources, etc.

### A. Agriculture and the law of land-use planning

With respect to comprehensive land-use planning there exists an important distincion between planning above the local level for the entire Federal Republic, for the *Länder* or the regions, and planning on the level of municipalities.

The legal base of the comprehensive land-use planning above the local level (*Raumordnung* and *Landesplanung*) is the Federal Act on Land-use Planning (*Raumordnungsgesetz*) of 8 April 1965, amended by the act of 19 July 1989. This Act is a basic act of the Federal Republic which has been implemented by laws (*Landesplanungsgesetze*) of the *Länder.* The Federal Act on Land-use Planning formulates certain principles that have a binding effect on the authorities of the Federal Republic and planning activities of the *Länder.* Agriculture is affected by several of these principles. The most important is the seventh principle (section 2,1), which contains a guarantee for the maintenance of a rustic agriculture (*bäuerliche Landwirtschaft*) as an efficient segment of the national economy. A rustic agriculture entails agriculture characterized by family farms dependent on the cultivation of soil with limited numbers of livestock. The seventh principle provides that a dependent rustic agriculture relying on the cultivation of the soil shall precede all other forms of farming. Also, the seventh principle restricts the conversion of agricultural land to other non-agricultural land uses. Good agricultural soils shall be preserved to a sufficient extent, and a conversion of agricultural land should give precedence to a use that is compatible with environmental conservation. The sixth principle of the Federal Act on Land-use Planning refers to rural areas. It establishes a policy to provide rural areas with a sufficient population density, an adequate infrastructure, a fitting economic efficiency with sufficient jobs also outside agriculture and forestry. In addition, agriculture is affected by the eighth principle, which is designed to protect, conserve, and develop natural resources and landscape including forestry and to protect soil and water resources. All of the principles of the Act may be completed and enlarged by legislation of the *Länder.*

The most important instrument of general comprehensive land-use planning on the level of a *Land* or on the level of the regions of the *Land* above the local level is the so-called *Landesplanung* (land-use planning of a *Land*). The land-use planning of a *Land* formulates objectives to implement the principles of the Federal Act on Land-use Planning. While the land-use planning of a *Land* comprises the whole area of the *Land,* regional planning limits itself to the various regions of the *Land.* Within the scope of the land-use planning of a *Land,* special interests such as agriculture may be considered. Thus the land-use planning of a *Land* may designate areas that should be used in a special manner because of the functions of the area concerned or preceding uses. This may include agricultural uses. In addition to comprehensive plans that combine various planning activities and measures, it is lawful to draw up plans that concern only particular areas or special uses. All these plans have the same binding effect for the authorities of the *Land* as the comprehensive land-use planning. An example is the so-called *Agrarleitplan* (agricultural land-use plan) in Bavaria, which is elaborated on the level of a district and regulates agricultural land uses.

## B. Agriculture and Federal Building Act

Comprehensive land-use planning in municipalities (*Bauleitplanung*) is based on the Federal Building Act (*Baugesetzbuch*) of 8 December 1986. This Act affects agriculture through the provisions for municipal area planning and procedures concerning permission for building construction.

The *Baugesetzbuch* establishes two types of local plans (*Bauleitpläne*), *Flächennutzungspläne* and *Bebauungspläne.* A *Flächennutzungsplan* (zoning plan) serves as preparatory planning through the designation of different land-uses for the foreseeable future of the entire area of a municipality. Thus, it is a zoning plan designating areas for housing, industrial activities, recreation, agriculture and forestry. As such, a zoning plan does not create obligations for private persons; it only establishes requirements for the municipality itself. This plan is the basis for a second type of municipal plan, the *Bebauungsplan* (alignment plan). A municipality is obliged to draw up alignment plans to conform with its zoning plans. An alignment plan refers only to some parts of the municipality, not to its whole area. It contains provisions for all types of land use, especially for building purposes, that are binding for private persons. The local plans must be adapted to further the aims of planning on the level of the *Land* or the region.

Agriculture and forestry may be affected by local plans in two respects. On the one hand, the principles of the local plans take in consideration the interests of agriculture and forestry. In this respect the Federal Building Act requires that soil must be used in a conserving and careful manner and that agricultural and forest lands may be designated and used for other purposes only to the extent necessary. In the zoning plans, as well as in the alignment plans, plots can be designated for agricultural and forest use. Designation of plots for agriculture or forestry guarantees that certain plots remain reserved for agricultural and forest use and are excluded from non-agricultural development.

On the other hand, the Federal Building Act may affect agriculture by requiring permission for the construction of buildings. The permissibility of building construction depends on whether a plot is situated within an area where an alignment plan is in force, within built-up areas (where there is no alignment plan in force), or within undeveloped areas (*Außenbereich*). Especially relevant for agriculture and forestry is the Federal Building Act prohibition in principle of the construction of buildings in an undeveloped area. However, there are some exemptions from this prohibition, especially for buildings that serve a farm. The regulations concerning the inadmissibility of building construction in the undeveloped area seek to reserve this area for agricultural and forest uses, for the preservation of nature and landscape, and for recreation (Götz, 1978, p. 242).

## C. Agriculture and special planning activities

Agriculture may be affected in a considerable manner by special planning (*Fachplanung*) when agricultural lands are used for special projects or in special preserves. Special projects would include construction of buildings, road construction and other projects proposed by public authorities or private entrepreneurs. Special planning may affect agricultural land in preserves destined to protect nature and landscape or water resources through the imposition of use restrictions. In this respect there is the question of the extent and manner by which farming may be taken in consideration under special plans. The comprehensive land-use planning of the *Land* pursues the aims of facilitating comprehensive plans above the local level and co-ordinating various special plans, although the comprehensive land-use planning of the *Land* may supersede or take priority over special plans. Various procedures and instruments serve to co-ordinate comprehensive land-use planning and special plans. The legislation provides a particular proceeding, the so-called *Raumordnungsverfahren*, to reconcile the different special plans with the principles and objectives of the comprehensive land-use planning of the *Land*. In this manner the principles of the comprehensive land-use planning concerning agriculture may be taken into account as against other non-agricultural special plans. Various laws contain special clauses that interlink the comprehensive land-use planning and special planning. Two types of clauses may be distinguished. First, clauses may limit themselves to the co-ordination of the various procedures by providing participation (information, hearing) to authorities of the comprehensive land-use planning in special projects. Other clauses may provide for co-ordination in a substantive manner by prescribing that the aims and the principles of general land-use planning must be observed. In a more direct manner, agricultural interests may be protected by participation of agricultural authorities in the proceedings concerning certain special projects.

In this way, agricultural interests may be taken in account within the scope of the planning of special projects that tend to impair agricultural land use. For example, if an intended project could be implemented without interference with an agricultural land use or in a manner that would diminish the adverse impact on an agricultural land use, it could lead to an objection to this planning. The deciding authority would need to consider these facts.

## III. Agriculture and the Law of Improving Agricultural Structure

### A. Changes of agricultural structure

Since the Second World War, agricultural structure has changed considerably. The number of farms in West Germany has decreased from about 1 650 000 in 1949 to about 630 000 in 1990. During the same time the amount of farmland has diminished from 13 340 000 ha to 11 790 000 ha. At present only 3.0% of all employed persons work in agriculture, and 3.4% work in agriculture, forestry, and fishery. Characteristic of West Germany is the high percentage of part-time farmers. In 1990 only 57.7% of the farms were cultivated by full-time farmers, while 42.3% of the farms were cultivated by part-time farmers (*Materialband*, 1991, Tables 2, 8, 11).

In East Germany the amount of farmland has diminished from 6 419 000 ha in 1960 to 6 165 000 ha in 1990 (*Materialband*, 1991, Table 169). The number of farms amounted in 1989 to only 8668, among them 4630 co-operative farms cultivating about 87% of the farmland, 580 state farms cultivating about 7% of the farmland and 3558 individual farms and farms owned by churches cultivating about 6% of the farmland. In East

Germany about 10% of all employed persons work in agriculture (*Agrarbericht*, 1991, p. 138–41).

During the last decades the functions of agriculture have also changed. While a priority of agricultural policy after the Second World War was to supply the population with foodstuffs and to increase the productivity of farming, at present the importance of this policy has decreased as a result of the surplus production. As a result of the use of agricultural lands for non-agricultural uses and the increasing importance of the environment, agriculture has gained a particular relevancy for the preservation of the cultivated landscape and recreation areas, the preservation and improvement of natural resources, and the contribution of agriculture to a sufficient population density in rural areas. At the same time the functions of rural areas have changed. Whereas rural areas had been seen as existing for agricultural and forest production and as reserve land for development, at present rural areas have gained a considerable relevancy for recreation, water supply, and other environmental purposes (Maichel, 1982, pp. 6–16).

## B. The common action (*Gemeinschaftsaufgabe*) improvement of agricultural structure and the protection of coasts

The improvement of agricultural structure as a part of federal agricultural policy is implemented on different levels. To co-ordinate development measures of the Federal Republic and the *Länder* in the field of the improvement of agricultural structure, an amendment of the Constitution in 1969 provided for Common Actions (*Gemeinschaftsaufgaben*) between the Federal Republic and the *Länder*. Within the scope of a Common Action, the Federal Republic and the *Länder* co-operate in planning and financing development measures. Thus the Federal Republic may participate in the planning and financing of measures for which the *Länder* as such as competent. The legal basis for the improvement of agricultural structure is the Federal Law on the Common Action Improvement of Agricultural Structure and Protection of Coasts of 3 September 1969, amended by the law of 21 July 1988.

A distinction exists between promotion measures above the level of individual farms (e.g. promotion of land consolidation, etc.) and individual farm development programmes (e.g. promotion of farm investments). For all development measures the regulations of the European Community may partly apply (especially Regulation no. 2328/91). Consequently the European Agricultural Guidance and Guarantee Fund may share in the expenses of certain measures. The financial promotion measures within the scope of the Common Action Improvement of Agricultural Structure are based on a common basic plan, which is made by a Planning Commission composed of representatives of the Federal Republic and the *Länder* for a period of 5 years and which is considered and adapted yearly to further changes. Decisions of the Planning Commission are made by a qualified majority. Sixty percent of the costs of projects submitted by the *Länder* to the Common Action Improvement of Agricultural Structure and Protection of Coasts are supported by the Federal Republic and 40% by the *Land* concerned, while the Federal Republic supports 70% of the costs of measures within the scope of the protection of coasts and setaside, and extensification programmes.

## C. Agricultural structure planning of the *Länder*

Agrarian structure plans made exclusively by the *Länder* have less relevancy than the basic plan within the scope of the Common Action Improvement of Agricultural Structure and Protection of Coasts. Several levels of agricultural structure planning within the *Länder* must be distinguished. First, there are agricultural structure plans on the level of the whole of a *Land.* Next there are agricultural structure plans on the regional level and development proposals for the improvement of structure in agriculture and forestry (*agrarstrukturelle Vorplanungen*) that generally apply to smaller areas. Finally agricultural structure plans may exist at a local level in the form of village development and village renewal plans (Maichel, 1982, pp. 46–94). Agricultural structure planning is defined by the competence of an agricultural authority and by reference to agricultural structure. Among the different agricultural structure plans of the *Länder*, a *Vorplanung* (development proposal for the improvement of structure in agriculture and forestry within a small area) is of particular importance. Actually, two types of agricultural development proposals exist, the one promoted by the Federal Law on the Common Action Improvement of Agricultural Structure and Protection of Coasts and the other implemented pursuant to section 38 of the Federal Land Consolidation Act (see below). An agricultural development proposal according to the Law of Land Consolidation tends to give greater weight to agricultural and farm economic interests within the land consolidation procedure. An agricultural development proposal according to the Law on the Common Action Improvement of Agricultural Structures and Protection of Coasts does not depend on the implementation of a definite project. Rather such a plan covers the areas of several villages. The two types of agricultural development proposals have no binding effect on private persons. They relate only to the administrative authorities within the scope of the *Landesplanung* and of special planning activities.

## D. The Land Consolidation Act

Land consolidation in Germany has a long history. At present the legal basis of land consolidation procedures is the Federal Land Consolidation Act (*Flurbereinigungsgesetz*) of 14 July 1953, amended by a law of 16 March 1976. The land consolidation procedure pursues the objectives of improving the production of agricultural commodities and working conditions in agriculture, promoting soil preservation and improvement (*Landeskultur*), and facilitating regional development (*Landentwicklung*). The term *Landeskultur* encompasses all of the economical and ecological aspects of agricultural and forest areas. The term *Landentwicklung* means the implementation of the aims provided by the comprehensive land-use planning of a *Land* for the area covered by the land consolidation procedure. It is the function of land consolidation to reorganize the area submitted to the land consolidation procedure, to consolidate scattered holdings according to modern farm economical aspects, to construct roads and other common and public constructions, to regulate watercourses, and to execute measures to protect or to improve the soil and the landscape. The Land Consolidation Office has to take into account the comprehensive land-use planning of the land, environmental protection, and other interests.

A distinction exists between the ordinary land consolidation procedure and four special procedures. A land consolidation procedure is ordered by the competent Land Consolidation Administration whenever conditions exist for the implementation of the land consolidation procedure and an objective interest of affected property owners. In Germany the implementation of a land consolidation procedure is not dependent on an affirmative vote of a majority of the property owners. In addition to the Land Consolidation Office, a public corporation composed of the property owners (*Teilnehmergemeinschaft*) takes part in the procedure. This public corporation may charge its members fees for the purposes of the land consolidation procedure. After commencement of the land consolidation procedure, the plots are evaluated. This evaluation serves as the basis for the assignment of new holdings to affected property owners. The evaluation of holdings is followed by a planning procedure relating to roads, other constructions in public or common interest, or watercourses. The plan relating to roads and watercourses (*Wege- und Gewässerplan*) must evaluate the ecological consequences of the implementation of the project and make proposals for ecological improvements (the so-called *landschaftspflegerischer Begleitplan*). The implementation of the plan relating to roads and watercourses (by altering or constructing public roads, regulating watercourses, constructions to preserve, or improve soil and landscape) forms the framework for the consolidation of fragmented holdings. The land consolidation procedure becomes finalized through a land consolidation plan that designates the consolidation measures concerning fragmented holdings. Its legal effect consists in a direct change of title of the holdings. The distribution and the assignment of plots to property owners is based on the principles of equality of value between the old and the new holdings. Pecuniary compensation is granted to a property owner only in exceptional circumstances, and the owner must agree to receive compensation in lieu of land.

In addition to the ordinary land consolidation procedure, the Land Consolidation Act authorizes four other types of procedures: a simplified land consolidation procedure, special land consolidation in connection with the expropriation of agricultural land for certain construction and projects (*Unternehmensflurbereinigung*), an accelerated land consolidation procedure, and a voluntary exchange of agricultural plots. In a simplified land consolidation procedure, there is no obligation to consider the construction of roads or alteration of watercourses. This procedure is available to alleviate the detrimental effects on farmers caused by construction or projects (e.g. roads, watercourses) or to facilitate the implementation of development measures, measures serving the preservation of nature and landscape, etc. Furthermore, the simplified land consolidation procedure is admissible in regions with a predominance of isolated farms or where an ordinary land consolidation procedure has already been executed.

The land consolidation procedure in connection with the expropriation of agricultural land in favour of certain construction and projects may be used if agricultural plots have been expropriated largely as result of particular construction or projects (e.g. the construction of motorways, railways, airports, etc.). The main objective of this procedure is to distribute the loss of agricultural land among several landowners to limit each owner's loss to a small area. At the same time this procedure reduces the detrimental effects of the project on farmers in the area.

In the absence of construction of new roads or alteration of watercourses, an accelerated land consolidation procedure is available. The accelerated procedure provides for more rapid improvement of agricultural production or for facilitating operational procedures of the farms and for incorporating measures for the preservation of nature and landscape. This procedure must be employed if several landowners or a Chamber of Agriculture (a public corporation founded on the compulsory membership of farmers) apply for it. The Land Consolidation Office may use this procedure if the Nature Preservation Administration applies for it and at the same time it serves the interests of the affected landowners.

A voluntary exchange of agricultural holdings of several landowners is possible with the participation of the Land Consolidation Office. A voluntary exchange of plots may serve to improve the structure of the farms or foster measures serving the preservation of nature and landscape.

The Federal Land Consolidation Act also provides for the consideration of ecological interests. Three of the special land consolidation procedures (simplified land consolidation procedure, accelerated land consolidation procedure, and voluntary exchange of plots) may be used as instruments for nature preservation and landscape management. In this case, nature conservation and landscape management serve as the major objective of the procedure.

The Federal Building Act regulates the relationship between measures serving to improve agricultural structure and comprehensive land-use planning at the local level by providing co-ordination between the local planning of the municipalities and land consolidation procedures.

## E. The Act on the Administrative Control of the Transfer of Ownership on Agricultural Holdings

The Act on the Administrative Control of the Transfer of Ownership on Agricultural Holdings (*Grundstückverkehrsgesetz*) of 28 July 1961 provides in principle for prior administrative authorization of the transfer of ownership of agricultural and forest holdings. The Act, literally designated as an act on measures concerning the improvement of agricultural structure and safeguards for agricultural and forest enterprises, pursues objectives to maintain viable farms, to maintain the results of a land consolidation and of other measures relating to the improvement of agricultural structure, and to make possible a sufficient increase of size of viable farms.

Legal transactions concerning agricultural holdings, in which the Federal Republic, a *Land* or a church participates, are not subject to prior administrative authorization; also transactions in the scope of a land consolidation procedure are exempt. Furthermore transactions involving agricultural plots within the field of a local alignment plan are not subject to authorization unless they are designated by the plan as agricultural or forest plots or unless the transaction concerns farm buildings. This fact reveals the priority of local planning over planning concerning the improvement of agricultural structure, because the Federal Act of 28 July 1961 aiming at safeguarding agricultural land use is not applicable in these cases.

In three situations administrative authorization may be refused. Refusal is possible if the transaction would lead to an unwanted distribution of agricultural or forest land, if the size of an agricultural or forest enterprise or plot would be diminished or a farm or plot would be fragmented in an deleterious manner, or if there is a serious disproportion between the price and the value of the holdings. An unwanted distribution of agricultural or forest land involves any transaction incompatible with measures tending to improve agricultural structure. Although it appeared unclear whether a non-farmer could be authorized to acquire agricultural holdings, in 1967 the Federal Constitutional Court decided that authorization might be refused to a non-farmer only if a farmer needed the land to increase the size of his farm and was willing to pay the price stipulated between the owner and the non-farmer (except when the price was raised excessively). Consequently, farmers may take priority over non-farmers. If part-time and full-time farmers compete for the acquisition of agricultural holdings, full-time farmers generally take priority over part-time farmers under the same conditions. A fragmentation of agricultural land occurs whenever a transfer causes a farm to lose its viability, if an agricultural plot would be smaller than 1 ha or a forest plot would be smaller than 3.5 ha, or if the transfer would lead to a new fragmentation of holdings after the implementation of a land consolidation procedure. A serious disproportion between the stipulated price and the value of the land is presumed if the price exceeds the value by more than 50%. The value is calculated using the comparable prices of agricultural plots for agricultural uses in the village. In exceptional circumstances authorization may be granted for the transfer of land to a non-farmer (e.g. transfer of the land for the purpose of extracting soil constituents). If the competent authority denies authorization, it is obliged to report the transfer to the land settlement corporation (*Siedlungsgesellschaft*), which may then exercise a legal right of preemption. The settlement corporations are organized as private companies on the basis of the Land Settlement Act of 11 August 1919, and they are charged with the public function of improving farm structure by acquiring agricultural lands and assigning them to interested farmers.

## F. The Act on the Administrative Control of Leasing Contracts

While the *Grundstückverkehrsgesetz* concerns only the transfer of ownership of agricultural and forest holdings, the so-called *Landpachtverkehrsgesetz* (Act on the Administrative Control of Leasing Contracts) of 8 November 1985 provides for administrative control of the conclusion and modification of leasing contracts relating to agricultural holdings. Leasing contracts relating to forest land are not so regulated. An agricultural landlord is obliged to report the conclusion and each modification of a leasing contract to the competent authority; a tenant may report on the leasing contract. While a transaction relating to the transfer of ownership of agricultural lands is suspended until the grant of authorization, a leasing contract is effective immediately at the moment of its conclusion. However, the competent authority may order the parties to modify or cancel the contract for reasons similar to those for refusal of a transfer according to the Act on the Administrative Control of the Transfer of Ownership on Agricultural Holdings. If the parties do not obey this order, the authority will cancel the contract, which operates prospectively. The administrative control of leasing contracts is not very efficient, because many landlords do not report the contract to the authority on account of the weak sanctions. In contrast with the Act on the Administrative Control of the Transfer of Ownership on Agricultural Holdings, the Act on the Administrative Control of Leasing Contracts provides generally for equal treatment of full-time farmers and part-time farmers with respect to land leases. In this manner the legislature acknowledged the increasing relevancy of the part-time farmers for establishing a viable population density in rural areas.

### G. Farms and succession law

In the Federal Republic of Germany, several Federal laws and laws of some of the *Länder* diverge from the fundamental principle of Civil Law of Succession involving equality of all heirs. This particular legislation authorizes the succession of a farm to a single heir who is then obliged to pay compensation to his co-heirs. The compensation is calculated on the basis of the value of turnover or of the taxable value, not of the commercial value of the farm. Thus the legislature has attempted to ensure the continued viability of farms during succession and to prevent the fragmentation of farms among co-heirs. This legislation concerns structure of ownership rather than agricultural land use. Therefore details of agricultural succession law will not be discussed.

## IV. Agricultural Land Use and Foodstuff Production

### A. Law of cultivation of agricultural holdings and control of conversion of agricultural into non-agricultural land uses

Agricultural land serves as the fundamental production factor for plant and animal foodstuffs with agricultural soil as the base for food supply. Previous scarcities of foodstuffs prompted the legislature to adopt provisions to help guarantee an adequate food supply by obliging farmers to cultivate agricultural land in accordance with good husbandry. If a farmer did not satisfy this legal obligation, the law provided sanctions, such as the compulsory leasing of the land to another person willing to cultivate the land in accordance with good husbandry. The recent surplus of certain agricultural products has obviated the justification for this legal obligation to cultivate agricultural land in accordance with good husbandry. Therefore the German legislature responded in 1961 by abrogating the law relating to the obligation of landowners and tenants to cultivate agricultural land in accordance with good husbandry. Legal obligations to cultivate land exist now only in the law of forestry and in the law of preservation of nature, where ecological interests and not the production of foodstuffs must be considered.

Nor does the German legislation impose an obligation on farmers to apply for approval if they want to convert from an agricultural to a non-agricultural land use. Legal obligations to apply for administrative authorization exist only with respect to the implementation of certain non-agricultural land uses (e.g. authorization referring to afforestation or to construction).

## B. Setaside and extensification programmes

Surplus production of agricultural produce reduces the need for administrative interventions in agricultural land use to foster food production. Further removed from such pro-food interventions are the setaside and extensification programmes of the European Community aimed at helping lower agricultural production to reduce the costs of the Common Agricultural Policy. In 1988 the Community provided a legal basis for setaside and extensification programmes to be implemented by the Member States in EC Regulation no. 1094/88 of 25 April 1988. The setaside and extensification programmes from Community Law are different from certain national measures aimed at taking agricultural land out of production and/or at extensification for purely ecological purposes. The Community measures differ from these ecologically motivated setaside and extensification programmes because their primary objective is market-oriented. The setaside and extensification programmes provided by the Community Law have been incorporated in the Common Action Improvement of Agricultural Structure and Coastal Protection by an amendment of the Act of 21 July 1988 and are consequently implemented within the scope of this procedure. Conditions for applying for a setaside or an extensification measure and the available financial funds of the budget are found in a special basic plan of the Common Action Improvement of the Agricultural Structure and Coastal Protection. The Federal Republic supports 70% of the necessary expenses. Arable land in a setaside programme may have the following uses: permanent fallow, fallow with rotation possibilities, afforestation, grazing for extensive livestock farming, or uses for non-agricultural purposes. Two methods are admissible for extensification: the quantitative decrease of production or the use of extensive production methods. The 'quantitative' method is currently being used only for wine (for other products only within the scope of pilot projects), in which the production must be reduced by at least 20%.

The Federal Republic has also followed community law in establishing a pension programme for the cessation of production. The Federal legislation has implemented EC regulation no. 1096/88 of 25 April 1988, establishing a Community Scheme to encourage the cessation of farming, by adopting the Act Aiming at Encouraging the Cessation of Farming of 21 February 1989. Farmers who are insured under the law of farmer's old age pension are eligible, provided they are at least 55 and have paid contributions to the agricultural pension fund for at least 180 calendar months. German law offers two possibilities, either transfer of the land to another holding or setaside. Setaside may take two forms, either discontinuation of agricultural use or afforestation.

### C. Agricultural land use and tenancy law

A tenancy contract covering agricultural lands is regulated in a special chapter of the Civil Code. There is no statutory minimum lease term. Under certain conditions, a tenancy contract may be extended by the agricultural tribunal up to a maximum term of 18 years (farms) or 12 years (plots). A tenant is legally obliged to cultivate leased land in an ordinary manner, and the right of a tenant to convert an agricultural use or to modify an existing use of land is limited. The conversion of an agricultural use of leased land to non-agricultural uses and the construction of a building need prior approval of the landlord. If tenants want to modify a current agricultural use of leased land (e.g. cessation of livestock farming), they need the prior approval of the landlord only in instances where the change has effect beyond the termination of the tenancy contract. If the landlord declines to approve a request to modify an agricultural use or to erect a building (but not a conversion from an agricultural to non-agricultural use), the tenant may appeal to the agricultural tribunal for approval. The Agricultural Court may give its approval if the requested change is appropriate to ensure or improve the profitability of the farm.

Landlords may pursue ecological aims by imposing limitations on farming for ecological purposes by certain clauses in the tenancy contract. This frequently occurs when a *Land* rents state-owned farms to a farmer (Hötzel, 1986, p. 174).

## V. Agricultural Land Use and Environmental Law

### A. The preservation of nature and landscape

Originally the prevervation of nature was only aimed at protecting certain nature reserves and natural monuments, as well as certain plant and animal species. The modern concept of preservation of nature has expanded considerably and includes the entire country instead of special protected areas. The new concept has led to the development of a particular system of planning aimed at preserving nature and landscape. Modern legislation also provides for the recreational needs of the population by introducing a right for everybody to tread on grounds belonging to a third person. The legal basis is a Federal Basic Act referring to the Protection of Nature of 20 December 1976 amended by an Act of 12 March 1987, which is completed by laws of the *Länder.*

The enlargement of nature protection to the entire Federal Republic of Germany and the increasing designation of reserves have augmented the possibilities for conflicts between farming and nature and preservation of the countryside. Farming plays three different roles in the environment. First, agriculture itself is the victim of environmental pollution (e.g. damages to forests caused by acid rain). Second, certain forms of intensive production (e.g. management of pesticides, use of manure and fertilizers, or livestock confinement systems) may cause considerable environmental damage to water resources, soil, air, animal and plant species. Finally, farming contributes to the shaping and preservation of historic landscapes that have developed over centuries from land cultivation. The functions of agriculture as well as the numerous possibilities for conflicts between farming and the environment have led to several particular provisions relating to agriculture within the scope of the nature preservation legislation. The Federal Law on Nature Preservation formulates the principle that farming satisfying the rules of ordinary cultivation is fundamentally important for preserving the cultivated landscape. This leads to a presumption that such farming conforms with the aims of legislation relating to nature preservation.

Provisions concerning disturbances of natural resources and the landscape may be relevant for farming under the protection afforded the whole area of Germany (outside the reserves). 'Disturbances of nature and landscape' are human activities that cause changes in land use or the shape of plots. Such disturbances – as far as avoidable – must be stopped or their adverse effects must be offset within a prescribed period by measures of nature preservation. If the adverse effects on nature and the landscape cannot be avoided or offset, the disturbance must be prohibited, provided that preservation of nature has priority. These provisions apply only if the intended project needs administrative authorization or is submitted in a report to a public administration. Farming is affected by these provisions of the law of nature preservation only to a limited extent. Production measures, such as the use of manure, fertilizers, or agricultural chemicals that do not lead to changes in land use or the shape of plots, need not be submitted for authorization or in a report. Furthermore, the Federal Act on Nature Preservation provides that land use within the scope of farming, forestry or fishery that is regular according to the Act does not constitute a disturbance of nature or the landscape. When determining whether farming is regular, ecological interests must be considered.

Legal obligations to cultivate land in an ecological manner may also affect farmers. The *Länder* may perform measures aimed at cultivating the land either at public expense or at the expense of the owner. Some laws of the *Länder* require owners or tenants to cultivate their land from an ecological point of view. Whenever an owner or tenant does not satisfy this obligation, the law may provide sanctions, such as compulsory leasing.

The designation of protected areas for nature preservation, safeguarding the countryside, or protecting natural monuments or trees, hedges, etc. may also affect farming. In this connection restrictions or even prohibitions may be imposed on farmers. Various provisions relating to the protection of plant and animal species may also interfere with farming.

Finally, the right of the public to tread on open unused farmland for purposes of recreation affects agriculture. However, the *Länder* may restrain this right for selected reasons, e.g. nature preservation, farming, etc.

## B. Law of Forestry

The legal basis of the Law of Forestry is the Federal Act on Forests of 2 May 1975. It is a basic law completed by laws of the *Länder.* As owners of woodland, many farmers are affected by the provisions of the law of forestry. According to the Federal Act on Forests, the forests have to serve three purposes: wood production, ecology and recreation. The Act has established forest planning. Prior authorization is required for uprooting or conversion of forest into a non-forestry land use. Likewise, the afforestation of plots is submitted to prior approval of the competent authorities. The law of forestry imposes on the owners of forests the obligation to cultivate the woods in accordance with good husbandry. Forests are open to public access for recreation. Forests may be designated as protected forests to prevent ecological damage and pollution, or forests may be designated as forests serving recreation. This designation leads to restrictions on cultivation.

## C. Law relating to water

The legal basis of the law relating to water is the Federal Act on Water Uses of 27 July 1957, amended by the law of 23 September 1986; the Act is completed by laws of the *Länder.* The Federal Act on Water Uses establishes public regulation of water supply and distribution of surface and underground waters. The use of water requires permission or concession from the Water Authority. Only to a limited extent may farmers use surface or underground water for agricultural purposes without permission or authorization.

The designation of protected water areas affects farming significantly. Protected water areas may be designated for purposes of water supply, for accumulation of underground water, to avoid detrimental runoff of precipitation water, or to avoid the dissemination of fertilizers, manure or agricultural chemicals into water. In water reserves certain agricultural activities may be prohibited or severely limited. If orders of a Water Authority establish stricter requirements restraining the ordinary cultivation of agricultural land for farmers in water reserves, as compared with other farmers, the Federal Act on Water Uses grants affected farmers a claim to a compensation payment. This is true even when the restrictions on farming do not represent an expropriation for which the Constitution prescribes the payment of compensation. The payment provided by the Federal Act on Water Uses is intended to compensate farmers for economical disadvantages caused by the restriction of their activities in water reserves.

Acts or facilities that damage surface or underground water result in absolute liability of the responsible person. The Water Law also includes provisions relating to drinking water. In this respect the EC directive of 15 July 1980 limiting the concentration of nitrate and plant protection products in drinking water is relevant for farming.

## D. The law of waste

The Federal Act relating to waste of 27 August 1986 concerns farming in two ways, the spreading of manure and the use of sewage sludge. In principle, wastes may only be deposited in special refuse dumps. The spreading of stable manure, semi-liquid manure, and dung water is exempted from the Act relating to Waste if their use does not exceed the usual extent of manuring. Four *Länder* (North-Rhine Westphalia, Lower Saxony, Schleswig-Holstein, and Bremen) have adopted so-called semi-liquid manure decrees that establish temporal and spatial restrictions on the use of semi-liquid manure and provide a maximum limit per ha for its use. This limit ranges between 2 (Schleswig-Holstein) and 3 (North-Rhine Westphalia) so-called units of manure, a unit of manure being calculated on the basis of the number and species of livestock.

The Waste Law provides for administrative control of the use of sludge and sewage, etc. on arable land. A Federal Regulation provides numerous prohibitions and limitations on sewage sludge manuring of plots (grassland, arable land, horticultural land, forest land). Regulations also govern the concentration of heavy metals in soil and sludge. In addition to the provisions of the Waste Law relating to manuring, the more strict provisions of the Law of Water Uses and the Law of Nature Preservation apply to certain reserves.

### E. The law of fertilizer

While the use of manure and sludge is regulated by the Law of Waste, the use of fertilizers is regulated by the Federal Act relating to Fertilizers of 15 November 1977. This Act regulates not only the putting into commerce of fertilizers, but also their use. A 1989 amendment to the Act provides that fertilizers may be used only according to the rules of good agricultural practice. This means that mineral fertilizing has to consider the kind, quantity and time needs of the plant and the soil, taking into account existing nutritive and organic substances in the soil, the conditions of locations and the crop ratio. The rules of a good agricultural practice may be finalized by a decree of the Federal Ministry of Agriculture. In water and nature reserves, further restrictions concerning the use of fertilizer may be established.

### F. The law of agricultural chemicals used in the production of crops

The new Federal Act relating to Plant Protection Products (*Pflanzenschutzgesetz*) of 15 September 1986 regulates both the introduction into trade and the use of agricultural chemicals used in the production of crops. The Act has increased consideration of ecological objectives by also taking in account the impact of agricultural chemicals on the health of man and animals, the resources of nature, and the avoidance of ecological damages. Such chemicals must be used only according to the rules of good agricultural practice so that the rules of integrated plant protection must be observed. A farmer cannot use agricultural chemicals if their application would be expected to cause damage to the health of man or animal, underground water, or natural resources. In nature reserves and in water reserves, the use of agricultural chemicals may be more restricted.

## VI. Compensation for Interferences with Agricultural Land Use

Disturbances of agricultural land-use have intensified during the last decades, particularly on account of limitations imposed for ecological purposes. These disturbances limit agricultural land-use and may constitute an expropriation for which an indemnity must be paid. The Constitution distinguishes between expropriations that are permitted only if the law provides compensation and general restrictions in conformity with the social function of property (*Sozialbindung*). Restrictions on individual property rights for the benefit of society must be tolerated by property owners without a claim for compensation. Generally, restrictions of agricultural land uses, especially for nature and water preservation, are acts in conformity with the social function of property. These restrictions incorporate the social function of agricultural property, which is dependent upon the situation and kind of agricultural plot. Ordinarily the farmer has to tolerate prohibitions and restrictions of prospective uses without compensation, whereas prohibitions and restrictions of uses already in existence that interfere with the legal position of the farmer may be acts of expropriation. Meanwhile, the Courts have enlarged the field of restrictions on individual property rights for the benefit of the society and have acknowledged that disturbances of existing uses must also be tolerated by the property owner without a claim to compensation if the prohibition or the restriction of a use is predominantly based on interests of environmental protection (Kloepfer, 1989, p. 565). Furthermore, the legislature can provide legal claims for compensation if farmers suffer economic detriments by disturbances of an agricultural land use. Thus, for example, the Federal Act on Water Uses has established a claim for compensation for farmers who suffer economic disadvantages as a result of the designation of a water reserve.

While a claim to an indemnity for expropriation or a claim for compensation payments is based on provisions of the Constitution or special law, the *Länder* may establish financial incentives through subsidies for farming activities that foster ecological demands. Thus, the *Länder* have established several environmental programmes to provide subsidies to farmers.

Moreover, the so-called 'contractual nature preservation' agreements (*Vertragsnaturschutz*) may become more and more relevant. *Vertragsnaturschutz* involves an agreement between the State and a farmer whereby the farmer chooses to cultivate his land for ecological purposes in exchange for a contractual claim to payment of a certain yearly sum as compensation for the restricted use of land.

## Conclusions

The law of agricultural land use is altered considerably by the changing functions of agricultural soil. Due to increasing surplus production, preservation of the agricultural soil as a production factor for foodstuffs has lost much of its relevancy. Consequently, special provisions aiming at maintaining the cultivation of arable lands were abolished in 1961. Replacing this primary function of agricultural soil are ecological and social functions concerning the preservation and safeguarding of nature, environment and resources, recreational needs of the population and the rural landscape. As a result of these developments, government interference has intensified, especially within the scope of the Nature Preservation Law and the Water

Law, where the designation of special reserves has greatly increased limitations on farming activities. Policies for the improvement of agricultural structure pursue the objectives of establishing and maintaining viable farms and establishing economical and social parity between agricultural and other sectors of the national economy and society. Financial measures, such as subsidies, have become increasingly important to implement these objectives. In addition, measures such as the administrative control of the transfer of ownership and the conclusion of tenancy contracts are significant.

Co-ordination between agriculture's need to cultivate the soil and the demands of the public or subgroups of society is also significant. This reveals an increasing interconnection among agriculture and other sectors of society and the economy. The law of general planning of land use contains several provisions to protect agricultural land use, but these provisions are not very efficient given the diminished importance of producing foodstuffs. In the future, ecological demands with respect to farming will become more relevant and will lead to stricter limitations and prohibitions of agricultural activities. It will be necessary to provide payments to farmers to compensate for the diminished income caused by stricter environmental regulations. These payments will be essential for maintaining agriculture's role in producing foodstuffs and other important functions with respect to rural areas and the preservation of the cultivated landscape.

## References

*Agrarbericht 1991 (Bundestags-Drucksache 12/70).* Heger, Bonn.

*Bodenschutzkonzeption der Bundesregierung vom 7.3.1985 (Bundestagsdrucksache 10/2977).* Heger, Bonn.

Götz, V. (1978) *Der Schutz des landwirtschaftlichen Bodens im Agrarrecht.* Deutsche zivil-, kollisions- und wirtschaftsrechtliche Beiträge zum X. Internationalen Kongreß für Rechtsvergleichung in Budapest, pp. 230–250. Mohr, Tübingen.

Götz, V., Kroeschell, K. and Winkler, W. (eds) (1981–82) *Handwörterbuch des Agrarrechts,* Vols 1–2. Erich Schmidt, Berlin.

Hötzel, H.-J. (1986) *Umweltvorschriften für die Landwirtschaft.* Ulmer Stuttgart.

Kloepfer, M. (1989) *Umweltrecht.* Beck, München.

Maichel, G. (1982) *Agrarstrukturelle Planung und räumliche Gesamtplanung.* Heymann, Köln.

*Materialband zum Agrarbericht 1991 der Bundesregierung (Bundestags-Drucksache 12/71).* Hager, Bonn.

Naturlandstiftung Hessen e.V. (ed.) (1987) *Naturschutzprogramme mit der Landwirtschaft.* Bad Nauheim.

*Statistisches Jahrbuch über Ernährung, Landwirtschaft und Forsten 1989.* Landwirtschaftsverlag, Münster-Hiltrup.

# 6

# AGRARIAN LAND LAW IN ITALY

Paola Porru

## I. Introduction

### A. Objectives of the chapter

In Italy the most ancient experience in land planning and management is found in the agricultural domain. Italian legislation, within the period running from the Unity of Italy (1861) to the First World War, yielded several measures aimed at the creation of environmental conditions as necessary elements of agricultural production, development, and improvement (water regulations, hydraulic public works, irrigation, land reclamation, forest and pasture regulations, water and forest works aimed at improving mountainous basins).

An organic legislation is still lacking. Only fragmentary, incomplete laws and laws relating to specific sectors are available, and this makes it very difficult to draw up an overall picture of general principles. Nonetheless, it is useful to examine the most relevant of these laws to understand to what extent public legal interventions can influence agricultural land matters (Perez, 1971; Desideri, 1978; Galloni, 1988).

These laws will be dealt with in the second part of this chapter, following a part devoted to general information about the legal nature of agricultural land, constitutional principles concerned with land ownership, an outline of public authorities operating in agriculture, and a discussion of the influence of the European Economic Community. The second part looks at the administrative structures that govern agricultural territory, such as Regions, *Comunità montane* (public bodies operating in mountainous areas), *Enti di sviluppo* (land development agencies), and then proceeds to a synthetic evaluation of their actions.

Furthermore, in the Italian legal system agricultural land has never had traditional legal relevance as such; in other words, land use for agriculture is not legally protected. This is proven by the fact that in urban environmental plans, which are significant for the identification of the basic instruments of land-use planning, land use for agriculture has always been, and largely still is, a merely residual use: agricultural land is the area that is not – or is not yet – suitable for serving towns. On the agricultural land, which on the maps normally appears as white space, a town can spread itself at will. (In fact, between 1970 and 1982, agricultural land decreased by over 1 500 000 ha.)

In the last few years some draft bills have been presented in Parliament to introduce a new principle in opposition to the residual one. According to this principle, lands for which plans did not provide a different use should be considered agricultural lands and be protected as such. Those draft bills have come to nothing; Italian legislation does not yet seem inclined to give general protection to agricultural land.

If a general law on agricultural land is lacking (or if general principles deriving from various laws are lacking), fragmentary rules of different origin and nature aim to protect the agricultural use of lands, albeit partially, temporarily, and often indirectly. These rules will be examined in part three of this chapter in connection with an outline of town planning legislation and environmental laws. Furthermore, this chapter will analyse the institutions of private agrarian law that affect, in most cases indirectly, agricultural land use.

## B. Legal nature of agricultural lands: public property, private property and the *usi civici* (rights belonging to the inhabitants of a community)

In Italy, ownership is public or private (article 42 of the Constitution). So far as land is concerned, public land belongs to the State, some territorial units (Regions, Provinces, *Comuni**) or public non-territorial agencies (for example, land development agencies; see section IIH). Private land belongs to physical persons and private agencies.

Within public lands, forests have particular relevance from a quality and a quantity point of view. They constitute, according to special laws, the forest heritage (*demanio forestale*), a form of public property of State and Regions. Consequently, such forests are inalienable and are subject to a special obligation of maintaining afforestation (Decreto-legge of 30 December 1923, n. 3267; Regulation of 16 May 1926, n. 1126).

*Uso civico* is a third category of land, which in a sense comes between private and public landownership. This land is characterized by the fact that the community of inhabitants of a *Comune* (not the *Comune* as an institution) enjoys some rights such as pasture, watering livestock, felling

---

*This term includes town, urban and rural districts.

timber for domestic use, sowing and gleaning, using water for irrigation, hunting and fishing, and the right to pick wild fruits. These rights constitute the *usi civici*; they affect either public lands (*terre comunali*, and in such cases are called *demani collettivi*) or private lands. *Usi civici*, whose origin goes back to a very ancient time, were considered perpetual rights, non-prescriptive and inalienable, existing even before the rights of property (public and private).

*Usi civici* are regulated by a law (law of 16 June 1927, n. 1766) which laid down a special procedure for their liquidation. The very complicated procedures in this law encountered much opposition. Consequently, a great many *usi civici* remain until today, and represent the essential bulwark for maintaining agricultural use on lands that constitute a relevant portion of our country. Recent statistics calculate about 5 million ha of a total territory of 30 million ha. Indeed, although this use is linked with an archaic concept of agriculture, it has allowed those lands to maintain until today a greater significance with regard to environmental issues.

## C. Article 44 of the Italian Constitution

The basic principles of agrarian land law are found in article 44 of the Italian Constitution, among the provisions related to property rights in the chapter delineating the rights and duties of Italian citizens.

The main goals of this article consist of securing a rational utilization of the soil and in establishing equitable social relations. To realize these aims, article 44 indicates to the ordinary legislator the following methods:

1. obligations on, and limitations to, private land ownership;
2. limits to its extent, which vary in the different regions of the country and according to diverse agricultural areas;
3. land reclamation;
4. transformation of large estates (*latifondo*);
5. reconstitution of productive units;
6. protection of small- and medium-sized holdings;
7. measures in favour of mountainous areas.

Since 1948 (when the Italian Constitution was enacted), these measures have represented the weft on which were woven legal interventions concerning the use and management of agricultural land. A part of article 44 is now obsolete, because the large estates at present no longer present a problem. Moreover, there are no lands to be reclaimed (on the contrary, in Italy it is now necessary to recreate marshes for environmental purposes).

The modernity of article 44 resides basically in the above-mentioned goals, for agricultural land law especially in the criterion of rationality that applies to the use of the soil. This criterion should encourage the use of soil according to its natural function, and if an area of land is naturally devoted to agriculture, this use should be taken into consideration. Indeed, as stated already, in ordinary legislation the Italian legislature does not emphasize the agricultural use of land.

It is important to point out that, as for land management, the principle of rational utilization of the soil can be adjusted to changing necessities. In the past, rational land use implied the maximum production; today, on the contrary, agricultural land should produce with a particular concern for environmental issues. Laws and regulations for nature conservation and environmental protection must operate according to this aim.

Finally, article 44 of the Italian Constitution concerns not only general principles in regard to agricultural land management and planning (those relevant in this context) but also general principles relating to agrarian contracts, farm business, and to overall agriculture legislation (Carrozza, 1988). In other words, the two main goals of the article (rational utilization of the soil and equitable social relations) should direct the whole agricultural legislative policy.

Although article 44 represents the fundamental provision in the matters dealt with, in this chapter we will refer to many laws already in force before the Republican Constitution enactment, either because they are still enforced (like the civil code of 1942) or because they have a profound effect on the present legal order (like legislation on land reclamation enacted in 1933).

## D. Public authorities operating in agriculture

Article 117 of Italian Constitution attributes to the Region's legislative power over several matters including agriculture, forestry, and town planning. Regions legislate on these matters 'within the limits of the fundamental principles established by the laws of the State' (article 117) and also exercise the related administrative functions (article 118). For this reason, their power is termed 'concurrent' authority (*competenza concorrente*). The power of establishing basic principles (even issuing special laws such as the *legge quadro* or *legge cornice*, i.e. frame laws that state general principles on specific matters) resides in the central State; Regions are entitled to issue detailed laws or some other laws to enforce those principles. Although the Italian Constitution was enacted in 1948, the regional order came into force only in the 1970s. Transfer of power from central authority, in particular from the Minister of Agriculture and Forestry (MAF), to Regions has been effected in two phases: in 1972 through various provisions (the Decreto Presidente della Repubblica (DPR) of 14 January 1972, no. 4, concerning agriculture) and in 1977 (because those provisions appeared not very effective) through enactment of a more organic law (DPR of 24 July 1977, n. 616). Thus, since the 1970s Regions have been entitled to management and planning on agricultural land; conversely, the State establishes general principles.

According to a principle confirmed several times by the Constitutional Court, the State maintains its competence in regulating private-law relations, even those involving subjects listed in article 117 of the Italian Constitution. Thus, the State continues to be empowered to legislate in regard to private property rights on agricultural holdings, to lay down contents, and to prescribe limitations to these rights (and also all the other private institutions: agricultural contracts, farm business, etc.).

In addition, five Italian Regions (Sicily, Sardinia, Valle d'Aosta, Trentino-Alto Adige and Friuli-Venezia Giulia), for reasons of their peculiar history, are provided with wider autonomy in accordance with special statutes adopted by constitutional law (they are called in fact *Regioni a statuto speciale*). These statutes assign exclusive, not merely concurrent, authority to them in some matters, including agriculture.

## E. The influence of the European Community

European Community legislation is discussed elsewhere in the present book (Chapter 1), to which we refer the reader. In the present context, however, its effects on the Italian legal system are discussed briefly.

The socio-structural 1972 directives (ns 159, 160, 161), effected in Italy by the law of 9 May 1975, no. 153, undoubtedly encouraged Italian agriculture to attain maximum levels of productivity. As a consequence, development of agricultural production occurred above all on fertile land in flat areas (causing serious ecological problems) to the detriment of other territories, notably marginal lands.

As far as marginal areas are concerned, those Community provisions aimed at preserving agricultural activities (Directive 75/268 of 28 April 1975, implemented in Italy by law of 10 May 1976, no. 352, and Regulation 85/797 of 12 May 1985) have not been very successful. The system of the grant of compensatory allowances to farmers in those areas is a mere assistance measure and in Italy insufficiently applied because of the administrative inefficiency and scant interest of Regions in undertaking co-financing.

Instruments introduced in the 1980s aimed at stabilization of agricultural surplus production have undoubtedly achieved some results and also in Italy where discrepancy between rich and poor agriculture is increasingly evident.

The effects of Regulation 88/1094 of 25 April 1988 should be stressed. This provides for the withdrawal of arable land from agricultural production areas (setaside) and thus contributes to the preservation of the agricultural use of lands. Areas withdrawn can in fact be used for pasture and special crops (chick-peas, lentils, and vetches) and must be managed to keep them in good agronomic condition and to protect the environment.

In Italy, setaside has been broadly applied, at least proportionally as compared with other member states (Winkler, 1989). Generally, however, it is applied on marginal lands with low productivity. This fact confirms the expectations since the outset about the ineffectiveness of this instrument in reducing production levels.

A great influence on Italian legislative thinking has been the EC system of planning recently adopted in our country. We refer particularly to integrated development programmes, PIM (Regulation 2088/85 of 23 July 1985), and to the reform of structural funds (Regulation 2052/88 of 24 June 1988). The important document issued by the Commission of the European Communities on *The Future of the Rural World* (Com. 88/501 of 28 July 1988) should be mentioned as well.

Leaving out of consideration the concrete consequences produced in Italy by the relative regulations, PIM substantially failed because of the planning inefficiency of many regions.

It is early to judge the effect of the reform of structural funds; their most important result has been in surpassing the traditional system of sectional planning and in imposing a system undoubtedly more rational and effective, the integrated planning system. (An analysis of CAP implementation in Italy has been published in the MAF review, *Agricoltura*, no. 206, April 1990.)

## II. Agricultural Land Planning and Management

### A. The *bonifica integrale* (integral land reclamation)

In Italy the first public interventions concerning agricultural land planning and management occurred, as noted earlier in this chapter, with the post-unity legislation and especially with the land reclamation laws (*legislazione di bonifica*). At the beginning this legislation was conceived only for hydraulic purposes, and only during fascism acquired a much greater and complex relevance.

The royal decree of 13 February 1933, no. 215, introduced the concept of integral land reclamation, which meant an organic complex of interventions, either public (such as hydraulic works, soil systematization, infrastructures) or private (land transformations) (Desideri, 1978). The *bonifica* legislation – some parts of which have been transposed in the Italian Civil Code of 1942 – is still partially in force.

Lands to be reclaimed are classified by the Ministry of Agriculture and

Forestry (MAF) within districts. Each district can be organized in co-operatives on the initiative of landowners. Representation within co-operatives operates on the basis of the multiple vote; votes are not calculated per head but on the extent of landownership. For each reclamation district, the Ministry of Agriculture and Forestry draws up a general plan that the co-operative implements. The plan sets out which works have to be charged to the State account and which ones to the members of co-operatives who are also required to carry out the works.

Co-operatives, moreover, are entitled, if necessary, to set up plans for amalgamation (*ricomposizione fondiaria*), to assemble two or more plots not adjoining but belonging to the same landowner.

It has often been thought that the *bonifica integrale*, which represents the first suitable system of land planning, did not achieve its goals, especially in southern Italy where the need for changes to rural land were more evident. The reasons for this failure basically reside in the law itself, which entrusted private individuals to implement general plans of reclamation. These plans often imposed obligations on, and limitations to, private landownership through expropriations contrary to the owners' own immediate interests.

Legislation on reclamation nowadays has little relevance. In addition to technical and political factors that brought about its failure, ecological reasons now demand the safeguarding of the few marshlands still existing. Moreoever, in general, it is desirable to maintain unchanged those lands that are uncultivated or extensively farmed and whose areas, under the logic of *bonifica* legislation, should have been transformed.

### B. The *riforma fondiaria* (agricultural land reform)

After the Second World War, under pressure from peasants' movements, the laws on agricultural land reform were enacted (Romagnoli, 1978). These laws, enacted in 1950, were created to achieve the basic goals of rational utilization of the soil and equitable social relations, according to the formulation of article 44 of Italian Constitution (see section IC).

They did not involve the entire Italian territory, but only 600 000 ha; in fact they applied only in those areas where the peasants' struggle had been harder and the hunger for land more desperate: i.e. some areas of Calabria (law of 12 May 1950, no. 250, called *legge Sila*), Sicily (regional law Sicilia of 27 December 1950, no. 104), and vast tracts of remaining Italian territory (law of 21 October 1950, n. 841, called *legge stralcio*, because it represented only a part of a general reform).

Special public agencies, called *Enti di riforma fondiaria*, were instituted to draw up and implement agricultural land transformation plans. These plans provided new allocations of land by means of expropriation with compensation for those private lands that were too extended or not properly farmed. The land expropriated was transformed and then granted to those who wished to work it with their own labour jointly with their family, with the object of securing the institution of peasant farm business. The allotments assigned varied in diverse agricultural areas and different parts of the country.

Granting of lands was realised by means of a special contract (*contratto di assegnazione*), which was like a deed of sale with reservation of ownership. The grantees paid the price of land in 30 yearly installments, after which they were fully entitled to the property.

Later, legislation provided the right to become owner of the allocated land in 15 years (law of 30 April 1976, n. 386). Nonetheless, limitations stated by the reform law remained for 30 years; among these limitations was the obligation to become members of co-operatives aimed at transformation and commercialization of agricultural products.

Within the phase of rural land settlement change, the *Enti di riforma* had to provide infrastructure (roads, waterworks, schools, etc.), build agricultural dwellings and transformation plants; and within the phase immediately subsequent they provided the institution of co-operatives.

Agricultural land reform enjoyed a mixture of success and failure. Land reform did not create only efficient farms. In fact, several marginal farms exist, because of either the small size of the granted holding or the lack of effective technical assistance. The phases of land expropriations and allocations having been accomplished in the 1950s, the 30-year limitations on lands and obligations imposed on the grantees are today no longer in force. Consequently these lands can be diverted from agricultural use.

## C. The *intervento straordinario nel mezzogiorno* (extraordinary measures in southern Italy)

The year of agricultural land reform, 1950, saw another important legislative intervention dealing particularly with southern Italy and greatly hastened by the bad economic situation traditionally existing in that area. This law (law of 10 August 1950, n. 646) provided southern Italy with an 'extraordinary' intervention (i.e. in addition to the ordinary law) consisting of special State financial allocations. The law operated until 1986 as basic legislation on which were drawn up subsequent legislative interventions.

Plans set up to operate for several years were provided from the beginning, and later special projects (aimed to attain specific objectives) were settled in sectors related to agriculture. These concerned such public works matters as resettlement of basins and watercourses in mountainous areas; land reclamation; irrigations and land transformation; equipment for agricultural products exploitation. Plan management was entrusted to the

*Cassa per il Mezzogiorno,* a special public body that continued operating until 1986 although, meanwhile, a part of its activities had moved within the jurisdiction of Regions.

Since substantial financial resources were available, this special intervention could have been a basic instrument for achieving organic management of southern territory. Actually, the plans and projects have substantially failed, and the 'extraordinary' intervention can be seen as a complex of fragmentary measures applying within a logic based mainly on a patronage system. This has strongly limited positive effects of some really important works such as the ones concerning irrigation.

In 1986, a new law (law of 1 March 1986, n. 64) regulated these matters by instituting an agency that could replace the *Cassa* (termed *Agenzia per la promozione dello sviluppo del Mezzogiorno*) aimed at promotion and development in southern Italy. Furthermore, the law states that the extraordinary intervention will become part of a 3-year plan, which will be implemented through a 1-year plan. New instruments were established to achieve an effective co-ordination within overall public interventions in southern Italy. It has been established to give more consideration to the role of CIPE (*Comitato Interministeriale della Programmazione Economica*), expressly created for carrying out economic planning.

On the other hand, the new law has greatly emphasized the role of Regions with a particular concern for their initiatives in farm business promotion (Annesi, 1986). In recent years, however, the extraordinary intervention in southern Italy has been mainly aimed at the industrial sector, because those involved in agriculture in southern Italy have been attracted to the European Community policy for less-favoured areas.

### D. Legislation on mountains and the Communità montane (mountain communities)

In Italy, since the early 1950s, special legislation has been concerned with mountainous areas as a whole (i.e. not only concerning specifically individual matters), as marginal areas requiring specific rules. This legislation, because of the peculiar features of mountains, mostly consists of measures for agricultural land management.

The law of 25 July 1952, n. 991, establishes the boundaries of mountain territory within which the Ministry of Agriculture and Forestry implements a programme of measures in favour of public and private subjects. Within the territory, reclamation mountain districts (*comprensori di bonifica*) can be identified, in which measures apply like those provided by reclamation laws (see section IIA).

A later law of 3 December 1971, n. 1102 still represents the basic law in this realm, although some sections have been modified by the law on the reform of local authorities (law of 8 June 1990, n. 142), which provides for identification of homogenous mountain zones within which are created the *Comunità montane* (local agencies directly governed by representatives elected by the Councils of the *Comuni* involved).

One of the basic tasks of *Comunità montana* is to set up and allow the implementation of a development plan; this is an integrated development programme enacted for many years and concerned with all productive sectors and services. As a result of the agricultural function of mountains, in the majority of cases the programme is essentially based on agriculture.

This plan establishes the objectives of economic development and also foresees various land-uses. Due to meagre financial allocations, however, the programmes were rarely put into effect. They cannot represent, as they could have done, a pattern of land planning and management, with particular concern for agricultural land.

## E. The *piani verdi* (green plans)

After the establishment of the European Community, the need to adapt Italian agriculture to a new situation and to promote a rapid modernization of agricultural structures, which at that time were very backward, induced Italy to initiate a system of planning.

Two basic laws, known as the first and second *piano verde* (green plan), were expressly enacted (respectively, law of 2 June 1961, n. 454 and law of 27 October 1966, n. 910). These laws were not real plans but only measures designed for 5 years and concerning only public expenses; they were implemented by MAF, which applied these rules separately from the other sectors of economic policy. This has occurred principally for two reasons: a law that could have provided an overall point of reference was missing, and the basic public authorities for achieving the plans were without real power (Desideri, 1978).

Under this legislation, the MAF should have drawn up plans for homogenous zones (known as *piani zonali*) aimed at identifying the objectives of agricultural development in the territory involved and defining the framework where public interventions and financial aid would be effected, thereby establishing the levels of interdependence and authority.

However, this instrument of land planning was never carried out; neither were the *piani di valorizzazione* that the agricultural development agencies (see section IIH) should have set up in their own territories in accordance with the law.

### F. The national agricultural plan

The 1970s were characterized by the search for instruments to reduce the continuous worsening of the agricultural and food balance in Italy. This phenomenon had been induced by the change of use affecting a relevant portion of agricultural land (i.e. the loss of agricultural land to urban development) and by the exodus of farm workers who abandoned millions of hectares, leaving a significant gap in social life and the economic viability of services in the countryside.

Two remedial laws were enacted. The first, called *quadrifoglio* (four-leaved clover) (law of 27 December 1977, n. 984), was supposed to represent the basis for an overall agricultural and food programme, and contained norms aimed at the co-ordination of public interventions on strategic sectors and on hill and mountain areas as well. The second (law of 4 August 1978, n. 440, on uncultivated lands) was intended to attract people, especially young people, back to the land.

Actually, with some exceptions (e.g. pig-breeding) the *quadrifoglio* did not attain its objectives of development as foreseen within the agricultural and food programme, perhaps because it was fundamentally a law on expenditure and not on planning. Moreover, the second law appeared to be an absolute failure because it was based on too weak assumptions.

It is not surprising, therefore, that in the 1980s the severe problem of surplus production in the EC arose. At the end of 1984, the Minister of Agriculture presented the national agricultural plan (in accordance with the law of 4 June 1984, n. 194), which adopted the new directions of the common agricultural policy: limits on production (milk), threshold guarantees (cereals, tomatoes, vegetable oils), and prohibitions on extending cultivation (vines). This approach, however, means that agricultural production tends to be localized in areas considered more suitable for attaining the objectives expressed in the new directions mentioned above, with severe consequences for hill, mountain, and southern areas.

The national agricultural plan, together with the national forestry plan issued in the same period, are financed by the law of 8 November 1986, n. 757. Although conceived with the purpose of carrying out programmed interventions (like the *piani verdi* in the 1960s and the *quadrifoglio* in the 1970s) this law can be still considered a law on expenditure and not on planning.

### G. Regional legislation

Since the regional order was effected, Italian Regions have been entitled to exercise the majority of the active administrative functions in agriculture and particularly, as noted earlier, those functions relating to agrarian land planning and management. Trend and co-ordination functions reside in the State, as do those of general planning (although often the State trespasses the sphere of regional competence). In effect, State laws relating to agriculture and enacted after the establishment of the Regions contain trends, co-ordinate interventions, and foresee expenses to be carried out by Regions in their own territory.

An overall evaluation of the way Regions have faced the problem of public intervention in agriculture and particularly of land planning and management would indicate that agriculture, at least in general, has not been considered an isolated sector, but in relation to a whole composed also of the other productive sectors and services. This means that Regions act in the perspective of integrated and global planning.

The instrument for this kind of planning is the district plan (*piano comprensoriale*), which concerns a territory of smaller size than the Regions and particularly suitable to achieve planning objectives. The district plan will normally be prepared by local authorities, to which the Regions delegate power to carry out and manage the plan.

Furthermore, some Regions provide the agricultural zone plan (*piano zonale agricolo*) as a facet of the *piano comprensoriale.* This agricultural zone plan is set up by agricultural unions and is supposed to provide the detailed basis for the development of the areas involved.

It is clear that regional statutes foresee a wide participation of public authorities and individuals in land planning and management policy. *Piano comprensoriale* and *piano zonale* theoretically represent the basic instruments of overall planning and management of rural territory. But, from an analysis of general principles (especially from regional statutes) and regional laws and acts, it is clear that only rarely have Regions created effective instruments of land planning. In fact, they have reproposed the pattern of diffuse financial intervention (so-called *intervento a pioggia*) on territory that was formerly covered by State legislation.

A few other reasons explain the failure of the regional planning policy: the concept of district is not very clear, and no state law regulates district authority (i.e. the authority concerned with the plan's design and management). Italian culture about planning is not yet in line with such a matter.

### H. *Enti di sviluppo* (agricultural development agencies)

Agricultural development agencies, which in Italian doctrine are classified as public law agencies without economic purposes but just furnishing services, were created in the 1960s when agricultural planning was clearly needed (see section IIE). Consequently public intervention in agriculture changed its orientation from an intervention basically conceived to attain landownership towards an intervention aimed at development. Thus, agricultural development agencies represent the instrument for achieving agricultural development policy by means of zone programmes and land resettlement (Serrani, 1978).

This purpose has been pursued by law since the first *piano verde* (law of 2 June 1961, n. 454) and the Decree of the President of the Italian Republic (DPR) of 23 June 1962, n. 948, which gradually established agricultural development agencies over almost the whole Italian territory. (On lands devoted to agricultural reform, they were created by transforming pre-existent reform agencies; on the other lands, they were instituted *ex novo*). They are required by law to carry out a number of measures such as reclamation, infrastructure, amalgamation and land resettlement, promotion of family farm business and co-operatives, technical assistance, and economic and agrarian improvement of lands.

As a consequence of regional system establishment, the law of 30 April 1976, n. 386 (which today, with various regional laws, represents the fundamental *legge quadro* (i.e. a law stating general principles) on land development agencies) provided for 'regionalization'. In this way, agricultural development agencies have become the technical and executive instruments through which Regions achieve their own agricultural policy and particularly their own choices for agrarian land planning and management.

Agricultural development agencies, however, can rarely succeed in practice in accomplishing their function of an instrument of regional agricultural planning because of the numerous tasks that they are required to carry out without any co-ordination.

Often (especially in some regional provisions and bills issued recently) a tendency has emerged to characterize the role of these agencies as strictly connected with land matters. In other words, their aim would be to achieve land transformation and amalgamation, purchase (or expropriation) and sale of lands in favour of those whom the law wishes to benefit; they would be intended to exercise all those functions at present carried out by the *Cassa per la formazione della proprietà contadina*, the public body responsible for the formation of peasant landownership (see section IIIC).

### I. *Agriturismo* (rural tourism)

The law of 5 December 1985, n. 730, regulating *agriturismo* (rural tourism), states that Regions, in harmony with directions of national and regional programmes and with territorial planning, have to draw up the *programma agrituristico e di rivitalizzazione* (rural tourism and development programme) in rural areas. It is a sectional programme because it affects only one sector and deals with a specific agricultural activity. *Agriturismo*, in fact, is considered by law as an agricultural activity (or more precisely as 'connected' to the main agricultural activity ex article 2135 of

Italian Civil Code); it results from combining recreational and agricultural uses of the countryside in some specific areas.

Such a programme establishes objectives of development to be attained in this sector, and determines which zones are of outstanding interest and suitable for exercising *agriturismo.* Within these zones, the *Comuni* together provide an integrated plan of extraordinary measures within which they show in detail everything that is essential in carrying out *agriturismo.*

The plan is approved by Regions, which also determine financial allocations, including those for individual farmers to promote their initiatives in this sector.

## III. Agricultural Land Use Protection

### A. Town planning legislation

It is now necessary to examine whether, and how, agricultural use of territory is taken into account by the legal system. First of all, town planning legislation is relevant because it regulates and determines the various land uses. As already noted, in Italian town planning (and even legislative) culture, agriculture is a purely residual use.

In town planning legislation from 1942 (law of 17 August 1942, n. 1150), agricultural use was not even provided. The fundamental instrument of planning, the *piano regolatore generale* set up by the *Comune,* concerned only the built-up areas. Also provided by this law were the *piani territoriali di coordinamento,* i.e. supra communal plans binding *Comuni.* These dealt with either built-up areas or uninhabited territory and could establish special uses in the territory itself. Such plans were rarely applied, due to the lack of sensitivity of administrative bodies towards planning.

Furthermore, in rural areas building was freely permitted (either for agricultural or non-agricultural purposes) and for this general reason a special licence (*licenza edilizia*) for building activities was not required.

Much later, legislation established a compulsory licence for any type of building (law of 6 August 1967, n. 765), and this extended the general *piano regolatore* (regulatory plan) to encompass all municipal territory (law of 19 November 1969, n. 1187, which modified article 7 of town planning law). Municipal territory is divided into zones (and therefore rural areas must also be indicated). Such a plan is required to determine what limitations and features should be followed within each zone.

From national legislative formulation, however, and even more from the enactment of plans, agricultural use of territory remains residual; rural zones are areas whose development comes after satisfying needs of expansion of built-up areas, of industrial settlements and road infrastructures. As a consequence, especially the most productive areas have been diverted from agricultural use.

The establishment of the powers of Regions (1970), which are assigned competence in town planning (in addition to agriculture and forestry and many other subjects listed in article 117 of the Italian Constitution), provoked a reversal of this tendency: in fact, within regional legislation agricultural land protection has been introduced.

This protection has two different aspects. On one hand, Regions aim to safeguard agricultural areas from building interventions unrelated to agriculture, particularly by drastically forbidding housing in forestry areas. On the other hand, Regions tend to avoid the discretionary power of the *Comuni* required to draw up urban plans, by establishing precise rules suitable for stopping and increasing expansion (urban sprawl made through *piani regolatori*) of the town into the countryside. For example, article 15 of the law Piemonte of 20 May 1980, n. 50, states that the *piano regolatore* can 'only exceptionally' convert soils devoted to specialized cultivations, irrigated or high productivity cultivations into non-agricultural uses.

Within regional legislation, this principle, unlike the residual one predominant until that time, means that the agricultural function of territory now finds positive juridical relevance within the legal system.

## B. Environmental legislation

Environmental legislation does not concern agricultural land use as such. Nonetheless it is necessary to deal with this matter because through environmental preservation it is possible to ensure agricultural land use. Furthermore, the most significant legal provisions on the environment directly affect agriculture and agricultural land use because they attempt to improve natural resources. It is therefore useful to examine environmental legislation through its more significant phases.

The starting point is the law of 1939 (law of 29 June 1939, n. 1497) on the protection of natural beauty and amenities, which until 1985 has been considered the only general instrument on land preservation. This law, which reflected the culture of that time, was founded on a purely aesthetic logic: territory was protected only exceptionally when it was possible, through special procedures, to ascertain the character of 'natural beauty' in each individual resource. Consequently, a specific obligation of non-building (i.e. *vincolo paesaggistico*) was imposed on each beauty-spot.

Agricultural land might then be taken into account if it could be included within the classification of 'natural beauty' considered picturesque in accordance with article 1 of the law of 1939. For such beauty-spots, public administration was given the power to draw up a *piano territoriale paesistico* (territorial landscape plan) to prevent the territory involved from being used in a way prejudicial to landscape maintenance. Such plans have rarely been applied, as the unfortunate damage to the Italian landscapes shows.

Only in 1985, when the so-called *legge Galasso* (law of 8 August 1985, n. 431) was enacted, was a provision available that considered environmental protection of territories in a modern framework (not merely aesthetic and focusing on the outstanding value of each individual natural resource).

According to this law, through *ex lege* application of the obligation of non-building (*vincolo paesaggistico*), large areas of land normally devoted to agricultural and forestry use (article 1) are also automatically protected. On these natural beauty-spots restriction of building is absolute, but temporary: it lasts until Regions draw up the *piani paesistici* (landscape plans) which, compared with the ones laid down in the law of 1939, have broader contents because they contain general directions of land settlement and use. Consequently, for the territories affected by the *vincolo paesaggistico* provided by the 1985 law, such plans are the fundamental instrument of general land planning and management as well as agricultural land use. Indeed, in light of the new overall concept of landscape and environment, some Regions applied the *piano paesistico* over the whole regional territory.

In 1989, after a debate that lasted for many years, a law on soil conservation and water improvement was enacted (law of 18 May 1989, n. 183) which, among other things, aims at re-organizing a set of instruments on the protection of soil and waters (until now regulated by fragmentary and disorganized legislation).

The law provides planning activities and programmes and a bundle of rules to be effective within catchment basins through the instrument of basin plans (*piani di bacino*), which are territorial, and sectional plans. Some of these rules affect agriculture indirectly (watercourses regulation, defending land from flooding, erosion and landslides prevention, improvement and rational use of waters, settlement of hydrogeologic obligations). Others directly affect agricultural aspects of territory, such as water and forest projects and works concerning agricultural land, forest and pasture measures, provisions on afforestation and reclamation, on water purification from agricultural pollution, and on rational utilization of manures and pesticides in agriculture (article 3). Furthermore, the law expressly establishes that basin plans ought to provide utilization programmes for agricultural and forest resources (article 17).

It is impossible to give an adequate appraisal of this law enacted such a short time ago, but it seems to be a law competent to face an environment by now seriously damaged and compromised.

Even within legislation on protected areas (natural parks) provisions on agricultural land protection exist. At the State level, in 1991 after 30 years of bills and discussions, the *legge quadro* on protected areas (law of 6 December 1991, no. 394) has been issued. This law, for the first time, states general principles on this specific matter and institutes a few new national parks, which join those already in existence.

Furthermore this law provides a park plan of a territorial nature to determine the use (also agricultural) of each area and a development programme on compatible economic activities, within which agricultural and forest activities would assume a more relevant role.

Also, within the limits of their powers, Regions have created various protected regional areas with the instruments of land planning and development programmes. These contain approximately the same rules provided by the bills mentioned above.

## C. Private law regulation

Private law instruments that directly or indirectly ensure the stability of agricultural use of lands will now be examined.

### 1. Legal obligation to farm

The direct instrument is provided by the legal obligation of farming use affecting land reform areas and, in some instances, lands acquired through public allocations granted for the creation and development of peasant landownership.

In the first case, this obligation, like the other limitations affecting areas of land reform for 30 years, is no longer in force because the last land allocations were accomplished more than 30 years ago (see section IIB). Consequently, there are no limitations on lands that can be diverted from agricultural use.

In the second case, the obligation of agricultural use remains. Italian legislation (decreto-legge of 24 February 1948, n. 114; decreto-legge of 5 March 1948, n. 121; law of 26 May 1965, n. 590; law of 14 August 1971, n. 817) states that manual workers, when they purchase an agricultural holding, are entitled to enjoy special credit facilities and fiscal benefits. The farmers involved are required not to own other holdings for fear that they might exhaust their own and their family's working capacity; in this case the land purchase must be accomplished only through a special public body (*Cassa per la formazione della proprietà contadina*) or through special agencies such as *Enti di sviluppo* (see section IIH). Even though laws are not very clear, the agricultural land use obligation exists *ex lege*; such an obligation, however, can be established in the purchase contract.

### 2. Protection of agrarian land use

Other private law instruments indirectly protect agrarian land use. Their immediate objective is to increase and rationalize agricultural activities on a holding; as a result they contribute to the stability of agricultural land use on the holdings involved.

Among these instruments is the obligation of indivisibility (*vincolo di indivisibilità*) of lands. The Italian Civil Code establishes this obligation as a general and permanent principle: no land can be parcelled out under a minimum size, called *minima unità colturale* (article 846). This provision, however, could never apply because legislation did not provide procedures for determining such a minimum unit.

Conversely the *vincolo di indivisibilità* set up for 30 years has been applied within land reform areas and still applies within lands purchased through funds assigned in favour of peasant land-ownership (law of 14 August 1971, n. 817, article 11). It applies now, in a general and permanent way, only within the province of Bolzano (Alto Adige), to the very ancient institution called *maso chiuso*, which presents a form of rural family householding of German origin.

Furthermore, in 1975, with family law reform, the family farm business institution (*impresa familiare*) was introduced in the Italian Civil Code. The provision regulating this institution (article 230 bis) provides a legal principle according to which undesirable subdivision of farms can be avoided. In case of distribution of the estate or of parcelling out of the farm (and therefore of the agricultural holding as well), members of the family working in the farm business are entitled to the right of pre-emption, i.e. they are entitled to purchase the farm.

With the object of implementing the principle set out in article 44 of the Constitution ('the law ... assists small and medium-sized holdings') various laws enacted since 1948 (law of 5 March 1948, n. 121) state that manual workers who purchase an agricultural holding are entitled to enjoy special credit facilities and fiscal benefits.

The agricultural land to be acquired must be suitable for an efficient holding. The farmer involved is not allowed to hold other holdings for fear that they might overstretch his own and his family's working capacity. The farmer and his family must be able to provide at least one-third of the labour necessary for working their landholdings; long-term loans (30 years) with very low rates of interest are made available.

The *Cassa per la formazione della proprietà contadina* instituted within the *Ministero dell'Agricoltura e Foreste* and the *Enti di sviluppo* provide these loans, arrange the sales to farm workers who fulfil the conditions required by law, stock the new holdings, and provide them with technical assistance.

In Italy most sales of agricultural holdings enjoy benefits provided by laws expressly aimed at the creation and development of peasant landownership.

## 3. Land resettlement

Besides the *vincolo di indivisibilità* (obligation of indivisibility), which aims to prevent the case of *minifondo* (i.e. a very small holding under the minimum size stated by law), remedial measures also exist. Among these is land amalgamation, regulated by the Italian Civil Code (article 849, etc.) and aimed at re-assembling in one single ownership (even through compulsory conveyance) holdings owned by few farmers that are too small individually to farm conveniently.

But for exceptional cases, this instrument has not been applied in practice because of complex procedures and small-holders' hostility. Conversely another measure is normally applied when an agricultural holding is put up for sale: if there is a neighbour owner-occupier, he is entitled to the right of pre-emption, i.e. the right to be preferred in the purchase on the same terms as a third party (law of 14 August 1971 n. 817 article 7).

The right of pre-emption has contributed, even though indirectly, to ensure maintenance of agricultural use of land. The same result is achieved by the other type of agrarian pre-emption, which does not aim to increase land units but to unify land ownership and farm business in the hands of one single individual who is an actual farmer: i.e. the pre-emption right of tenant-farmers and share-croppers (*mezzadria* and *colonia parziaria*), when the holding they are farming is put on sale (law of 26 May 1965, n. 590 article 8).

With some exceptions at the local level (e.g. in Friuli-Venezia Giulia), the broader design of land resettlement, conceived within Italian legislation when land development agencies were given the powers to operate in this matter (DPR of 23 June 1962, n. 948), appears to be a failure.

## 4. Agricultural contracts

Until the 1950s, agricultural contracts were common and of various natures. They were regulated by custom, which usually protected the interests of the stronger party, i.e. the owner.

During the last 130 years the most common forms of agricultural contracts were regulated by the civil codes of 1865 and 1942. These contracts – i.e. tenancy and share-cropping (*mezzadria* and *colonia parziaria*) – were all considered as contracts of lease on the basis of the French pattern, by the 1865 code. Only in the early 1930s, during the period of fascism, did *mezzadria* and *colonia parziaria* become autonomous from tenancy, and a category of agricultural contracts based on a form of partnership between landowners granting land and farmers was created. This category differs from tenancy because the latter is not based on a partnership but on an exchange of service, while the former was regulated by the civil code of 1942.

*Mezzadria* involves the farming of an agricultural holding provided with a farm house. This form of land tenure was widely used in the well-populated countryside. It is based on a partnership between a landowner granting to the *mezzadro* and his family the enjoyment of the landowner's own holding provided with fixed equipment and often with livestock. Both parties aim to share the profits and produce of the holding and they, in accordance with the Civil Code, have to share these equally. The *mezzadro* and family use their own labour, and they must reside in the house on the farm. Furthermore, the Civil Code imposes the obligation on the *mezzadro* to farm the holding in a proper manner and to maintain an efficient standard of production, at the same time keeping the holding in a condition that will enable similar standards to be maintained in the future. As regards the management of the farm business within *mezzadria*, both partners are supposed to be farmers and consequently to operate in common. However, the real head of the farm business is the grantor-landowner who is given a greater power in making decisions, contracting debts, etc.

*Colonia parziaria* is also a form of land tenure based on produce and profit-sharing and is generally very similar to *mezzadria*. However, a few differences between the two contracts exist. First, in the *colonia parziaria*, the relationship can be created between a landowner and one farmer or more, not necessarily involving the whole family as under *mezzadria*. Furthermore, the landowner grants only land and not the equipped holding; in fact, this form of land tenure used to apply especially in depopulated country. *Colonia parziaria* is aimed at sharing produce and profits between the parties, but this matter is regulated by covenants and custom, and not by the Civil Code as under *mezzadria*. Finally, decisions are made by the landlord; thus there appears to be a much stronger dependence of the tenant-*colono*.

Today *mezzadria* and *colonia parziaria* are considerably undermined. According to current opinion, this is due to the feudal connotation of these contracts, relying essentially on the exploitation of farmers' labour. In fact, throughout the history of these forms of tenure, the worker has been considered the weaker party of the relationship, and the Civil Code of 1942 confirms this statement.

Subsequently, specific agrarian laws – and especially the law of 15 September 1964, n. 756 and article 8 of the law of 26 May 1965, n. 590 – provided measures in favour of the workers (for example, by increasing their share of the association's profits, by granting them wider autonomy in carrying on improvements on the agricultural holding, by giving them the possibility of enjoying a special right of pre-emption in case of sale of the farm).

These laws, at the same time, prohibited the creation of new contracts of *mezzadria* and *colonia parziaria*, establishing that agricultural contracts regulated by custom should have been included among the contracts already governed by law; in fact, statutes provide a better guarantee than custom for the weaker party.

The last phase in the process of reform of agricultural contracts is expressed in the law of 3 May 1982, n. 203, which converted all the agricultural contracts other than tenancy into one single type, i.e. the agricultural tenancy. Consequently, today it is possible to draw up only agricultural tenancies; if another contract is created it will be converted into a tenancy.

Legislation on agricultural contracts contains strong restrictions and limitations on private property to protect the position of tenant-farmers within land tenure. In particular, since the post-war period, provisions on the duration of tenure have extended agricultural contracts with tenant-farmers often and repeatedly. The basic reform law of 1982 established terms for contract expiration and, in general, set a minimum duration of 15 years for new agricultural leases. In addition, other provisions regulate rent, which is anchored to objective and equitable parameters (*equo canone*), and improvements, allowing the tenant to invest profitably in agricultural land.

It is clear that post-war provisions, especially those on contractual duration, have ensured that farmers and their families remain on land. These provisions have helped, albeit not decisively, to maintain the agricultural use of holdings that are objects of agricultural contracts.

## Conclusions

Italy lacks overall legislation to protect and preserve agrarian land. This deficit has induced a very big change of use from agriculture to some other extra-agricultural uses, which especially involved the most fertile lands and, very often, lands of particular environmental relevance. Moreover, Italian legislation on agricultural land planning is fragmentary and disorganized, due to the great number of agencies and public bodies empowered to carry out planning. Even though the powers of these agencies and bodies are theoretically different, in practice they intersect and are superimposed upon one another. Overall guidance and co-ordination is required especially at regional level, in accordance with the specific role assigned to Regions by the Constitution.

Italian experience on agricultural development programmes has substantially failed. Two kinds of fundamental reasons explain this failure: the assistance approach and the sectional method. In fact, agriculture has been traditionally conceived as a sector closed in itself where financing interventions have been aimed above all at obtaining social consent. Conversely, it is required that planning be tightly linked to selection of objectives and to an idea of integrated development (essential elements appearing only very recently as effects of methodological choices of the European Community).

Legal measures in areas of special environmental interest can be considered a new type of instrument of land planning and management; these areas obviously serve as a pattern for agricultural development as well.

The democratic principle of participation of local authorities and groups in choices of land planning and management presents in itself a basic reason for the effectiveness of these choices. If, in Italy, planning application has been a failure, it is also because the parties involved are insufficiently planning-minded. Effectiveness of land planning and management, including that of agricultural land, cannot be achieved by limiting participation, but rather by rendering it more secure and stronger.

## References


Annesi, M. (1986) Il nuovo intervento straordinario nel Mezzogiorno. In: *Rivista trimestrale di diritto pubblico.* Giuffrè, Milano, p. 981.

Carrozza, A. (1988) *Lezionidi diritto agrario. Elementi di teoria generale.* Giuffré, Milano.

Desideri, C. (1978) La programmazione in agricoltura. In: Irti, N. (ed.) *Diritto agrario italiano.* UTET, Torino, pp. 435–87.

Galloni, G. (1988) *Istituzioni di diritto agrario e legislazione rurale,* 2nd edn. Edagricole, Bologna, pp. 260–73.

Morbidelli, G. (1983) Edilizia rurale. In: Carrozza, A. (ed.) *Dizionario del diritto agrario.* Giuffrè, Milano, p. 337.

Perez, R. (1971) *Aspetti giuridici della pianificazione in agricoltura.* Giuffré, Milano.

Porru, P.M. (1987) Diritto al paesaggio: Considerazioni sulla disciplina vigente. In: *Atti del XVII Incontro C.E.S.E.T., Firenze, 3–4 April 1987.*

Romagnoli, E. (1978) Riforma fondiaria e riforma agraria. In: Irti, N. (ed.) *Diritto agrario italiano,* UTET, Torino, pp. 557–69.

Serrani, D. (1978) L'amministrazione pubblica dell'agricoltura: organi e strutture. In: Irti, N. (ed.) *Diritto agrario italiano,* UTET, Torino. p. 511.

Winkler, W. (1989) Le gel des terres dans les Communautés Européennes. In: *Reports of the XVth European Agricultural Law Congress, Ghent. Belgium, 2–4 October 1989,* Vol II, p. 689.

# 7

# AGRARIAN LAND LAW IN THE NETHERLANDS

Wim Brussaard

## I. Introduction

### A. Agrarian land in the Netherlands

The Netherlands is a small and densely populated country. In an area of a little more than 4 million ha live 15 million inhabitants. Half of the total area of the Netherlands is cultivated land (1.1 million ha are used for grassland, 0.8 million ha for arable farming, and 0.1 million ha for horticulture). Although farmers make up less than 6% of the Dutch working population, agriculture contributes approximately 25% to the annual exports and so considerably to the Dutch economy. The Netherlands has an intensive agricultural industry that produces for consumption at home and abroad. As a result the Dutch have to share their country with some 14 million pigs, 4.7 million cattle, and 93 million chickens. This gives rise to a serious environmental problem (see section IVC).

As a result of Holland's high population density the Dutch countryside is the site of intense competition between conflicting interests, such as urbanization and industrialization, infrastructure developments, outdoor recreation, nature conservation and – of course – agriculture. During the 1970s the annual loss of farmland to other purposes was about 10000 ha; during more recent years, about 5000 ha. So the Dutch have to be careful with their land. They have adopted stringent measures to control the allocation of land for different purposes in a system of physical planning (see section II).

### B. Administrative context

In the administrative organization of the Netherlands there are three levels of government: central government, twelve provinces and some 700 municipalities. Each level has its own specific, politically constituted bodies: the State General (Parliament) and Government; Provincial Council and Provincial Executive; and Municipal Council and Municipal Executive.

The relations between these three levels of administration are determined by the decentralized unitary state – decentralized because the different territorial parts of the state (provinces and municipalities) have independent legislative and administrative powers, while the unity of the state is maintained by supervision of higher authorities over the exercise of these powers. In principle, each level of administration is free to conduct a policy of its own and to promulgate its own regulations, provided that it does not come into conflict with the policy or regulations of a higher authority. In case of conflict, central government has powers to undo the decisions of the lower authorities.

On the national level the government and parliament exercise legislative power jointly, but the government can regulate in many areas by decree (called *Algemene maatregel van bestuur*), when such regulation is authorized by statute.

## C. Land-use policy

To realize land-use policies the government (national and provincial, as well as municipal) can try to influence land owners and users, for instance by land-use plans (see section IIA2) or by offering management agreements (see section IIIB). In some situations the goals of government policy can only be achieved when the government has control of the land, to make sure that public works are realized or that the present situation is maintained. First of all this can be done by buying the necessary land. In rural areas the purchase of agricultural land for non-urban purposes is a task of the Bureau for Agricultural Land Management (*Bureau beheer landbouwgronden*). The Bureau has the status of a juridical person. It is in charge of the acquisition, temporary management, and transfer of real property as required to carry out specific laws or regulations, such as in land development areas and reserve areas (see sections IIIA and B).

If the government cannot obtain the necessary land in an amicable way, in certain situations it has the right of compulsory purchase. The largest percentage of all compulsory purchases in the Netherlands takes place on the basis of a land-use plan. In land development areas, too, there is the right of compulsory purchase. The procedure leading to compulsory purchase has many time limitations that may not be exceeded, to prevent the landowner from being kept in uncertainty for too long. The first part of the procedure serves to establish the plots for which purchase by the government will be necessary. In judging this issue the Crown tries to establish whether the owner of a plot is prepared to realize and also capable of realizing what the designated land-use objective is. If this is the case, the compulsory purchase will usually not be approved. After the decision of the Crown, the compulsory purchase claim can be brought before the Court (an independent judge), but first the municipality or other government must make one final attempt to purchase the land by way of amicable agreement. In this second part of the procedure the Court checks whether the formal requirements of the first part have been complied with, proclaims the compulsory purchase, and determines the amount of compensation (established by experts). The real value of the property, that is the market value of the premises, with certain correction factors, has to be paid to the owner (Brussaard, 1987, pp. 27–8).

For the realization of certain public works (for instance, pipelines and powerlines) compulsory purchase of the land will not be convenient, because such a measure would reach much further than necessary. In that case the government can oblige the owner to allow the work to be carried out on his land, again with compensation.

## II. Physical Planning Law

In the Netherlands the physical planning legislation plays an important role in the designation of land uses. Physical planning (or spatial planning) can be described as 'the search for and the establishment of the best possible mutual adaptation of space and society, for the benefit of society' (*Oriënteringsnota*). This physical planning is based on the Physical Planning Act (*Wet op de Ruimtelijke Ordening*, Stb. 1962, p. 286), a law that applies to rural as well as urban areas. This law gives the national, provincial and municipal governments the responsibility of establishing the goals for the use of real estate. (This paragraph is partly adapted from Grossman and Brussaard, 1988.)

### A. Instruments of physical planning

#### *1. National and provincial instruments*

At the national level, the Minister of Housing, Physical Planning and Environment is responsible for the preparation of government policy on physical planning. The most important documents expressing this policy are the successive reports on physical planning, which contain the main outlines and principles of national spatial policy. The *Fourth Report Extra* (the most recent) was published in 1990.

Besides these more general reports, government policy on physical planning also can be expressed in plans for specific aspects of national spatial policy. Such plans can consist of Structural Outline Sketches, Structural Outline Plans, and concrete policy decisions that are important for national spatial policy. Both reports and plans are adopted according to the procedure for national physical planning of key decisions (a special procedure used for particularly important spatial decisions on the national level).

A Structural Outline Sketch (*Structuurschets*) provides insight into possible developments that in the long term can be significant for national spatial policy. A Structural Outline Plan (*Structuurschema*) contains main outlines and principles that are generally important for national spatial policy, but directed to a specific sector of that policy. So far eleven structural outline plans have been published. For the rural areas, the most important are the Structural Outline Plans on land development, nature and landscape conservation, and outdoor recreation. Structural Outline Sketches and Structural Outline Plans are revised regularly after an operational period of 5–10 years, in the light of intervening developments.

At the provincial level the Regional Plan (*streekplan*) is the most important instrument by which the provincial administration can articulate its spatial policy. Such a plan indicates the main outlines of the future development of the entire province or a part of the province. All spatially relevant measures within a plan area are weighed in a Regional Plan. The plan also indicates the extent to which the Provincial Executive is allowed to deviate from the plan. The Executive cannot deviate from decisions designated as essential; to deviate from these decisions, the plan must be revised.

A Regional Plan is meant to steer the provincial planning process. Although it has no direct legal consequences, it has particular administrative significance as a guide for the province's own policy and for the assessment of the policy of municipal authorities. Thus, the Regional Plan provides the basis for the Provincial Executive's policy for approving municipal Land-use Plans and for issuing directives. The Regional Plan, however, can also give direction outside the direct field of physical planning. For example, a Land Development Plan or Programme must be evaluated in connection with provincial spatial policy as set out in the Regional Plan, before it is established by the Provincial Council (see section IIIA1).

Although provinces are not obliged to make Regional Plans, such plans currently exist for practically all the Netherlands.

### *2. The local Land-use Plan*

The municipal administrative level has two plan models to express its spatial policy: the Structure Plan (*structuurplan*) and the Land-use Plan (*bestemmingsplan*). In a Structure Plan, the Municipal Council indicates the future development of that municipality or a part of it. The making of a Structure Plan is not obligatory.

The Land-use Plan (*bestemmingsplan*) has a different nature and significance. It is the only plan regulated by the Physical Planning Act that is directly binding on the citizen. Thus, it reaches much further than other plan models. Practically all physical planning decisions at the municipal level are in one way or another linked with the Land-use Plan. Consequently, the plan is the more important physical planning instrument at the municipal level.

A Land-use Plan indicates, insofar as necessary for satisfactory policy, the appropriate use or designation (*bestemming*) for the land involved in the plan. If necessary, the plan also provides instructions for the use of land, buildings, and structures in the plan area. The Municipal Council is obliged to establish a Land-use Plan for the rural area of the municipality. Within the built-up area the plan is optional.

What the Land-use Plan intends to regulate is expressed in the system of land-use designations on the map and in the goal description provided for each designation. Such a land use can be singular (for example, agricultural area, traffic goals) or plural in character (for example, agricultural area combined with water collection; nature conservation combined with outdoor recreation). Land-use designations and goal descriptions are further elaborated in the instructions for use, indicating what is allowed and, especially, what is not allowed within a specific land-use objective. They can contain provisions that prohibit, but may not contain injunctions. The instructions should restrict the most appropriate use only for urgent reasons. They should not contain requirements concerning the structure of agricultural businesses. This means that the municipal government is not allowed to make regulations on the size of agricultural holdings. Among their other provisions, instructions often indicate the types of works or projects for which a construction permit will be required.

Because the Land-use Plan directly binds the citizen, it can impose restrictions on the citizen's right to use property through, for example, building and construction permit requirements and instructions for use. Government agencies (for example, land development authorities), are bound by the Land-use Plan and need a permit from the Municipal Executive for buildings and other constructions. Moreover, land can be compulsorily purchased on the basis of the Land-use Plan (see section IC). Compulsory purchase is possible both to execute a Land-use Plan (for example, urban and village expansions) and to keep an existing situation (for example, nature reserves) in agreement with the plan.

As a result of these significant legal consequences, the Physical Planning Act bases establishment of the plan on a thorough procedure with many legal protections. The procedure involves two administrative levels: the Municipal Council establishes the plan, and the Provincial Executive approves it. In addition, there is the subsequent possibility of an appeal to a third level, the Crown. This appeal to the Crown suspends the effectiveness of the plan.

Apart from the possibility of compulsory purchase, a Land-use Plan is realized and maintained by building and construction permits.

Construction of buildings is allowed only in conjunction with a building permit issued by the Municipal Executive. If a building would be in conflict with a Land-use Plan, the Executive must refuse the permit.

A construction permit for the execution of works or projects is needed only if explicitly required in a Land-use Plan. Construction permits may be required only insofar as necessary to prevent a terrain from becoming less suitable for the realization of a land-use designation assigned to it or to maintain and protect an already realized land use. Thus the plan can require a construction permit for such activities as cutting hedges, digging ditches, levelling land, or paving roads. Here too the permit must be refused if the construction would be in conflict with a Land-use Plan.

In addition, a Land-use Plan can simply prohibit the execution of certain building works and projects and certain types of use, if these activities in all circumstances would entail a threat to the desired land use.

## B. Spatial policy between administrative levels

The establishment of spatial policy in the Netherlands is characterized by a process of consultation. Thus, lower authorities normally influence the establishment of spatial policy of higher authorities and *vice versa.* This influence usually takes the form of direct consultations, sometimes prescribed compulsorily by law or regulation. At the same time, every authority can express its views on plans of other authorities through objection procedures and public inquiry. This process of consultation also means that the various administrative levels will be well informed about the spatial policy at other levels.

This climate of co-operation helps to ensure that the spatial policy of lower authorities will remain within the limits set by the policy of the higher authorities. However, the lower authority is not obliged to remain within these limits. In accordance with the principle of decentralized administration in the Netherlands, the lower authorities are in principle free to determine the contents of their own policy and plans. Insofar as the lower authority could conflict with the policy of the higher authority in an unacceptable manner, the higher authority may interfere by orders or directives.

For example, the Minister of Housing, Physical Planning and Environment can issue an order to oblige the Provincial Council to establish or to revise a Regional Plan within a certain time. Insofar as the correct execution of government policy requires establishment or revision of physical planning measures, the Minister can, in such an order, issue directives on the contents of the Regional Plan. Thus, a directive is more than an order. An order instructs only that a plan must be established or revised; a directive specifies the contents of that plan or its revision. After the Minister has issued an order and a directive, the Provincial Council is obliged to establish a Regional Plan or to revise it in accordance with the directive given. If the Council fails, the Minister will establish or revise the plan at provincial expense. Because it involves significant interference, this power of directive has been used sparingly.

The Minister also possesses similar powers with respect to the municipal administrative level, if correct execution of central government policy requires establishment or revision of a Land-use Plan.

In addition to these specific physical planning instruments, annulment (a general administrative–judicial instrument) is significant in the context of physical planning. The Crown can annul the decisions of lower authorities (Provincial Executive, Provincial Council, and Municipal Executive) if they are in conflict with the law or the public good.

The elaboration of provincial spatial policy at the municipal level (which is usually based on the Regional Plan) will also take place primarily through consultation. The most important instrument to ensure implementation of the provincial administration's policy is the requirement that municipal Land-use Plans be subject to the approval of the Provincial Executive. If the Provincial Executive completely or partly withholds its consent to a Land-use Plan, the Municipal Council must establish a new plan within a year, taking into account the Provincial Executive's decision.

Like the Minister at the national level, the Provincial Executive has the power to order the Municipal Council to establish or revise a Land-use Plan within a specific time. Moreover, to the extent that supra-municipal interests require, the order can include directives on the contents of the plan. Provincial administrations have made moderate use of their directive powers.

## III. Agrarian Land Legislation

### A. Land development

In the Netherlands from 1924 onwards there has been legislation to encourage agricultural development of rural areas, financed by the government. This legislation was intended primarily for agricultural purposes by providing land consolidation and thus improving agrarian productivity conditions. However, in the 1960s and 1970s, societal developments led to changes in the functions and value of rural areas, such as expansion of towns, increasing mobility, higher recreational needs, and the enhanced value assigned to nature and landscape. New legislation was framed, recognizing both agricultural and non-agricultural claims on land in rural areas, especially nature and landscape values and outdoor recreation. This Land Development Act (*Landinrichtingswet*, Stb. 1985, p. 299) came into force in 1985. (This paragraph is partly adapted from Grossman and Brussaard, 1988.)

### *1. Instruments of land development*

In the Land Development Act physical planning policy is taken as guidance for land-development decisions. This is formulated in article 4 of the Land Development Act: 'Land development strives toward the improvement of the countryside in conformity with the functions of that area, as they are specified in the framework of physical planning.' That the countryside must accommodate several land-use functions is elaborated by the provision in the law that land development can include, but is not limited to, measures and provisions for arable agriculture, horticulture, and forestry; for nature and landscape; for infrastructure; for open air recreation; and for cultural history. The close correspondence of land development with physical planning is implemented in the law by numerous requirements for co-ordination of land-development decisions with physical planning decisions and decision-making authorities.

Land development in the Netherlands takes place in the context of comprehensive policy planning, articulated in the Structural Outline Plan for Land Development. This plan delineates the main principles governing national land development policy and provides special insight into the spatial aspects of that policy. Thus, this document stands at the intersection of physical planning policy and land-development policy. It therefore is adopted in accordance with the procedure for national physical planning key decisions (see section IIA1).

Because the Land Development Act is designed to accommodate varied interests, these require different land-development approaches and different decision-making processes. Thus, the law includes four statutory types of land development:

**1.** Consolidation (*ruilverkaveling*), modelled after methods long used in the Netherlands and other West European countries, is intended for areas in which agriculture is the primary function and in which other functions are less important. It usually involves re-allocation of land in the entire area. The decision to proceed with consolidation needs the approval of a majority of the landowners or users.
**2.** Redevelopment (*herinrichting*) is a new method and is intended for areas in which important non-agricultural functions must co-exist with agri-

culture. Thus this method is appropriate for areas within the urban sphere of influence or with important nature and landscape values. Reallocation of land will normally occur in a redevelopment area, but redevelopment can also proceed without reallocation.
**3.** Adaptation (*aanpassingsinrichting*) is also new and is derived from German legislation (*Flurbereinigungsgesetz*). It is designed to be used in conjunction with an infrastructural improvement or development (a road or a canal) to modify the unfavourable land-use effects of that project.
**4.** Consolidation by agreement (*ruilverkaveling bij overeenkomst*), the oldest method of consolidation, regulates a procedure by which three or more landowners voluntarily exchange land to achieve better parcelling.

The choice between consolidation and redevelopment is especially difficult and closely related to physical planning policy. Therefore the Structural Outline Plan for Land Development provides general guidelines for that choice.

The decision-making about land development involves a complicated and time-consuming procedure, which can take some 10 to 20 years. This procedure is initiated with a written request to the Minister of Agriculture, Nature Management and Fisheries, submitted by a government or other public body, an eligible organization, or a group of landowners and users representing together at least 30% of the ground involved. If the land development is consistent with the land development and physical planning policy, and if land development in the area is desirable, the Minister places the area on the List of Land Development Projects in Preparation (*Voorbereidingsschema Landinrichting*). The list is annually amended, on recommendation of the provincial governments. An important part of the provincial evaluation process involves ensuring that land development will be consistent with provincial spatial policy. The provincial government also recommends the appropriate type of land development and the preferred method of preparation. After an area is placed on the list, a local land development commission is appointed, which is responsible for the preparation and implementation of the land development project.

The Land Development Act authorizes two methods of preparation for land development: simplified and phased. The simplified method involves immediate preparation of a Land Development Plan, which serves as the basis for a decision as well as the guide for implementing the project. In areas where problems are complicated and especially where non-agricultural functions are significant, first a rather general Land Development Program is prepared on which the decision is based, followed by a plan that guides the implementation. In practice, the majority of land development projects will use simplified preparation. This is particularly appropriate for consolidation areas, where a detailed plan is necessary for landowners and users to vote meaningfully on the project.

The preparing of the Land Development Plan or Program by the local commission is based on extensive research. Here, too, careful co-ordination with physical planning policy is prescribed. Thus, the plan or programme must be examined in light of its consistency with the spatial policy of the province, normally expressed in a Regional Plan. Often this plan will give direction to the decisions made about the Land Development Plan or Program. In addition, the Land Development Act requires consultation about a proposed plan or programme with municipal authorities. This consultation should identify possible conflicts with the local Land-use Plans (see section IIA2). After several opportunities for public comment, the provincial government makes a decision about establishing the plan or programme and chooses between consolidation and redevelopment.

When a land development project has been identified as redevelopment, the decision to proceed with the project is made by the provincial government at the time the plan is established. In case of consolidation, landowners and tenants have the opportunity to vote on the project. In the election, a decision to proceed with the consolidation results if there is an affirmative vote of *either* a majority of the number of votes *or* a majority of the amount of ground surface represented in the election.

### 2. Implementation

After the decision about redevelopment or consolidation, a rather lengthy process of implementation starts. This process involves public as well as private components. The public aspects include acquisition of land for a number of agricultural and non-agricultural purposes. This land will be used for public infrastructure facilities (roads and watercourses) as well as for nature or landscape protection and recreation. In addition, some land is needed to increase the size of farms and to make the land exchange operate more smoothly.

The Land Development Act provides mechanisms for both voluntary and involuntary transfers. As a general principle in land development, each owner of land within a block has the right to receive, in the reparcelling and reallocation, land of the same type and agricultural value as the land that owner contributed to the project. This general principle is modified, however, for the purpose of obtaining ground for public purposes. To affect owners fairly, the law permits a reduction (*korting*) in the value of land that each owner is entitled to receive in the reallocation. Owners receive compensation for this reduction. The reduction should be used only when necessary; most of the land needed should be obtained through voluntary sale.

The public purposes for which land acquired through reduction can be used are specified by law. For land development projects involving redevelopment, the reduction can be used only for public roads and watercourses.

Other public purposes can be achieved by using compulsory purchase if the required ground cannot be obtained through voluntary sale. Compulsory purchase is not available in consolidation.

The final stage in the construction of facilities for public purposes in land development areas is the establishment of the Delimitation Plan (*begrenzingenplan*) and the finalization of the related provisions for ownership, management, and maintenance of public facilities. The Delimitation Plan is the official administrative-cadastral document that describes the situation concerning roads, watercourses, and other public areas within the block.

Land development involves a process of land exchange combined with improvement of access, water management, and parcelling. Landowners are required to contribute to the cost of the land development process in an amount related both to the benefits received from the project and to the increased value of land received through the Reallocation Plan (*plan van toedeling*). Thus, the law prescribes a two-stage process of land valuation designed to establish the initial value of parcels in the development block as well as the enhanced value of that land after redevelopment.

The Reallocation Plan, which establishes the reallocation of parcels of farmland, is one of the last stages of the land development process. Landowners and users have the opportunity to state their wishes with respect to the Reallocation Plan. The plan is formulated by the local commission, but actually designed by the Land Registry Office (*kadaster*), which has detailed records concerning geographic and legal aspects of landownership. Actual transfer of ownership pursuant to the plan occurs through the deed of reallocation, which vests title to property in the new owners.

As the implementation phase is lengthy, it is often necessary for ground to be available for use by an individual or an entity other than the recognized owner or user long before the land registry record of land ownership is adjusted. The Land Development Act thus permits interim use of land within the land development block pursuant to a formally adopted plan of temporary use. Under such a plan, for example, public works or facilities may be constructed on land not yet actually owned by the government, and provisions for maintaining landscape and nature values may be made early in the execution process. The owner or user of that land is compensated either with other land or with money.

## B. Management agreements

Rural areas in the Netherlands must fulfil various purposes. Therefore, Dutch land-use policy distinguishes between situations involving integration or separation of land uses. Integration has particular relevance for agricultural land with special landscape or natural values: that is some 500000 to 700000 ha (one-quarter to one-third of all cultivated land in the Netherlands). Characteristic of these areas is the direct connection between the natural conditions and the farming situation. On one hand, existing landscape and nature values are threatened there by agricultural developments; on the other hand, those values can only exist together with certain forms of agrarian land use.

In 1975, the Dutch government introduced in the Relationship Report (*Relatienota*) a policy programme for specialized agricultural land management. The report distinguishes two types of areas:

**1.** Management areas: areas where maintaining the present nature and landscape values is just as important as continuing the agricultural use and production. In these areas, integration of land-use functions is the goal. Therefore, farmers are offered the opportunity to enter voluntary contractual management agreements (*beheersovereenkomsten*), under which they will receive financial compensation for adapting their farming practices to the requirements of nature and landscape preservation.
**2.** Reserve areas: areas where the values of nature and landscape are so high that effective agricultural production will be impossible in the long run. The goal in these areas therefore is to end farming entirely by purchasing the land. Farmers cannot be forced to sell, but if they offer their land for sale, the government has an obligation to purchase. In the meantime, farmers in reserve areas have the opportunity to enter transitional management agreements.

So the *Relatienota* policy has two goals: the maintenance and development of nature and landscape values in the most vulnerable agrarian cultural landscapes by adaptation of agricultural management, and the financial subsidization of the position of farmers who carry out the farm business in those areas. This policy is limited to a number of geographically defined regions of particular value and vulnerability (up to 200000 ha). The instruments to carry out this policy are embodied in the Decree on Management Agreements (*Regeling beheersovereenkomsten 1988*, Stcrt. 1988, p. 149), which also incorporates the Dutch translation of the EC programme for farming in less favoured areas (Directive 75/268 on mountain and hill farming and farming in less favoured areas).

For every province the Minister of Agriculture, Nature Management and Fisheries has indicated the number of hectares to which the *Relatienota* policy will be applicable. It then becomes the responsibility of the provincial governments to establish the boundaries of the areas, indicate which areas are management areas and which are reserve areas, and establish a Management Plan for each area. This plan indicates the range of possible practices (actions to be taken or to be omitted in the area) and the corresponding compensations. In every management area there is a limited number of packets of management provisions, depending on the management goals for that area (for instance maintenance of natural handicaps, protection of nearby nature reserves, botanical management, meadowbird management, migratory bird management, or maintenance of landscape).

Once the Management Plan for an area is established, farmers can enter into management agreements. Such an agreement is a private contract between an individual farmer and the government. A management agreement lists the packet of specific management treatments (measures to be taken and activities to be avoided) to which the farmer is obligated and the compensation he will receive. Participating farmers can choose only from the management packets indicated in the plan. The government is not obligated to contract for parcels that would not further the management goals. A management agreement is normally entered for a duration of 6 years, and is presumed to be renewed for the next 6-year period unless a party gives notice before the end of the period. The government's right to end the agreement, however, is limited. The farmer can also end an agreement after a trial period of one year (Grossman, 1988).

The implementation of management agreements had a very slow start. The procedure for establishing the management plans was lengthy, and farmers were reluctant to enter management agreements. Now farmers are getting increasingly interested in entering management agreements. (Section IIIB is partly adapted from Grossman and Brussaard, 1988.)

## C. Setaside

In 1988, the European Community introduced the setaside regulations (EC Regulation no. 1094/88). These regulations aim to stimulate farmers to take arable land out of production and at the same time to maintain the agricultural productivity of that land. The regulation is applicable on land on which crops are cultivated for which a European market regulation exists. If farmers meet certain conditions, they can get financial compensation. In the Dutch translation of this regulation (*Beschikking ter zake van het uit produktie nemen van bouwland*, Stcrt. 1988, p. 158) farmers who want to make use of this possibility have to be younger than 65 years and are obliged to keep their land out of production for a period of 5 years. They have the choice of three possible measures:

1. laying fallow the land, with a possibility of crop rotation;
2. afforesting; or
3. use for non-agricultural purposes.

In the case of laying fallow, farmers have to meet several obligations. They are not allowed to use organic waste matter or animal manure, and only the insecticides, pesticides, and herbicides approved by the Minister of

Agriculture are allowed. Furthermore, the land must be cultivated with a 'green manure', i.e. a conservation cover crop, like clover or marigolds. This green manure may not be removed from the land or used for animal feed or commercial purposes. It is to be ploughed under at the end of the setaside period or when the land is put into use again for crop rotation within that period.

In the case of afforestation the land must be afforested with quick-growing trees. Although the explanatory note to the regulation presumes that afforesting land is an agricultural activity, in fact a problem may exist, because the designation of land uses in a Land-use Plan is a municipal concern. Certain parts in the north of Holland are characteristic for their treeless and open landscape, and especially the farmers in this part of the country are in trouble now because of decreasing prices. If they should want to afforest their land, it is possible that municipal physical planning regulations would prevent them from doing so.

If farmers agree to use their land for non-agricultural purposes (the third possibility the regulation offers), they are not allowed to use the land for the production of any form of vegetable or animal products (Brussaard, 1991, pp. 1533–4).

The compensation the farmer gets paid for setting aside his land is 700 ECU (European Currency Unit) per hectare per year in the case of laying fallow and afforesting, and 300 ECU in the case of non-agricultural use.

## D. Land lease

Thirty-five percent of Dutch agricultural land is leased. The acreage under lease is declining: in 1970, still 48% of the land was leased. However, as approximately 54% of all Dutch farm holdings are totally or partly leased, land lease is still of great importance for a majority of farmers.

Land lease is regulated by the Agricultural Lease Act (*Pachtwet*, Stb. 1958, p. 37). The Act aims to protect the lessee (who is supposed to be in a weaker position) as well as to protect the common good of agriculture in general. The heart of the Act is the regulation of the agricultural lease contract, which deviates on essential points from the normal contract rules in the Civil Code, and involves a substantial amount of government influence.

In the Agricultural Lease Act an agricultural lease contract is defined as: every contract, in any form and under any name, in which one party takes upon it to provide the other party, in return for a compensation, the use of land or a farm, for agricultural purposes. As soon as a contract fits within the terms of this definition, the rules of the Agricultural Lease Act apply, even though the parties may have given another name to their agreement and even if they have no written agreement. In accordance with the Act an agricultural lease contract must be concluded in writing and approved by a Land Control Board (*Grondkamer*). These boards are administrative bodies, entrusted by the government with the control of the enforcement of the Act; they are situated in each of the twelve provinces of the Netherlands. The Land Control Boards examine, among other things, whether the lease contract complies with the agricultural lease standards given by government (along with the maximum rent), and whether the contract contains 'excessive obligations' from an agricultural point of view for the lessee. The Boards can approve, change or nullify the lease contract. They can modify the rent and other obligations of the lessee. Nullification is only allowed if there are no possibilities to change the contract within the law. Decisions of the boards can be brought in appeal to the Central Land Control Board (*Centrale Grondkamer*).

The legal duration of an agricultural lease contract is 12 years for a farm and 6 years for land without farm buildings. Contracts for a longer period are allowed; for a shorter period, only under extraordinary circumstances and with approval of the Land Control Board. Lease contracts concluded for the normal duration are *de jure* continued for a period of 6 years, unless one of the parties informs the other party, within a certain period before the termination of the contract, that he or she does not wish to prolong the contract. The lessee can oppose such a non-renewal notice. Verbal lease contracts, or written lease contracts that are not offered for approval to the Land Control Board, are valid for an indefinite period and cannot be terminated by either one of the parties. Termination is possible again when the contract is changed in writing and approved by the Land Control Board.

Disputes about agricultural land lease cases are heard by special law courts in two instances: the Tenancy Tribunal (*Pachtkamer*), one with every cantonal court and consisting of a cantonal judge and two lay experts; and in appeal the Tenancy Tribunal of the Court of Appeal at Arnhem, consisting of three judges and two lay experts. In the case of a non-renewal notice, the lessee can request the Tenancy Tribunal to continue the contract. The Tribunal decides on the request in accordance with the principles of equity, provided that the Agricultural Lease Act makes no exception. The Act mentions several exceptions: refusal of renewal is obligatory if the lessee has seriously failed his obligations, if the lessor wants to use the leased object for purposes other than agriculture and that use is in accordance with the common agricultural good, and if the lessor or spouse wants to use the leased object personally for an agricultural purpose. However, the latter case is again decided according to equity when refusal or renewal would seriously endanger the foundations of the social position of the lessee, and the personal use is not of overriding importance for the lessor or for the people who derive their rights from the lessor. If the interest of both lessee and lessor are deemed to be of equal importance, continuation is refused.

If the lessor wants to sell the leased property, it has to be offered first to the lessee. If the parties cannot agree on a price, the lessor can ask the Land Control Board to value the leased object. The board has to base its valuation on the leased status of the object. This reduces its value generally by about 45%. As a result of the rather low maximum rents prescribed by the government, and the far-reaching protection of the lessee, the value of an object in leased condition is about 55% of its value if it were not leased.

So the Agricultural Lease Act offers a system with strong influence from government policy. The powers of the Land Control Boards can interfere significantly with the intentions of the contracting parties. For example, this system makes it difficult to insert in agricultural lease contracts obligations for the lessee directed at the maintenance of nature and landscape, because this would mean an 'excessive obligation' from an agricultural point of view, even when the lessee will agree with such an obligation. Therefore a bill was introduced in Parliament to amend the Agricultural Lease Act (Tweede Kamer, 1987–1988, 20617, n. 1–2). This amendment will make it possible for lessees to agree to lease contract obligations (with compensation) to maintain the values of nature and landscape. This will open another opportunity for nature and landscape protection in agricultural means, which until now was mainly based on management agreements (see section IIIB) (Walda, 1991).

At the same time the government started a discussion about a further liberalization of the land lease system. The government proposals involve, among other things, the introduction of a new kind of land lease, the 'extraordinary lease', on which the approval by the Land Control Boards and the other limitations will not be applicable (De Hoog, 1991).

## IV. Nature and Environment in Rural Areas

### A. Forestry

The object of the Dutch forest legislation is to maintain a forest acreage of reasonable dimension and quality. In accordance with the Forestry Act (*Boswet*, Stb. 1961, p. 256) the owner of a wood or trees that have been cut down or have perished otherwise (for instance through storm or fire) is obliged to plant the same area of trees again. This obligation must be fulfilled on the same spot or, with permission of the head of the Forestry Department, somewhere else. Before starting to fell a wood or some trees, the owner has to inform the head of the Forestry Department. In exceptional situations, to protect natural and scenic beauty, the Minister of Agriculture, Nature Management and Fisheries can prohibit the cutting down of woods and trees for a maximum period of 5 years. The obligations to inform and to plant, and the possibility of a prohibition to cut down trees do not apply in case the trees have to be cut down for the realization of public works in conformity with a Land-use Plan (see section IIA2).

For the protection of woods with natural scientific significance, the Nature Conservation Act (see section IVB), rather than the Forestry Act, is the appropriate instrument.

## B. Nature conservation

The oldest nature conservation legislation in the Netherlands is the 1928 Nature Protection Act (*Natuurschoonwet*, Stb. 1928, p. 205). This Act seeks to support country estates whose continued existence is desirable from a viewpoint of scenic beauty, by offering tax benefits. The Minister of Agriculture, Nature Management and Fisheries, together with the Minister of Finance, selects the country estates for which the Act is applicable. When the owner maintains his estate for 25 years, the value on which the owner must pay annual capital-tax is reduced to half, and even to nil if the estate is open to the public too.

Since 1968 the Netherlands has had a Nature Conservation Act (*Natuurbeschermingswet*, Stb. 1967, p. 572). This Act makes it possible to protect nature areas by designating them as 'protected nature areas' (*beschermd natuurmonument*) or as 'State nature areas' (*Staatsnatuurmonument*). Such a designation has certain legal consequences.

Nature areas are described by the Act as: terrains and waters, which are of common interest for their natural beauty or their natural scientific significance. Agricultural grounds can be part of such terrains and waters in certain situations: when those grounds have sufficient intrinsic nature value to justify a designation under the Nature Conservation Act, or when they are an integral part of the designated nature area.

The decision about designation of protected nature areas is made by the Minister of Agriculture, Nature Management and Fisheries, in agreement with the Minister of Housing, Physical Planning and Environment. After that decision the owner needs a licence from the Minister of Agriculture for all actions that are harmful or disfiguring for the area. The Minister, in agreement with the owner, can draw up a management plan to maintain or restore the natural beauty or natural scientific significance.

Areas that are already owned by the government can be designated as State nature areas.

## C. Soil protection

The use of agricultural land also is regulated from an environmental point of view. The most important law here is the Soil Protection Act. This act came into force in 1987 and authorizes the national government to issue decrees on various aspects relating to soil protection. Until now, the main regulations on this point concern manure.

The Netherlands has a serious manure problem. The Dutch livestock industry, which is concentrated in the eastern and southern parts of the country, produces a gigantic quantity of animal manure. Livestock farmers have been spreading most of this manure for years on their own lands, or it was spread in the immediate surroundings. This has often resulted in an overdosing, sometimes extreme, of minerals (nitrogen, phosphate, and potassium) and heavy metals (copper, cadmium, and zinc) found in the manure. This overdosing causes serious harm both to the agricultural sector and to the environment, such as decline in soil fertility, decrease in quality of crops, health hazards for livestock, decline in quality of groundwater, deposition of potentially acidifying substances, and stench nuisance. This problem has given rise to an elaborate system of manure regulation (based on the Soil Protection Act in conjunction with the Fertilizer Act) regulating the use of animal manure, the trade in fertilizing products, the removal of surplus manure, and the production of animal manure. Since 1987 this legislation has applied to manure produced by cattle, pigs, chickens, and turkeys (because these animal types produced by far the greatest part of the total animal manure in the Netherlands), but from 1992 the manure regulations also apply to ducks, rabbits, sheep, goats, minks and foxes. The manure legislation standardizes the use and the production of manure in relation to the quantity of phosphate found in the manure.

With respect to the use of animal manure on agricultural land, this matter is regulated by a government Decree on the Application of Animal Manure (*Besluit gebruik dierlijke meststoffen*, Stb. 1987, p. 114). This decree establishes standards for the maximum quantities of manure (expressed in kilograms of phosphate) that may be applied on agricultural land per hectare per year. Since the extent to which phosphate is absorbed from the soil can differ with various crops, a distinction has been made between grassland, fodder cropland (i.e. land on which corn is cultivated), and arable land. These standards are implemented in a number of phases, because implementation of a final standard at short notice would have lead to enormous manure surpluses and serious problems for the livestock industry. The final standards, when the amount of manure applied will be in equilibrium with the amount the soil can digest, must be reached before the year 2000. The decree includes rules that allow fewer phosphates to be applied on phosphate-saturated ground, and more on ground with little phosphate. The inventory of phosphate-saturated grounds that has been drawn up recently indicates that in the areas where the livestock industry is concentrated 60% of all agricultural land is saturated with phosphate already. As the use of animal manure in autumn and winter carries extra risks of nitrogen and phosphate leaching and running off to groundwater or surface water, the manure legislation also has provisions about manure spreading during those periods. Here too, the implementation of these provisions is phased: by the end of 1994 the prohibition to spread manure for the majority of all grounds will last from 1 September until 31 January. In connection with the evaporation of ammonia that may occur when manure is applied, the regulation also contains provisions about incorporation of the spread manure into the soil (Brussaard and Grossman, 1990, pp. 91–5).

The Soil Protection Act also gives the provincial governments the possibility to designate soil protection areas, in conjunction with their physical planning policy. In those areas the provincial states can draw up rules to protect the chemical, physical, and biological qualities of the soil.

## Conclusion

The picture of Dutch agrarian land law shows, in some aspects, similarity to that of other West European countries. In the Netherlands also land uses are influenced by physical planning legislation, although that influence, via the Land-use Plan, may be stronger than in other countries. Also the tradition of land consolidation and land lease is, with differences, shared by neighbouring countries, and the rules about setaside are based on the same EC regulation.

Where the Netherlands differs greatly from other countries is in interweaving agriculture and nature and landscape conservation. The recent legislation on land development offers possibilities of a new approach to the use of rural areas, and the same applies to the management agreement.

On one subject the Dutch legislation is unique: the elaborate system of regulations concerning the manure problem. The Dutch hope to lose that extraordinary position as soon as possible.

## References

Brussaard, W. (1987) *The Rules of Physical Planning 1986.* Ministry of Housing, Physical Planning and Environment, The Hague.

Brussaard, W. (1991) Protecting agricultural resources in Europe: A report from the Netherlands. *Indian Law Review,* 24, 1525–42.

Brussaard, W. and Grossman, M.R. (1990) Legislation to abate pollution from manure: The Dutch approach. *North Carolina Journal of International Law and Commercial Regulation,* 15, 85–114.

Grossman, M.R. (1988) Management agreements in Dutch agricultural law: The contractual integration of agriculture and conservation. *Denver Journal of International Law and Policy,* 16, 95–138.

Grossman, M.R. and Brussaard, W. (1988) Planning, development, and management: Three steps in the legal protection of Dutch agricultural land. *Washburn Law Journal*, 28, 86–149.

De Hoog, P.A. (1991) Het wetsvoorstel tot liberalisering van de Pachtwet. *Agrarisch Recht*, 51, 314–30.

Walda, H.C.A. (1991) Nature and landscape conservation as a branch of agricultural industry: A second life for the Land Lease Act? In: F. von Benda-Beckmann and M. van der Velde (eds), *Law as a Resource in Agrarian Struggles*. Wageningen Studies in Sociology WSS 33, Agricultural University, Wageningen, pp. 169–89.

8

# AGRARIAN LAND LAW IN NORWAY

Torgeir Austenå

## I. Introduction

Norway, the western part of the Scandinavian peninsula, covers 324000 $km^2$, approximately 42% of the peninsula. More than 70% of the land area is covered with mountains and mountainous plateaus, glaciers and freshwater lakes. Almost 25% of the land is covered with forests, and only 970000 ha, or about 3% of the whole country, is agricultural land. Approximately 30% of Norwegian territory lies north of the Arctic Circle. Approximately 6.6 million ha is productive forest area. The population of Norway is 4.2 million.

The degree of self-sufficiency in terms of calories (the share produced in Norwegian agriculture) is expected to be 49% for 1990. In 1987 there were 97802 holdings with at least 0.5 ha of agricultural area.

## II. A Survey of the Norwegian Legal and Administrative System

As a background to the account of Norwegian agrarian land law it is necessary to outline the main characteristics of the Norwegian legal and administrative system. Norwegian law is neither civil law (in the English sense) nor common law (in the English sense). The Nordic laws, which are closely related, have developed on a national basis, but the impact of borrowings from other countries, in particular on the Continent, are substantial in many respects.

The Constitution of 17 May 1814, which can be amended only in accordance with a strict procedure, is the supreme source of law. All other law should in principle derive from the Constitution; this includes statutes passed in accordance with the rules of the Constitution and regulations in accordance with authority granted in a statute. Norway does not yet have a comprehensive codification of the civil law. Norwegian law remains, therefore, a number of statutes covering different sectors, sometimes with overlap, causing constructional problems. However, law comprises much more than statutes. Important parts of the civil law are regulated by customs or by so-called general principles of law, which may be extracted from one or more statutes and/or judgements found in the writings of legal scholars. Furthermore, it should be noted that the courts have the power to develop the law. A decision of the Supreme Court is considered binding on the lower courts, and, indeed, on the Supreme Court itself.

For civil cases (as opposed to criminal cases), the court structure is in principle very simple. There are about 100 District Courts in the first instance, having full jurisdiction in matters of civil and administrative law (as well as criminal law). An appeal from a District Court in a civil case lies to one of the five regional Courts of Appeal. Finally, a decision of a Court of Appeal may be brought before the Supreme Court. Both the Court of Appeal and the Supreme Court have the same competence as the District Court, i.e. they may review a case in its entirety, both as regards facts and law.

The Parliament (the *Storting*) has supreme legislative and budgetary powers in the kingdom of Norway. The Members of Parliament are elected by general election every fourth year. Parliament passes laws and approves the annual financial budget. Besides the office of Prime Minister there are seventeen Ministries, which prepare legislative proposals and exercise executive powers.

In the field of law, the king (i.e. the government) is often empowered to give Orders in Council. This authority is often delegated further to the relevant Ministry, and the Minister often delegates authority further to a civil servant of higher rank. In this chapter, the term Ministry means either the Minister or a civil servant with authority. In both cases the Minister is responsible to the Parliament.

The legislators do not use the terms land law or agricultural law. Agricultural law is a practical term for specific legal rules concerning farming activities. Moreover, characterizing a rule as belonging to land law has no particular legal significance. A specific rule may also be dealt with in administrative law, or criminal law, as the case may be.

Agrarian policy is applied through the administrative and political system. The Ministry of Agriculture is the highest authority in administration of the Land Act of 18 March 1955 and the Act of Forestry and Forest Protection of 21 May 1965.

The Ministry of Local Government and Labour deals with housing and building policy. The Housing and Building Department deals with site policy, housing programmes, rationalization and research within the building industry, financing of housing, and administrative matters in connection with housing; it is also responsible for building legislation. (For more information refer to: *Housing, Building and Planning in Norway*, published by the Norwegian Ministry of Local Government and Labour, Oslo, 1987.)

The Ministry of Environment is responsible for planning, pollution control, nature conservation, and the conservation of cultural heritage. These are regarded as essential elements in physical planning.

Local state administration is of primary importance at the county level. The County Governor has general control of municipalities, planning and building control, and environmental issues. At the County level, the County Agricultural Board has the administrative and executive role for the Land Act and the Act of Forestry and Forest Protection. The agricultural administration at the county level plays an important role in planning, because it controls the use of agricultural land for non-agricultural purposes. The state road administration also plays a role in general planning at a county level.

The eighteen county communes (municipalities) correspond geographically to the county districts of the state administration. The city of Oslo (with approximately 450000 inhabitants) is a municipality, but also functions as a county commune. The area of the counties vary from 2000 $km^2$ to almost 50000 $km^2$ with an average of 18000 $km^2$. The population varies from approximately 75000 to 400000 inhabitants, with an average of 200000.

The county communes play a role in planning and development. The county communes are primarily responsible for hospitals and other related health services, upper secondary schools and certain intermediate roads. The county communes have a taxation right although relatively strict limitations are set by the state. County communes do not have any authority over municipalities.

The County Council is elected for a 4-year period. The Council elects a County Executive Committee and a Chairperson from among its members. It also appoints a Chief Executive Officer. The Chairperson and the Chief Executive Officer have normal full-time positions.

The 448 municipalities are the most important local governing bodies, and all land in Norway is part of a municipality. Their populations vary from 450000 inhabitants to less than 1000, and their area varies from a few square kilometres to almost 10000 $km^2$. The average population density is 9000 inhabitants per 700 $km^2$.

Municipalities are the main planning authorities, responsible for building permission and control. In the housing field, the municipality carries out the purchase and development of some land, housing programmes and other important functions related to the financing of housing and housing subsidies.

In each municipality there are political bodies with roles in the administration of agricultural law. The municipalities are led by a Municipal Council, elected by popular vote for a 4-year period. The Council elects an Executive Committee and a Chairperson from among its members and appoints a Municipal Executive. To take care of agriculture and forestry, the Municipal Council elects the Agricultural Board.

Norwegian municipalities have a high degree of authority although they are subject to control by the Ministry of Local Government and Labour and the County Governor. Municipalities have the right to impose taxes on income and fixed property, but like the county communes are subject to limitations set by the state.

## III. The Agrarian Land Legislation

### A. The planning legislation

The purpose of the Planning and Building Act of 14 June 1985 (PBA) is to co-ordinate the activity of the state, the county, and the municipality and further give the basis for decisions about use and conservation of resources. In Norway, the PBA is the main authority for regulating land use, agricultural land included. On the national level, the government may set general aims and principles and specify guidelines for physical, economic and social developments. These have to be followed by the counties and municipalities in their planning activities.

The county commune prepares plans for the county; these are continually reviewed and updated. County planning is intended to co-ordinate the national and county communes' physical, economic, social, and cultural activities, as well as the municipalities' similar activities.

The County Plan defines the objectives and long-term guidelines for development in the county. It also draws up a co-ordinated programme for the activities of the national and county commune sectors and shows how these objectives may be achieved. The programme includes the municipal sectors in matters of major importance to the county or where large parts of the municipal sectors are concerned. In local municipal planning, the municipality has to follow the guidelines for planning and use of land in the County Plan in every case where the Municipal Plan has implications outside the municipal boundaries or where an individual municipality is unable to solve an issue within its own jurisdiction and the issue has to be considered jointly by the several municipalities it affects.

The Municipal Plan describes objectives for development in the municipality and provides guidelines for sector planning. The land-use part of the plan designates areas for building, agriculture, nature, outdoor recreation, extraction of raw materials, defense, and areas that are or will be reserved for a specific purpose. This part of the plan covers the use and protection of watercourses and sea areas, as well as important links in the communication system.

Generally, planning provisions are the same regarding agricultural and non-agricultural areas. However, the law contains a number of stipulations protecting agricultural areas against non-agricultural uses. Rather often land is designated as agricultural land, even if the main objective is to reserve it for recreation or nature.

### B. The Act on Nature Conservation (19 June 1970)

This act contains rules on four different plans, giving the possibility of creating national parks, landscape protected areas, nature reserves, and nature relics (sections 3, 5, 8, and 11). During the last 10–15 years, there have been several court cases in which farmers claimed damages for restrictions on farmland and forest. Only in a few exceptional cases will a farmer receive compensation (Backer, 1986).

### C. The Land Consolidation Act (21 December 1979)

For farming and agriculture, the legislation governing land consolidation and reallocation has been of great importance from the first act in 1821 to the present Land Consolidation Act. Land consolidation is basically designed to solve problems in rural areas, mainly in agriculture and forestry. Similar problems in urban or semi-urban areas are meant to be solved by other planning or regulation systems. Moreover, land consolidation is designed to solve problems in the private sector.

The Land Consolidation Act is in a way a planning act, but much more than that. The overall aim of land consolidation is to increase the net income from agricultural holdings by planning the structure of the farms in a certain district. Roughly, this may be obtained by increasing the volume of production, lowering the cost of production, or both. This simple aim must be in connection with the general policy for agricultural and forest production in Norway. Unfavourable climate, small holdings and other conditions lead to high production costs for most agricultural products. The volume of production is, more or less, limited by the domestic market.

In the 1970s it was possible to expand production of some agricultural products. In that situation, land consolidation was implemented both to increase production and to lower the cost of production both in agriculture and forestry. Along with improved economy for agricultural production, this soon led to over-production of some products. Consequently the aim of land consolidation in the 1980s is only to decrease the cost of production in agriculture. In forestry, the aims still are both to increase production and to lower the costs.

The present Land Consolidation Act, section 2, gives a list of actions that the land consolidation may include. Among these are the traditional actions of dissolving systems of joint ownership or use into systems of individual ownership, improving the use of holdings by reallocation of parcels, and prescribing rules for joint use of areas, roads, rivers, etc. The main elements in land consolidation are:

**1.** land pooling, reallocation and redistribution, according to the value of each holding;
**2.** acquisition of land on the part of government agencies, before or during the process, partly for public infrastructure, but mainly for redistribution (selling) to private owners (enlargement);
**3.** planning and implementation of joint infrastructure projects like roads and drainage, and distribution of the costs and maintenance involved;
**4.** eliminating outdated usufruct rights, and stipulating the compensation;
**5.** dividing holdings held in various kind of joint ownership;
**6.** establishing mutual regulations between owners of individual plots or between shareholders in joint ownership of various kinds, with regard to the use of the holdings. This is an alternative to dividing the land held in joint ownership and could also be an alternative to more complete reallocation in the case of individually-held plots.

The measures in a land consolidation scheme could include the following:

**1.** Eliminating dependency altogether, or at least reducing it to a minimum. This is the solution of classical land consolidation, aiming at individualizing the holdings, the land and the management as much as possible.
**2.** Improving the situation by changing and regulating the relationships; adjusting the dependency in accordance with the demands from efficient land-use management.
**3.** Introducing or formalizing rules for co-operation where no such rules exist, to regulate dependency, minimizing disadvantages and maximizing advantages.

A land consolidation procedure can only be started after request or application. Usually a farmer or a group of farmers applies for land consolidation. The owner of registered property or a perpetual right of use may apply for land consolidation, and application from one single owner is enough to start the proceedings. The Ministry of Agriculture, however, may apply for land consolidation in some cases: if land consolidation could make investment subsidies more efficient, if the application is necessary to lower the costs or to improve the effect of the land consolidation, if the State has bought agricultural land for reallocating (selling) it to enlarge existing holdings, and finally ‘when it is necessary in the public interest’.

Land consolidation cannot be effected if the costs and disadvantages involved exceed the benefits accruing to each individual property. This reflects the importance of the private owner and the economy of the holding. Money compensation for disadvantages is limited to very small amounts. The main rule is that compensation should be given in land, usufruct rights, or other 'real values'. This imposes some restrictions on the use of land consolidation for solving problems other than those of commercial agriculture or forestry, and, of course, for using it for public planning purposes.

The Land Consolidation Service is a special administrative body that implements the Consolidation Act. The Service is administered by the Ministry of Agriculture. The core of the Service is the Land Consolidation Court, the decision-making body, consisting of the Land Consolidation Judge (a professional surveyor) and two lay-persons plus a small technical staff. The decision of this body is a decision of court and not of an administrative body, elected board of involved landowners, or politically elected (public) authority. The Court has authority to change the relations between the participating individual parties.

To avoid conflicts between Land Consolidation Court decisions and decisions from other public planning authorities, the Court has to consult these authorities when the Court's actions are likely to affect matters under their jurisdiction. Even if it is not directly stated in the act, this implies that the Court has a co-ordinating position when various public authorities have different interests or power to decide in matters affecting the consolidation plan. The Court should also call on experts from other authorities if necessary, even if this is not stated formally in the law.

There are several important sector planning authorities in Norway, and the formal connection between sector planning law and land consolidation law is rather poorly developed. This causes problems of co-ordination. The Land Consolidation Court must inform or consult other authorities and should not decide or presuppose future decisions of public authorities. The Court must, of course, consider national policy, national economy, technology, etc. as framework for its actions.

### D. The Act of Concession and Public Pre-emption in Respect of the Acquisition of Real Property (the Concession Act) (31 May 1974) (Austenå, 1978; Falkanger, 1987)

The general rule in Norway is that one cannot acquire real property without concession granted by the king. The powers of the king (i.e. the government) have been delegated to the Ministry of Agriculture and even further down in the administrative hierarchy. 'Real property' is real property of any kind, regardless of size, value, and location.

The purpose of the Act is to regulate and control the sales of real property to protect areas suitable for agricultural production and to secure owner and user relations that are most beneficial for society, i.e. to take care of agriculture and forestry.

Sales are binding even if no approval is given, but buyers are not entitled to keep the properties; they have to sell them to buyers who either need no concession or to whom concession may be granted. Failing this, the state may order the property to be sold in a compulsory auction, with the price risk resting on the first buyer who did not get a concession.

The general rule for when concession is necessary is broad (section 2). There are, however, some exemptions, based partly on the nature of the property and partly on the status of the acquirer (sections 5 and 6). Of the status-related exemptions, the most important is that the spouse of the owner and the close family do not need a concession for acquiring the property, but if the property is a farm or a forest, then the acquirer has to settle on the property and run it for at least 5 years.

The question whether to grant a concession is evaluated on a broad basis, taking into account a number of political, economic, industrial, and demographic factors. The administration could, for example, deny the concession if there is reason to believe that the acquirer intends primarily to invest in real property, and especially if the acquisition is a short-term investment. A concession may be made subject to conditions, for example, that the acquirer must settle on the property or that the property must be used for a specific purpose (Falkanger, 1986b).

The right of pre-emption for the State and the municipality was introduced in the concession legislation in 1909 and has thereafter been an element in all legislation of this type. (Austenå, 1976). In this respect, the 1974 act is undoubtedly the most extensive. The right of pre-emption can be used only when an owner has decided to sell the land and a binding contract has been written.

Using pre-emption, the State or the municipality then takes over the buyer's position. The State can use this right to acquire land suitable for agriculture and thereafter convey it to a farmer whose farm is too small to produce a sufficient living as a farmer. When a property is acquired for agricultural purposes and the State finds that the contract price is too high, the State may demand that the court establish the price, based on the utility value as an agricultural property. The intention of Parliament is clearly to keep the price of farmland lower than the price of other types of land.

## E. The Land Act (18 March 1955)

The purpose of the Land Act of 18 March 1955 is to ensure that all land with forest and mountain and related features is used for the greatest benefit to society and to those whose occupation is in agriculture (Falkanger, 1986a, pp. 128–32). Accordingly, the owner has an obligation to preserve cultivated land, keep it in proper condition, and actually use it for farming (sections 53 and 54). In each municipality a Land Board controls the farmers' use of land, registers misuse, and each year sends a report to the County Agricultural Board. The Land Board also recommends the steps to be taken to facilitate profitable operation.

If the County Agricultural Board finds the land kept in improper condition or lying fallow, it may instruct the owner on the steps necessary to ensure that the land, depending on the circumstances, produces a reasonable yield. A time limit shall be set for carrying out the instructions. The owner may also be ordered to lease the land for a period of normally not less than 5 years. If more far-reaching measures or investments are necessary to ensure a satisfactory level of production from the land, and the lessee and owner cannot agree on this, the question may be taken up with the County Agricultural Board before the measures are initiated (section 53).

When conditions mentioned in the Act (section 6) are satisfied and the County Agricultural Board makes a proposal to that effect, the State may expropriate the property to transfer it to others who will undertake to run it properly. The decision rests with the king.

Cultivated and tillable land cannot be used for purposes that are not directed towards agricultural production (section 54). In special cases the County Agricultural Board may grant dispensation if, after an overall assessment of the circumstances, they consider that the agricultural interests should give way. In this connection the County Agricultural Board may require the submission of alternative solutions. The County Agricultural Board may make it a condition that a corresponding acreage of open land be cultivated, if that possibility exists. The Land Board and the County Agricultural Board shall ensure that the provisions of this section are observed.

Property that is or can be used for agriculture or forestry may not be subdivided without approval of the County Agricultural Board (section 55). This rule also applies on land subject to farm tenancy leases, site leases, and similar leases or user-rights in any part of the property, when those rights are instituted for a period exceeding 10 years or when they cannot be revoked by the owner (lessor). The County Agricultural Board can only grant its approval for subdivision if it is justifiable in terms of commercial viability or if important community interests render it desirable.

## F. The Act of Tenancy (25 June 1965)

Leasing of agricultural land without buildings is free and not regulated for a period of ten years: a longer period has to be approved by the County Agricultural Board (Land Act, 18 March 1955). The agreement for leasing a farm with buildings has to be written and the rent must be in the form of money not in duties. The rent fixing is free between the parties, but it can be fixed by the Municipal Agricultural Board if there is disagreement.

In Norway, there is no provision for indexing of rents, but this can be incorporated into a lease. If the rent is unreasonably high, it may be unlawful according to section 18 of the Act of Controlling and Regulating of Prices, Profit and Competition (26 June 1953).

## G. The Forestry Act (21 May 1965)

The dominant tree species in Norway are Norway spruce, Scots pine and birch. Approximately 77% of the productive forest area is privately owned and consists mostly of smaller woods belonging to farms. Both forestry and farming are considered agricultural activities and form a unit in national agricultural policy. In forest areas throughout the country, everybody has free access for various recreational and outdoor activities.

The Forestry Act has as its objective to increase the productivity of forest land and to promote afforestation and forest protection. Its purposes are to obtain satisfactory results for those employed in forestry, to secure an effective and regular supply of raw material for industry, and to secure the forest as a source of recreation for the population. Under the Act, logging operations must be planned and carried out with reasonable consideration of the natural environment and recreational activities. Once the operations have been competed, care shall be taken not to obstruct the public use of paths, ski tracks, or other routes. If, in the opinion of the Forest Authority, a forest owner has planned, commenced, or carried out regeneration felling (including clear felling) in a way or to an extent that harms recreational interests or the natural environment, the Ministry of Agriculture may, on the recommendation of the County Agricultural Board, prohibit or limit further regeneration felling in that forest for a specified period.

To the extent necessary to prevent substantial harm or inconvenience to the recreational interests or substantial damage to the natural environment, including pollution of important water resources, the Ministry of Agriculture may refuse or give conditional permission to plant on land without trees. The decision is made on recommendation of the County Agricultural Board (section 17). The same procedure is to be followed if there are questions of changing tree species, drainage, fertilization, and use of chemicals, etc.

Where forest areas of particular value to recreational interests and nature conservation are concerned, the king may establish other and more far-reaching restrictions on forestry (section 17b).

### H. The Pollution Control Act (13 March 1984)

This Act is intended to protect the external environment from pollution, reduce existing pollution, and promote improved treatments of waste. The duty to avoid pollution is somewhat limited (section 8). Normal pollution from fishing, agriculture, and forestry is permitted to the extent that special regulations have not been issued pursuant to article 9, under which the Ministry of Environment has regulated storing and spreading of manure from husbandry (Regulations 1 March 1989). A farmer is obliged to have one acre per cow on which to spread manure (section 4). In one county, this regulation had consequences for about 60% of farmers raising livestock.

### I. The Act Regulating Rearing of Domestic Animals (13 June 1975)

This Act gives authority to regulate the size of each unit in husbandry. Without permission from the Ministry of Agriculture, no one can establish, increase, rebuild, renovate, take over or hire an establishment for breeding pigs and poultry if the total production capacity would exceed a stipulated limit. The limits today are a stock of 700 pigs, 42000 broilers and 8000 turkeys a year. The limit for hens is a stock of 2300 at the same time. One of the reasons for the Act is to ensure that the breeder has enough farmland for spreading the manure. Another reason is to avoid agricultural production in 'industrial complexes'.

### J. The Wildlife Act (29 May 1981)

The purpose of this Act is to ensure that wildlife and its habitats are managed in a way that preserves the productivity of nature and diversity of species. Within this framework, wildlife may be harvested for the benefit of agriculture and outdoor recreation. According to this Act (section 27), the landowner has the sole right to hunt and trap within the limitations laid down in the Act and in its regulations. To secure the economic foundation of the farm property, the hunting rights may not be detached from the property for a period of more than 10 years at a time, except when the hunting rights follow the user-rights to the property.

### L. The Act of Pesticides (5 April 1963)

According to this Act pesticides cannot be sold or used in any form for business activities without approval from proper authorities. Production and import of pesticides are not allowed without approval from the Ministry of Agriculture. Permission can be given in certain conditions, and for some types of pesticides permission can be given for free production and trade. Use of pesticides can also be regulated by means of standards in the Pollution Control Act. Furthermore, the Act of Forestry (section 17), gives power to stop the use of pesticides. This has so far not been done.

### M. The Open-air Recreation Act (28 June 1957)

According to this Act, everyone has the right to free passage on foot on uncultivated land all the year around, when this is done considerately and with due care. On cultivated land anyone may walk when the ground is frozen or covered by snow, but not between 30 April and 14 October.

## IV. The Agrarian Land Legislation and Government Policy

**1.** The main objectives of Norwegian agrarian policy have, for some decades, been: **(a)** to secure self-sufficiency of food and timber for the wood products industry; **(b)** to stabilize the base for settlements in areas with a weak economy; **(c)** to secure efficient, long-range, and justifiable resource exploitation; and **(d)** to secure farmers' economic and social conditions.

**2.** Areas suitable for agriculture are small in Norway. To achieve the goals mentioned above it has been, and still is, important to protect arable land. Rules in the Land Act and the planning legislation have been the means to achieve this goal.

**3.** An important part of the policy is to secure the economic base for people living in the agrarian districts. The price for farm products is to a great extent stipulated in an agreement between the State and the two main organizations for farmers. If the State and the organizations cannot agree, the Parliament will set the prices. The agreement covers not only prices but also other economic means to secure the use of agricultural land and the conditions in agricultural districts. The State has also established banks to help farmers buy farms and farmland, build houses, and buy necessary machinery for the farm. It is cheaper to borrow from this bank than from the ordinary finance market.

**4.** An important part of agrarian policy during the last few decades has been to bring up and stabilize farmers' income and living conditions to the average of industrial workers. To achieve this, the government has transferred money from the national budget through the agreement between the State and farmers' organizations mentioned above. Great weight is given to regionalization of the aid to districts with decreasing population and unfavourable conditions for agriculture. The strong farmers' co-operative organizations have played an important role in this policy.

Another important point of the policy is to reserve the Norwegian market for agrarian products for Norwegian farmers. Import of farm products is allowed as far as necessary to supplement Norwegian food production. Import restrictions make possible long-term planning of agriculture that is independent of fluctuation in world market prices.

**5.** To secure farm population in all districts of Norway the government uses, besides financial transfers, the rules in the Land Act, the Concession Act, and the Allodial Act (28 June 1974).

The allodial right is a special Norwegian legal institution with roots in our first written codes from the 11th century. The core of the right is to secure the relatives of the present owner the right to take over the ancestral farm when the owner transfers the farm to a person outside the circle of persons with allodial right. Persons have such right if either of their parents, grandparents, or a brother or sister of his parents has owned the farm with allodial right. The children of the present owner have highest priority, and the oldest girl or boy has the first right. Until 1975, boys were always ranked above girls (Falkanger, 1984). Persons who take over a farm pursuant to their allodial right are obliged to live on and run the farm for 5 years. If they take over the farm from a buyer outside the circle with allodial right, they have to live on and run the farm for 10 years (the Allodial Act, section 27).

The Land Act gives authority to secure sufficient farmland for active farmers; the Concession Act makes it possible to keep the price of farmland lower than the market price and to ensure that the owner of the farm really lives on the farm and uses it for farm production.

**6.** A condition for the policy to secure the farmers' income and economic welfare is increased productivity and an efficient use of the agricultural resources of the country. These demands have led to increased use of feed grain, fertilizer, chemicals, intensive felling of forests, and heavily increased mechanization. This again has led to damage to the environment and conflicts with interests of other groups using the environment for recreation. By means of the legislation mentioned in section III of this chapter, these conflicts can be resolved.

## V. Evaluation of the Agrarian Land Legislation

The legislation securing arable land for agricultural purposes has, as a whole, been successful. Use of arable land for densely built-up areas, roads, and other purposes has decreased.

The aim of being self-sufficient in food has been achieved for husbandry products, most vegetables, feed grains, and half the grain used for human consumption.

The government has not managed to bring the income of all farmers up to the level of an average industrial income. In fact, the gap has increased during recent years.

The key problems for the agrarian legislation today are the demands for internationalization of trade with agricultural products, reduction of transfer of economic resources to agricultural activities, and reduction of agricultural production to avoid damage to the environment. For Norway, with a hard climate and marginal conditions for agriculture, development could lead to an increased movement of people from the districts to the centres and the end of agrarian activities in many districts.

## References

Austenå, T. (1976) *Løsningsrettigheter. Forkjøps-tilbuds- og kjøperett til fast eiendom.* Universitetsforlaget, Oslo.

Austenå, T. (1978) *Konsesjonsreglane for fast eigedom.* Det Norske Samlaget, Oslo.

Bachke, A. and Steinsholt, H. (1988) *Land Consolidation in Norway.* National report on Expert Meeting on Land Consolidation in the Federal Republic of Germany, April 1988. Bundesministerium für Ernährung, Landwirtschaft und Forsten.

Backer, I.L. (1986) *Naturvern og naturinngrep.* Universitetsforlaget, Oslo.

Falkanger, T. (1984) *Odelsretten og åsetesretten.* Universitetsforlaget, Oslo.

Falkanger, T. (1986a) *Eierrådighet og samfunnskontroll.* Universitetsforlaget, Oslo.

Falkanger, T. (1986b) Planning law in Norway. In Garner, J.F. and Gravells, N.P. (eds), *Planning Law in Western Europe.* Elsevier Science Publishers B.V., North-Holland.

Falkanger, T. (1987) Acquisition of real property and state approval (concession). *Scandinavian Studies in Law,* 1987, pp. 57–79.

# 9

# AGRICULTURAL TENURE, LAND USE AND CONSERVATION IN THE UNITED KINGDOM

Christopher P. Rodgers

## I. Introduction

The volume of legislation imposing restrictions on the use of agricultural land in the UK has grown considerably in recent years. This is due in part to the impact of European Community policy, e.g. in the introduction of the setaside programme and conservation measures. A number of differing legal mechanisms are currently employed to impose restrictions on agricultural land use in the UK.

**1.** The policy pursued by UK conservation legislation has always been to encourage the voluntary participation by landowners and farmers in conservation measures. This has, hitherto, been achieved by providing for the designation of certain areas of the countryside for special protection, and empowering the statutory nature conservancy bodies (such as the Nature Conservancy Council) to conclude management agreements with landowners whereby the latter undertake to comply with stated conservation measures in their use of the land. So, for example, the NCC can designate land a 'site of special scientific interest' (SSSI) under the terms of the Wildlife and Countryside Act 1981. This has the effect of prohibiting damaging agricultural operations specified in the designation, until a management agreement can be concluded. The voluntary principle to conservation management has been extended in the UK by the implementation of EC Council Directive No. 797 of 1985 on the Improvement of Agricultural Structures. The Agricultural Act 1986 now enables the Minister of Agriculture to designate 'environmentally sensitive areas' within which management agreements and grant aid will be available to promote traditional and non-intensive farming techniques. The legislation applicable to conservation management is considered in more detail below.

**2.** The use of management agreements is supplemented in some situations by the use of planning control. Although the use of land for agriculture is, in the UK, outside the control of the planning legislation, certain kinds of agricultural development (erection of buildings, etc.) will be illegal if carried out without planning permission from the local planning authority. The use of compulsion to restrict agricultural operations in this way is reserved primarily for areas of national significance, e.g. special planning controls apply to agricultural operations in National Parks. Implementation of EC Council Directive No. 337 of 1985 (the Environmental Assessment Directive) now means, further, that some kinds of agricultural development will be subjected to an environmental assessment before planning permission can be granted.

**3.** Certain aspects of agricultural practice are subjected to regulation under legislation concerned with the prevention of pollution. This is the case, for instance, with facilities for the storage of silage and sewage sludge. The quality and design of such facilities are regulated under the terms of the Water Resources Act 1991, with a view to preventing poisonous or noxious substances from polluting watercourses, rivers, or water supply. Pollution of controlled waters, as a consequence of agricultural operations, can also constitute a criminal offence in some circumstances. The voluntary principle is also evident, however, in the increasing use of agricultural grants to encourage the adoption of conservation measures by farmers. The Farm and Conservation Grant Scheme 1991, for instance, provides grant aid to encourage farmers to introduce fixed equipment and improvements specifically aimed at preventing pollution and conserving the environment.

**4.** Implementation of EC Council Regulation No. 1094 of 1988, designed to encourage the setaside of arable land, has led to the introduction of regulations providing for grant aid to be paid to farmers taking arable land out of production. The setaside programme has been supplemented in the UK context by additional legislation (in the form of the Farm Diversification Scheme) providing grant aid for farmers and landowners in other sectors of the agriculture industry wishing to diversify into alternative ancillary uses of land.

Many of the specifically legal problems associated with the implementation of restrictions on agricultural land use arise from the distinctive structure of land tenure in the UK. It may, therefore, be apposite to consider the system of land tenure in the UK before discussing the relevant conservation measures in detail.

## II. Agricultural Land Tenure in the UK

The landlord and tenant system has always been a distinctive feature of the agriculture industry in the UK. It is a system which, however, has been in steady decline for many years. A comprehensive study of land tenure in the UK was conducted in the late 1970s by the Committee of Inquiry into the Acquisition and Occupancy of Agricultural Land (the Northfield Committee). Their report, published in 1979, concluded that the area of agricultural land subject to commercial tenancies had fallen from 88% in 1908 to little more than 35–40% by 1979. This decline was predicted to continue. More recently, the Ministry of Agriculture has itself put the figure for tenanted land at 36% (Agricultural Tenancy Law – Proposals for Reform, 1991). Although in decline, the landlord–tenant system obviously retains considerable importance. Clearly, any study of the effectiveness of conservation legislation in the UK must take account of the legislative policy underlying the tenancy legislation, and the interaction of a tenant's rights and duties thereunder with conservation objectives and restrictions on land-use. Additionally, it is important to an understanding of the various arrangements by which land is held outside the landlord–tenant system in the UK, e.g. under share farming or partnership arrangements.

Agricultural land tenure in England and Wales is governed by the Agricultural Holdings Act 1986. This confers on tenants of farmland extensive rights to security of tenure, control of rents, and compensation on termination of tenancy. The 1986 Act applies whenever the 'substantial' use to which the land let is put is agricultural. It may apply, therefore, where there are ancillary non-agricultural uses of the land concerned. If the tenant changes the use of land substantially to non-agricultural activities, however, the effect may be to abandon unilaterally the protection of the Agricultural Holdings Act 1986 (*Weatherall* v. *Smith* (1980), *Hickson & Welch Ltd.* v. *Cann* (1977)). This is an important consideration where tenants are diversifying their enterprise into non-agricultural business uses, e.g. pursuant to the farm diversification of setaside schemes.

Historically, most tenancies of farmland in the UK have been held on periodic annual tenancies. The 1986 Act confers security of tenure by converting any interest by which land is let for less than a tenancy from year to year into an annual tenancy with protection. Similarly, a contractual licence to occupy agricultural land is converted by statute into a yearly tenancy (1986 Act, section 2(2)(b)). The only caveat to this rule is that a licence, to be protected, must confer on the occupant exclusive possession of the land for agricultural purposes. One of the primary considerations in the use of share farming and partnership arrangements in the UK is that they provide a flexible medium for conducting an agricultural enterprise, but without conferring exclusive possession on the working farmer. The provisions of the Agricultural Holdings Act 1986 can therefore be avoided, provided always that the 'share' farming arrangement is not in substance a sham. Express exceptions to the security of tenure provisions exist for short-term grazing or mowing agreements, and for other temporary arrangements where the Ministry of Agriculture has consented to a letting for those purposes (1986 Act, sections 2(1) and 5). Where the Agricultural Holdings Act 1986 applies, it confers security of tenure by controlling the operation of any notice to quit given by the landlord. The notice must be of at least 12 months' duration ending on a term date of the tenancy, and the tenant can refer it to an agricultural land tribunal. The tribunal can only consent to the notice taking effect on stated grounds, e.g. where tenants have been guilty of bad husbandry or landlords would suffer the greater hardship if possession were refused them. If the tenant has committed breaches of tenancy, become bankrupt, or the land is required for development, the tribunal jurisdiction is excluded. In this event the tenant's only recourse is to demand arbitration on the facts alleged in the notice to quit[1].

A central feature of the Agricultural Holdings Act is that the extensive rights it confers on tenants are all predicated on the assumption that the tenant is farming efficiently and maintaining the optimum level of agricultural production for the holding concerned. The policy underlying the 1986 Act is therefore one of maximizing agricultural production. This is at variance with the legislative policy underlying the various conservation and setaside measures that have been introduced in the UK in recent years and has caused problems in the implementation of conservation policy where land is tenanted. That the tenant's rights are conditional on maintaining an efficient level of production is evident from the terms of the 1986 Act itself.

## A. Security of tenure

Landlords can request tribunal consent to a notice to quit on the grounds that it would be in the interests of good husbandry for them to repossess the land concerned. Additionally, if tenants are farming badly they can obtain a certificate of bad husbandry from an agricultural land tribunal. This will then entitle them to give notice to quit without being subject to the requirement of tribunal consent (1986 Act, Sched. 3, Case C and para.9). If landlords claim the tenant is in breach of the terms of the tenancy, the tenants' conduct is similarly to be judged according to whether s/he has acted in accordance with the rules of good husbandry. The 'rules' of good husbandry are set out in section 11 to the Agriculture Act 1947, and reflect the agricultural policy of the immediate post-war period. They require, for instance, that a tenant maintain an adequate stocking level and adopt efficient measures for the control of pests and other infestations. If the farm includes arable land, an efficient system of cropping must be employed.

### B. Rent control

Under the current rent formula, introduced in 1984 and now set out in Schedule 2 of the 1986 Act, an arbitrator fixing an agricultural rent must have regard to the 'productive capacity' and 'related earning capacity' of the holding. The productive capacity is defined as its productive capacity 'on the assumption that it is in the occupation of a competent tenant practising a system of farming suitable to the holding'. Earning capacity, similarly, is defined by reference to the extent to which a reasonably competent tenant, practising such a system of farming, could profit from farming the holding. Whatever the implications of conservation management policy, therefore, the rent will be determined as that which a reasonably competent farmer, practising an efficient method of agricultural production, would expect to pay.

### C. Improvements

The 1986 Act gives tenants the right to claim compensation for any improvements they have effected to the holding during their tenancy. The improvements for which compensation can be claimed are specified in schedule 7 to the 1986 Act, and are mostly agricultural in nature. Compensation can, however, be claimed for the erection of buildings and other permanent structures. It is not clear whether compensation can be claimed for non-agricultural buildings and structures, e.g. those erected pursuant to a diversification plan funded by grant aid. The measure of compensation is fixed by the 1986 Act as 'the amount equal to the increase attributable to the improvement in the value of the agricultural holding *as a holding*' (1986 Act, section 66(1); *italics added*). This would indicate that compensation is only available for agricultural buildings, etc. that enhance the rental value of the farm as a farm, and not for buildings erected for non-agricultural use – unless there is some express agreement as to compensation with the landowner. This rule, clearly, is another potent disincentive to farmers considering the options for diversification and for setaside of farmland.

As will become apparent, some of the relevant UK conservation legislation does make specific provision for landlord–tenant matters. On the whole, however, the legislation does not take adequate account of the distinctive legal problems to which this form of land tenure gives rise. Neither, as we will see, is UK conservation legislation consistent in its treatment of landlord and tenant issues. This is one major defect in the UK legislation governing land use and conservation management, and one which will have to be removed if the efficiency of conservation management measures is to be improved.

## III. Conservation and Land Management

The primary mechanism by which legally binding controls have been imposed on agricultural land use in the United Kingdom has been the use of management agreements with landowners and farmers, in areas designated as worthy of special protection on conservation grounds.

### A. Legislative protection of designated sites

The following areas are designated for special protection under a variety of legislative measures.

#### *1. Sites of Special Scientific Interest*

These are designated by the Nature Conservancy Council (and now its successors[2]) under powers contained in the Wildlife and Countryside Act, 1981. When notifying the owner or occupier of farmland that it has been designated an SSSI, the NCC must specify the flora, fauna, or geological/physiographical features by reason of which the land is of special interest and any operations that the Council believes would be likely to damage the flora, fauna, or other features of the site (1981 Act, section 28(4)). This can encompass a wide range of agricultural operations such as land reclamation, ploughing wildlife habitats, reseeding, and erecting agricultural buildings on sensitive sites.

The main import of designation under the 1981 Act is to prohibit the carrying out of agricultural operations specified in the designation order, unless they are carried out with the NCC's consent or under a management agreement. If farmers propose to carry out a prohibited operation, they must give the NCC 4 months' notice of their intention to do so. Prior notification enables the NCC to negotiate for the conclusion of a management agreement protecting the site. If a management agreement is not concluded, the operations can only be prohibited if the Secretary of State has consulted the NCC and has made a 'nature conservation order' under section 29 of the 1981 Act.

The making of a nature conservation order places considerable restrictions on the carrying out of agricultural operations on the land concerned. Once an order has been made, no person can carry out any operations specified in the order that are, in the opinion of the Secretary of State, likely to destroy or damage the flora, fauna, or geological or physiographical features of the site. The prohibitions contained in a nature conservation order are wider than those in an SSSI designation, in that they extend to actions by third parties, and not simply the owners and occupiers of the site itself.

### *2. Environmentally Sensitive Areas (ESAs)*

The Agricultural Act 1986 implements in UK law the requirements of Title V of the European Community Directive on Improving the Efficiency of Agricultural Structures. Section 18 of the 1986 Act empowers the Minister of Agriculture to designate an area of land an 'environmentally sensitive area'. Designation is by order made by Statutory Instrument.

Designation enables the Minister to enter into management agreements with farmers and landowners within the ESA area under the 1986 Act. The terms of proposed management agreements within an ESA area are set out in the designation orders made under section 18. These, in most cases, seek to impose positive obligations on participants in an ESA scheme to adopt traditional and non-intensive farming methods, e.g. by restricting the application of fertilizers and herbicides/pesticides, and by fixing maximum stocking levels. The conservation objectives of the ESA scheme thus proceed along strictly voluntary lines, there being no residual powers of compulsion vested in the Minister to compel landowners to enter into management agreements. In this respect the scheme differs from the regime applicable to SSSIs, where the NCC has, in some instances, power to acquire land compulsorily if a satisfactory management agreement is not concluded. Fourteen ESA designations have been made using these provisions.

### *3. National parks*

These are designated by the Countryside Commission under powers in the National Parks and Access to the Countryside Act 1949. The conservation functions of designation are, in the case of national parks, chiefly pursued through planning law, rather than the use of management agreements – although land within a designated national park may also, for instance, be within an SSSI in respect of which management agreements will be available. Furthermore, agricultural development within a National Park has for some time been subjected to special planning requirements for prior notification and approval (as to siting and design) if it consists of the erection, extension, or alteration of a building or the formation/alteration of a private right of way. These restrictions ensure that planning authorities retain control of the design, appearance, and location of agricultural buildings erected within a designated National Park. Following consultation as to the extension of the regime applicable in National Parks, prior notification has now been made a general requirement prior to the erection of most new agricultural buildings, whether or not they are situated within a National Park. Parallel provisions already apply to buildings and other operations for the purposes of Forestry. Additionally, special provisions apply to control agricultural operations on moor and heath within a designated national park (1981 Act, section 42).

### *4. Areas of Outstanding Natural Beauty (AONBs)*

AONBs are designated by the Countryside Commission under the National Parks and Access to the Countryside Act 1949. Control of environmental policy in AONBs rests with local authorities and is conducted largely through the medium of planning control, rather than management agreements. Local planning authorities also have power to make by-laws to protect land in an AONB. The Countryside Commission must be consulted on development plans in an AONB, as in a National Park, and they have power to give advice on development proposals.

### *5. Nature reserves*

Nature reserves are designated by the relevant Nature Conservancy Council under provisions in sections 15–17 National Parks and Access to the Countryside Act 1949. The latter provides that the NCC may enter into a management agreement with any owner, lessee or occupier of land that they consider should be managed as a nature reserve in the national interest. The agreement can impose such restrictions as seem expedient on the exercise of rights over the land, and provide for the management of the land in a manner appropriate to achieve the satisfactory maintenance of the land as a nature reserve. The agreement can also bind the NCC to defray some or all of the cost of managing the land, and may make provision for the payment of compensation to the owner or occupier for the effect of any agreed restrictions on the agricultural use of the land.

The conclusion of satisfactory management agreements is the primary mode of protecting such areas. Where no satisfactory agreement can be achieved, however, the NCC enjoys powers of compulsory acquisition.

The use of management agreements to protect the environment in nature reserves is supplemented by section 20 of the 1949 Act, which confers on the NCC the power to make by-laws for the protection of the reserve. These may, *inter alia*, prohibit or restrict entry to or movement within a reserve of people, animals, or vehicles, and restrict the killing of animals or destruction of vegetation.

### *6. Limestone pavement orders*

The Wildlife and Countryside Act 1981 includes special rules for the protection of 'limestone pavements'. These are areas of limestone wholly or partly exposed on the surface of the ground, which have been fissured by natural erosion. They are a feature of certain parts of the country only, and are by their nature especially vulnerable to damage from unsympathetic agricultural operations. Section 34 of the 1981 Act therefore provides in the first instance that if the NCC or the Countryside Commission believe that a limestone pavement is of special interest by reason of its flora, fauna, or geological/physiographical features, they must notify the planning authority in whose area the land is situated. If the planning authority or the Secretary of State believe the character or appearance of the land would be likely to be adversely affected by the removal or disturbance of the limestone, they have power to make a 'limestone pavement order' protecting the site. This will designate the site a recognized limestone pavement and prohibit the removal or disturbance of limestone on or in it. The making of an order has the effect of absolutely prohibiting agricultural operations likely to damage, or involve the removal of, limestone; there is no dispensation, for instance, for agricultural operations carried out in an emergency. The only available defence is that the operations were sanctioned by planning permission granted under Part III of the Town and Country Planning Act, 1990. In this respect, the regime applicable to designated limestone pavements is more rigorous than that applied, for instance, to Sites of Special Scientific Interest.

### *7. Nitrate Sensitive Areas*

The Water Resources Act 1991 confers on the Minister of Agriculture power, by order, to designate an area a 'nitrate-sensitive area' with a view to achieving the prevention or control of the entry of nitrates into controlled waters as a result of agricultural activities (1991 Act, section 94). The designation mechanism is applied in a more flexible manner by the 1991 Act than in previous countryside legislation. The Minister is empowered, following designation, to enter into management agreements with owners and/or occupiers of affected land on a voluntary basis. Additionally, however, the Minister has power when designating nitrate-sensitive areas to impose requirements, restrictions, and prohibitions on agricultural practices. Where restrictions are imposed by order, the Minister may pay compensation to affected owners and occupiers, but is not obliged to do so.

Ten 'voluntary' nitrate-sensitive areas have initially been designated under these provisions, as part of the 'pilot' nitrate sensitive areas scheme. The Nitrate-Sensitive Areas (Designation) Order 1990 provides for voluntary management agreements to be concluded within the designated areas to control nitrate pollution of watercourses and other controlled waters. The compulsory powers of direction available to the Minister remain available, however, to reinforce the voluntary approach if this is deemed appropriate.

### *8. Water protection zones*

The Water Resources Act 1991 also makes provision for the designation (by the Secretary of State) of 'water protection zones' with a view to preventing or controlling the entry of poisonous, noxious, or pollutant material into controlled waters (1991 Act, section 93). A designation under these provisions can impose restrictions and prohibition on specified agricultural activities, but not (it should be noted) positive obligations as to management and cultivation. Management agreements are not the favoured mechanism for the control of pollution in water protection zones, and are not available under the 1991 Act.

## B. Management agreements

The legislation providing for the designation and protection of special areas (above) makes provision for different classes of management agreement in different areas and under different conservation schemes. They are available in the following situations.

### *1. Nature reserves*

The National Parks and Access to the Countryside Act 1949 gives the NCC power to enter into an agreement to secure the management of land as a nature reserve, but only where they consider it would be in the national interest that it should be so managed. An agreement can be made with 'every owner, lessee or occupier' of agricultural land and can impose such conditions as seem to the NCC to be expedient. The agreement is intended to limit the exercise of legal rights of exploitation and use of the land by the owner or tenant in occupation.

### *2. Sites of Special Scientific Interest*

Power to enter into management agreements where land is included in a notified SSSI is conferred on the relevant conservancy council by section 15 of the Countryside Act 1968. The NCC can now also offer an agreement to the occupier of land adjacent to a designated SSSI where this is, for instance, necessary to protect the site itself (Environmental Protection Act

1990, Schedule 9, para. 4). It has recently been held in *Sweet* v. *Secretary of State and Nature Conservancy Council* (1989), that a designation under the 1981 Act can include land that forms a 'single environment' with a site considered of special interest or importance within the meaning of the 1981 Act. A management agreement may therefore be available to restrict agricultural operations on land adjacent or near the site of primary interest, but which forms part of a single wildlife habitat.

In practice, the NCC will commonly offer a management agreement where the owner or occupier has notified the intention to carry out agricultural operations prohibited by the order designating the site an SSSI. One major weakness of the regime applicable to SSSIs is that if a management agreement cannot be concluded, the only recourse currently open to the NCC is to seek the imposition of a nature conservation order. Damaging agricultural operations can only be prevented if the NCC invokes its powers of compulsory purchase, if all else fails.

### *3. Refusal of capital grant*

Where an application is made to the Ministry of Agriculture for a capital grant (for instance, to finance agricultural improvements), but this is refused after objections by the NCC or local authorities, the latter can in some circumstances be compelled to offer a management agreement.

By virtue of section 32 of the Wildlife and Countryside Act 1981, when considering an application for capital grant to finance operations on land notified as an SSSI, the Minister must exercise his or her functions so as to further the conservation of the flora, fauna, or geological/physiographical features by reason of which the land is of special interest. Furthermore the Minister cannot make a grant without first considering the terms of the NCC's objections (if any). Similar provisions apply to applications for capital grant to carry out operations on land within a national park.

Where the application for grant is refused, the NCC (or other objecting body) must within 3 months of receiving notice of refusal, offer to enter into a management agreement with the applicant. This must make provision for restrictions to be placed on the activities in respect of which the grant has been refused, and make provision for payments to the applicant.

### *4. Environmentally Sensitive Areas*

The Agriculture Act 1986 confers on the Minister of Agriculture power to enter into a management agreement with 'any person having an interest in agricultural land' wholly or partly within a designated ESA area. The terms of each individual management agreement (including rates of payment) will be specified in the designation order itself. By virtue of section 18(4) the designation order may specify the requirements as to agricultural practices, methods, and operations, and the installation or use of equipment, which must be included in management agreements. It may also specify the minimum period for which agreements are to impose such restrictions on farming methods and/or a fixed period for which agreements are to run. The designation orders made under the 1986 Act invariably provide for a flat-rate payment per hectare to be paid to participating farmers and landowners for a 5-year agreement. Where agreements have been entered in a designated area, the Act imposes a duty on the Minister to arrange for the effect, on the area as a whole, of the performance of the agreements to be kept under review, and for this information (where appropriate) to be published.

Management agreements under the 1986 Act commonly impose restrictions as to the application of herbicides, pesticides, and certain fertilizers, and provide for maximum stocking levels to prevent over-grazing. The prescriptions naturally vary according to the predominant form of agriculture (livestock farming, arable, etc.) current in the locality.

### *5. General powers*

Section 39 of the Wildlife and Countryside Act 1981 confers a general power to enter into management agreements upon county and local planning authorities. The use of this power is actively encouraged by central government, although it is, of course, subject to the financial constraints within which local government operates. (See Department of Environment Circular 27/1987, especially paras 39(k) and 40.)

### *6. Nitrate Sensitive Areas*

The terms on which management agreements are available in the ten designated NSAs are laid down in considerable detail in the Nitrate Sensitive Areas (Designation) Order 1990. Two types of agreement are available. Farmers and landowners can opt for either a 'basic scheme agreement' or a 'premium scheme agreement' with enhanced levels of grant (1990 Order, article 5 and Schedules 1 and 2). The terms on which both types agreement may be entered into are set out in detail in Schedules 1 and 2 of the designation order. The principal objective of basic scheme agreements is to impose restrictions on the use of nitrates on arable crops. The 1990 order provides, for instance, that an agreement must stipulate that a farmer shall not apply in a single application inorganic fertilizer in excess of that containing 120 kg of nitrogen per hectare, and shall not apply to certain crops more than specified amounts of inorganic nitrogen fertilizer. Some positive obligations are also to be imposed, however; e.g. slurry or liquid sludge must be stored in a way that will avoid the entry of nitrates into controlled waters. Where a premium scheme agreement is sought, a participating farmer will be obliged to cease arable production altogether and establish a grassland sward by 1 October next following the conclusion of the management agreement. The farmer will, further, be obliged to opt for one of four alternative modes of management and to comply with the detailed obligations laid down in Schedule 2 of the 1990 Order. The latter enables a farmer to opt for conversion to unfertilized and ungrazed grassland, to grassland with grazing (with or without limited application of fertilizers), or for conversion of arable land to grassland with woodland. Premium scheme agreements also impose more extensive positive obligations as to land management on the participating farmer or landowner.

## C. Management agreements and agricultural tenure

A common theme of the various designating measures is that they empower the NCC, Minister, or local authority (whichever applies) to enter into management agreements with any person having an 'interest' in the land to which the agreement relates[3]. The classes of potential participants are therefore defined by reference to the categories of estate and interest in land recognized in English land law. This fails to take account, however, of the special nature of many of the arrangements by which agricultural land is held (such as share farming), or, indeed, of the impact of the tenancy protection legislation on the rights and duties of many agricultural occupiers.

An agreement can clearly be concluded in most cases with a tenant occupying land within a designated area or any other person having a sufficient legal interest to be able to guarantee performance of the obligations in the proposed management agreement. It is common, however, for land to be occupied for agricultural purposes under a variety of arrangements, many of which do not create an 'interest' in land in the required sense, e.g. a share farmer occupying under a joint venture arrangement will have no legal 'interest' in the land. The ability of the parties to a joint venture to participate in management agreements will ultimately depend upon the terms of the joint venture contract.

Special problems arise where a management agreement is sought with a tenant or someone occupying under some lesser form of interest (such as a licence) which is caught by the Agricultural Holdings Act 1986. The failure of current legislation to address the impact of conservation obligations on the rights and duties of landlord and tenant *inter se* inevitably creates practical problems in the implementation of conservation policy.

In the first place, the differing conservation measures make different provisions as to the formal requirements to be satisfied by a tenant wishing to enter into a management agreement. The Water Resources Act 1991 makes it a precondition that a tenant wishing to conclude a management agreement in a Nitrate Sensitive Area obtain the landlord's written consent prior to doing so (1991 Act, section 95(2)). On the other hand the Environmentally Sensitive Areas provisions require only that written notice be given to a landlord prior to the conclusion of an agreement (1986 Act, section 18(6)). Other conservation legislation makes no provision whatever for the landlord/tenant relationship, e.g. the SSSI provision in the Wildlife and Countryside Act 1981. There would appear to be no coherent policy reason for the different treatment of landlord and tenant matters in the different statutes.

Where a management agreement is concluded in an SSSI, or by a local authority using its general powers, the concurrence of the landlord will be necessary to secure the long-term protection of the site. Ministerial guidance issued to the NCC indicates that before offering a management agreement they should require the tenant to notify the owner of the land of the proposed operations which gave rise to the management agreement offer, of the area it will cover, and whether or not the offer of an agreement is likely to be accepted (Department of Environment Circular no. 41 of 1983, paras 7 and 8). Although notification alone is required, tenants will in practice be well advised to obtain their landlord's consent before concluding an agreement. Performance of the obligations in a management agreement could put the tenant in breach of the rules of good husbandry and entitle the landlord to give notice to quit. If the rules have been incorporated as an express term of the tenancy, moreover, landlords may be able to claim breach of the tenancy agreement itself, thereby furnishing themselves with an additional (and stronger) ground on which to serve notice to quit. The policy of the NCC in such cases is therefore to conclude a complementary agreement with landlords or to include their interest in the principal agreement in return for a nominal payment (Nature Conservancy Council, 1988). The landlords' position is otherwise protected by the Agricultural Holdings Act itself; e.g. they will be entitled to receive a proportion of grant monies paid to the tenants on rent review.

Similar considerations apply to agreements concluded in environmentally sensitive areas under the Agriculture Act 1986. Although a tenant's only duty is to notify the owner, he or she will be well advised to obtain the latter's consent to avoid potential problems of breach of tenancy. In practice this means that negotiations between landlord and tenant as to apportionment of grant monies may delay the implementation of conservation management schemes. The problem is recognized by the Agricultural Holdings Act 1986, insofar as the latter provides the tenant with a defence to claims of breach of tenancy, but only if the tenancy agreement (or some other agreement with the landlord) includes an express covenant allowing the tenant to farm in accordance with stated conservation objectives (1986 Act, Schedule 3 paras 10(1)(d) and 11(2)). If landlords are unwilling to grant tenancy agreements on such terms, there is no legal mechanism by which they can be compelled to do so.

## IV. Control of Agricultural Development

Agricultural operations and the use of land and/or buildings for agricultural purposes enjoy special privileges under the UK planning legislation. The Town and Country Planning Act 1990 provides, in general, that planning permission is required before any 'development' involving land or buildings can take place. Development is defined in wide terms to include 'the carrying out of building, engineering, mining, or other operations in, on, over and under land, or the making of any material change in the use of any buildings or other land' (1990 Act, section 55(1)[4]). Any operation which involves 'development', thus defined, requires planning permission under the 1990 Act before it can be carried out lawfully.

Control of agricultural development is provided for under the terms of the 1990 Act itself and the Town and Country Planning General Development Order 1988. Certain kinds of agricultural activity are exempted from the requirement of planning permission. Firstly, section 55(2)(e) of the 1990 Act exempts from the definition of 'development' the use of land or existing buildings for agriculture, or a change of use of land or buildings to agricultural use. This provision therefore exempts from planning control a change of use of land or buildings from a non-agricultural to an agricultural use (irrespective of the nature of the proposed agricultural user). (See, e.g. *McKellan* v. *Minister of Housing and Local Government* (1966).) It also exempts from planning control a change in the use of land or buildings from one agricultural use to another. If, however, it is proposed to erect new structures or buildings, or to modify existing ones, this may constitute a development requiring planning permission. In this event, the terms of the General Development Order (below) will need to be considered to ascertain whether automatic planning permission is thereby granted for the development proposed. For a development requiring permission to occur, there must be an activity resulting in some physical alteration to the land itself, with a degree of permanence (*Restormel B.C.* v. *Secretary of State* (1982)). It has been held, for instance, that merely placing an existing object (such as a caravan) onto agricultural land will not constitute development, provided the object/structure concerned is intended for agricultural use (*Wealdon D.C.* v. *Secretary of State* (1988)). Where no building or other operations are involved, planning permission will not be required unless there is a 'material' change of use to a non-agricultural use of the whole or part of the land and/or buildings included in the agricultural unit. Activities incidental to the farming of a holding will not constitute a material change of use, e.g. retail selling of vegetables and other produce of the holding itself. If ancillary business activities are not strictly ancillary to the farming of the holding, however, a material change of use may have occurred, e.g. where a 'lairage' for the storage and transport of livestock raised on other holdings is erected on the subject holding (as in *Warnock* v. *Secretary of State* (1980)).

The exemption of agricultural use from planning control is supplemented by Schedule 2, Part 6 of the Town and Country Planning General Development Order 1988. This grants automatic planning permission for a wide range of operations involving development on agricultural holdings of 5 ha or more, including the erection and modification of buildings, excavation and engineering operations. These 'permitted' development rights are subjected by the 1988 Order to conditions, with the intention of restricting and regulating large-scale developments on agricultural land, and especially those constituting potential nuisances to adjoining occupiers and the public at large. The development rights granted by the 1988 order are divided into three classes. Schedule 2, Class A, the most important, gives permission for the erection, extension, or alteration of a building, or for any excavation or engineering operations, 'reasonably necessary' for the purposes of agriculture within an agricultural unit. In order to prevent intensive development of small parcels of land, however, development cannot be carried out on land less than 1 ha in extent. For the purpose of calculating the ground area of the development no account is taken of separate parcels of land on which development is proposed. Permission does not extend to the erection, extension, or alteration of a dwelling, nor to any other building or structure not 'designed for the purposes of agriculture'.

Additional restrictions apply to livestock units and other buildings erected under Class A, in that development is not permitted if the ground area to be covered would exceed 465 $m^2$. For this purpose, the ground area of the proposed development is taken together with that of any other structure or building which is (or would be) within 90 m of the curtilage of the proposed development and which has been erected within the preceding 2 years (Class A, para. 3(1)(b)). This provision is intended to prevent intensive development of, e.g. livestock units. It can, however, be circumvented by 'spacing' units or buildings at more than 90 m, and/or staging development at 2-yearly intervals. Special rules also apply to developments near roads and aerodromes. Development is not permitted if the height of any building or structure within 3 km of the perimeter of an aerodrome would exceed 3 m. Similarly, if any part of a proposed development is within 25 m of the metalled portion of a classified road then the whole development is unauthorized.

Where development is permitted under the terms of the General Development Order it may also be subjected to conditions, e.g. if it involves the erection of livestock units, or slurry or sewage facilities. Development is not permitted if it would consist of the erection of buildings or structures to be used for the accommodation of livestock or for the storage of sewage sludge or slurry, if the proposed structure is, or could be, within 400 m of the curtilage of a dwelling on adjoining land. Where a permitted development is carried out within 400 m of a protected building, furthermore, the Order imposes the condition that any building or structure erected cannot be used to house livestock, or to store sewage sludge or slurry, within 5 years of the development. This provision is intended to prevent the erection of agricultural buildings using permitted rights under Class A and their subsequent conversion to livestock use or slurry storage. The Order also places restrictions on the bringing of waste material onto agricultural land; this is permitted only if it is intended for permitted building works or the creation of a hard surface. The excavation of minerals necessary for farming the holding concerned is also granted deemed permission. Class B of Schedule 6 to the 1988 Order grants more restricted development rights for holdings of less than 5 ha. Special development rights apply to operations connected with fish farming, and the construction of ponds, etc. for use in connection with fish farming and shellfish farming.

The consequences of the existing exemptions for agricultural use and the deemed permission granted by the 1988 order (above), is that an application for planning permission is not necessary for many kinds of agricultural development. Where no permission is required, however, prior notification of the erection of buildings must now be given to the local planning authority, which has a certain measure of control over the design, layout and appearance of the proposed erections. Where planning permission is required, moreover, the control of agricultural operations in the interests of environmental protection has now been enhanced by the implementation in UK law of the European Community directive on Environmental Impact Assessment (Council Directive (EC) no. 337 of 1985). This requires member states to subject certain kinds of agricultural operation to an environment assessment, prior to giving planning permission for the operation, where they consider it could result in a significant effect on the environment. The directive has been implemented in UK law by incorporating its requirements into the existing consent procedures for major agricultural developments.

**1.** As we have seen, many kinds of agricultural development are outside the control of UK planning legislation. The Agriculture Act 1986 now requires the Minister, however, to take into account the environmental impact of proposed developments when assessing applications for capital grants to finance improvements, etc. on individual holdings. There is a question whether the UK legislation satisfies the terms of the directive, in that no environmental assessment is provided for if a landowner or farmer undertakes a damaging development without applying for grant aid.

**2.** Where planning permission is required, the Town and Country Planning (Assessment of Environmental Effects) Regulations 1988[5] now require the local planning authority to have regard for the likely environmental effects of the development when deciding whether to grant permission. This requirement applies where the authority (or the Secretary of State) considers that the development would be likely to have a 'significant' effect on the environment by virtue of its nature, size, or location. Where environmental assessment is applied, the applicant for planning permission is required to submit an Environmental Statement of the project's likely effects, with supporting evidence, to the planning authority. This requirement is likely to apply chiefly to major agricultural projects. Those specified by the regulations include water management schemes, poultry and pig rearing, salmon hatcheries, and land reclamation from the sea. Ministerial guidance has been issued which indicates, for instance, that new pig rearing installations will not require environmental assessment unless they are designed to house more than 400 sows or 5000 fattening pigs, and that poultry rearing installations should only be subjected to assessment if intended to house more than 100000 broilers or 50000 layers, turkeys or other poultry (Department of Environment, Circular no. 15 of 1988, para. 20 and App.A). It is unlikely, therefore, that the introduction of environmental assessment in UK law will have a great impact on the majority of mixed agricultural enterprises.

## V. Setaside of Farmland and Diversification

The European Community programme for the setaside of arable land was introduced in the UK by the Set Aside Regulations 1988. The setaside scheme, intended as it is to encourage cessation of arable production and diversification into non-arable enterprises, should be viewed against a background of increased emphasis in domestic UK legislation on the diversification of agricultural enterprises. This has been manifested in legislation, making grants available to all sectors of agriculture to diversify into non-agricultural enterprises, e.g. the Farm Diversification Scheme 1987, considered below.

The setaside scheme for arable crops operates in the UK on strictly voluntary principles. Under the 1988 regulations, participation in the scheme and grant payments are available to producers who occupy arable land as either an owner or tenant, and have occupied the holding concerned for at least 12 months. Participation by tenants is limited to those occupying under a tenancy from year to year (the usual arrangement), or under a fixed-term lease with at least 5 years unexpired. The land to be setaside must, furthermore, have been in arable production during the 'reference period', i.e. 1 July 1987 to 30 June 1988. The definition of qualifying applicants by reference to the categories of property interest recognized in English law (lessees, freehold owners, etc.) means that some commonly encountered arrangements, such as share farming contracts, may not confer a right of participation on the working farmer. In order to receive grant payments under the scheme, an applicant must undertake for a 5-year period to setaside and withdraw from production an area of arable land of at least 20% of the arable land on the holding during the reference period. The area setaside cannot, moreover, exceed the total area used for arable production during the reference period. These basic requirements, which must be met by all applicants, implement the terms of Council Regulation (EC) No. 1094 of 1988 as to the broad features of national setaside schemes.

In addition to these fundamental obligations, the UK regulations require the applicant for setaside to opt for one of four optional uses of the land concerned. Land withdrawn from production can either be used as permanent or rotational fallow, grazed fallow, converted to woodland, or used for non-agricultural purposes during the setaside period. Following criticism of the scheme on, *inter alia*, conservation grounds, amendments were introduced in 1990 to enhance the environmental protection of setaside land, and to introduce greater flexibility in an applicant's choice of optional uses (Setaside (Amendment) Regulations 1990). The new requirements apply to applications made after 1 October 1990. So, for instance, land which has been setaside for non-agricultural purposes or woodland can now also be put to a combined use with either grazed fallow or permanent/rotational fallow.

The UK regulations specify detailed obligations to be undertaken by applicants opting for each of the setaside 'options'.

**1.** Where an applicant sets land aside to fallow, he will have to comply with the obligations specified in Schedule 2 to the 1988 regulations. The latter require, following amendments introduced in 1990, that plant cover be cut at least twice a year, and that unimproved grassland, moor, heath, and vernacular buildings be maintained. Plant cover must be established immediately following the commencement of setaside, and the application of fertilizers, slurry and manure is authorized in limited circumstances only. Cuttings cannot be used for feeding livestock.

**2.** A limited 'grazed fallow' option was introduced in 1990, under which applicants who had livestock during the reference period can opt to graze on their holding no more than the equivalent number of livestock units on the land during that period. If no livestock were kept during the reference period, setaside land can only be used as grazed fallow for deer and goats up to one livestock unit per forage hectare. Where the grazed fallow option is pursued, the applicant's obligations are more onerous than under the permanent or rotational fallow options. The area to be grown must be sown and maintained as grassland throughout the setaside period, and fertilizers, herbicides, and pesticides cannot be applied more than 12 months after sowing. Grass cover can be cut once a year (but not more), and cuttings can be fed to livestock – although not sold. Environmental features such as vernacular buildings and stone walls must be maintained.

**3.** If applicants opt to convert setaside land to woodland, they must maintain the land as permanent or rotational fallow until planting commences.

**4.** Similarly, if land is to be put to a permitted non-agricultural use, it must be maintained as permanent or rotational fallow, subject to the restrictions appropriate thereto (above) until the new use commences. The UK regulations do not specify those non-agricultural uses which qualify for grant aid, and any non-agricultural diversification may in principle qualify. Certain non-agricultural uses are excepted, however, chiefly on environmental grounds. Thus land setaside cannot be used for mineral extraction or the erection of industrial buildings, or for the erection of buildings intended for retail or wholesale sale of goods, residential use, office accommodation or storage and distribution.

The setaside scheme has met with a very limited degree of success in the UK. Ministry of Agriculture statistics indicate that, in the 3 years to 1991 during which the scheme has operated, 3794 applications have been received and approximately 3.5% of the total UK arable land (totalling 131543 ha) has been setaside and taken out of production (Ministry of Agriculture (1990), Release 397/90). The setaside provisions, however, operate strictly within the confines of existing consent procedures for non-agricultural development and the rules governing land tenure and farm leases. The latter give rise to problems and may act as a disincentive to certain categories of occupiers wishing to participate. Planning permission will be required, for instance, for the non-agricultural use of setaside land and for developments not falling within the terms of the General Development Order (above). Similarly, where applicants hold land under a tenancy agreement, setting land aside to permanent or (possibly) rotational fallow could constitute a breach of the rules of good husbandry and entitle the landowners to forfeit the tenants' interest. Turning land over to a non-agricultural use would also constitute a breach of most farm leases. This is a facet of English property law which, as we have seen, also causes problems in the implementation of conservation management policy.

The setaside scheme for arable land is, insofar as it promotes the conversion of land to non-agricultural uses, an instrument of diversification, albeit limited to arable holdings. Public policy has recently moved strongly in favour of encouraging diversification into ancillary farm businesses and non-agricultural uses in all sectors of British agriculture, however. The voluntary principle is again prominent. The Farm Diversification Scheme 1987 makes provision for grant aid for capital expenditure incurred in diversifying farm businesses, up to a maximum of 25% of qualifying expenditure. This is complemented by the Farm Business Non-Capital Grant Scheme 1988, which makes grant aid available for revenue expenditure incurred in diversifying and marketing agricultural products and services, e.g. the preparation of marketing and feasibility plans. The ancillary farm businesses which will qualify for grant aid are specified in similar terms in the 1987 and 1988 regulations, and include the following: farm-based industries (e.g. craft manufacture, food processing, repair/renovation of agriculture machinery), farm shops, retail sales of fruit and vegetables, provision of sports and recreational facilities, educational facilities, livery and the provision of ponies or horses for hire. Letting land or building for any of these purposes will also qualify. As with the setaside scheme, however, diversification must be viewed against the general law as to planning consent and land tenure. The need for planning permission must be considered before erecting buildings or commencing activities not in themselves strictly 'agricultural', e.g. the running of educational courses or selling produce in a manner not strictly incidental to the principal agricultural enterprise. Where a holding is leased, furthermore, the terms of the Agricultural Holdings Act 1986 will need to be considered. The applicant will need to ensure that diversification will not involve breaches of his tenancy agreement. As already mentioned (above, section II6), there is also a question whether compensation can be claimed for improvements (such as the erection of buildings) that are not agricultural in nature. Here, once again, the tenure and planning laws fail to take account of the public policy interest in encouraging diversification and the reduction of agricultural production.

## VI. Postscript: A New Era of Regulation?

It will be apparent from the foregoing that agriculture in the UK has, hitherto, been largely exempted from legal controls of a regulatory or mandatory nature. There are no legal restrictions on the ownership of agricultural land or on the minimum size of holdings, and conservation measures have largely been introduced within a voluntary framework. Control of pollution from agriculture is now, however, assuming a more prominent place in domestic public policy, and this is reflected in an increasing volume of anti-pollution legislation controlling certain agricultural land uses. These measures are regulatory in nature and not voluntary, *c.f.* the existing countryside legislation discussed above. It is already an offence to knowingly permit or cause the discharge of noxious or polluting substances into ponds, rivers and watercourses (Water Resources Act, 1991, sections 85 and 96). This criminal sanction has recently been supplemented by regulations, made under the Water Act 1989, setting compulsory minimum standards for silage, slurry and agricultural fuel oil installations (Control of Pollution etc. Regulations 1990). Breach of these requirements is a criminal offence carrying a substantial fine on conviction. Extension of the planning laws to require notification of a farmer's intention to erect or modify agricultural buildings also represents a major change in policy, and will give the public planning authorities greater control of the siting and design of buildings and other agricultural operations. Whether these measures represent a fundamental change in legal policy towards agriculture remains to be seen. They do, however, clearly impose substantial additional burdens on the agriculture industry in the UK at a time of economic difficulty and contraction.

## Notes

1. This is provided by section 26(2) and Schedule 3 to the 1986 Act, and the Agricultural Holdings (Arbitration Notices) Order 1987, SI 1987 No. 710.
2. The Nature Conservancy Council for England, Nature Conservancy Council for Scotland and the Countryside Council for Wales. These bodies are established by the Environmental Protection Act 1990, and by virtue of section 132 assume the designation functions of the (former) Nature Conservancy Council.
3. See, e.g. section 18(3) Agriculture Act 1986 in respect of environmentally sensitive areas. Also section 15 Countryside Act 1968 (SSSIs), section 39 Wildlife and Countryside Act 1981.
4. 'Development' also includes the demolition and alteration of existing buildings: Planning and Compensation Act 1991, section 13(1).
5. The Planning and Compensation Act 1991, section 15, has now introduced provisions enabling the Secretary of State to make regulations stipulating the consideration to be given, before planning permission is granted for the specified class of development, to the likely environmental effects of the development.

## References

Agricultural Holdings (Arbitration on Notices) Order 1987, SI 1987 No. 710.

Control of Pollution (Silage, Slurry and Agricultural Fuel Oil) Regs. 1991, SI 1991 No. 325.

Department of the Environment (1983) Circular 41/1983.

Department of the Environment (1987) Circular 27/1987.

*Hickson & Welch Ltd.* v. *Cann* (1977) 40 Property and Compensation Reports 218 (Note).

*McKellan* v. *Minister of Housing and Local Government* (1966) 198 *Estates Gazette* 683.

Ministry of Agriculture, Fisheries and Food, 'Set Aside: Third Year Take Up' (Joint Announcement by the Agriculture Departments, 17 December 1990, MAFF release 397/1990).

Ministry of Agriculture, Fisheries and Food, 'Agricultural Tenancy Law – Proposals for Reform' (Joint Announcement by the Agriculture Departments, 12 February 1991, MAFF release 45/1991).

Nitrate Sensitive Areas (Designation) Order 1990, SI 1990 Nos 1013 and 1187.

Report of the Committee of Inquiry into the Acquisition and Occupancy of Agricultural Land (1979) Cmnd. 7599 (HMSO).

*Restormel Borough Council* v. *Secretary of State* (1982). *Journal of Planning Law* 785.

Set Aside Regulations 1988, SI 1988 No. 1352.

Set Aside (Amendment) Regulations 1990, SI 1990 No. 1716.

*Sweet* v. *Secretary of State and Nature Conservancy Council* (1989) Journal of Planning and Environmental Law 927.

Town and Country Planning General Development Order 1988, SI 1988 No. 1813.

Town and Country Planning General Development (Amendment No. 2) Order 1991, SI 1991 No. 2268.

*Warnock* v. *Secretary of State* (1980) *Journal of Planning Law* 590.

*Wealdon District Council* v. *Secretary of State* (1988) 56 *Planning and Compensation Reports* 286.

*Weatherall* v. *Smith* (1980) 2 *All England Law Reports* 530.

# 10

# Agricultural Land-use Law in the United States

Margaret Rosso Grossman

## I. Introduction

### A. The context for agricultural land law

The law that governs agricultural land in the United States forms part of the complex body of law that results from a common law system with a federal government. Law comes from a number of separate, but interrelated sources. Federal and state constitutions provide overarching principles, while state and federal statutes and local ordinances are enacted by legislative bodies and are often implemented by administrative agencies, which promulgate regulations. Decisions of courts, organized in both federal and state systems, develop common law doctrines and play an important role in interpreting statutes, regulations, and constitutional provisions.

The interrelationship of state and federal law reflects in part the constitutional allocation of powers to the federal and state governments. Under the US Constitution, Congress is vested with certain enumerated powers (US Constitution article I, section 1). Among these is the power derived from the Commerce Clause (article I, section 8, clause 3), which authorizes a wide spectrum of federal regulation, including much of the federal law that governs agriculture. In addition, Congress has authority to enact all laws necessary and proper for carrying out its constitutional powers (article I, section 8, clause 18).

The Constitution also ensures that individual states retain some measure of sovereignty. Powers not delegated to the federal government or otherwise prohibited to the states are reserved to the states or to the people (amendment X). One important power that resides in state government is the so-called 'police power', which gives state governments the authority to legislate to protect the public health, safety, and welfare. Used for a variety of state regulatory schemes, the police power is the basis for many state laws that regulate agriculture and the use of agricultural land. Moreover, some aspects of state police power are often delegated to county and municipal governments.

By granting specific powers to the federal government and reserving others to the states, the Constitution restricts the regulatory authority of the federal government. Since the early years of the nation, the nature of this relationship between federal and state powers has been subject to debate. Even in the recent past, issues of 'federalism' have continued to provoke conflict between the federal and state governments. The direct coercion the federal government can exert over states is limited; states can co-operate voluntarily (or induced by incentives) with the federal government.

The doctrine of pre-emption delineates the extent of federal power to exclude state governments from an area of legislation and the constitutional inability of states to enter some areas of legislation (Freeman, 1972). This doctrine, based on the Supremacy Clause (article VI, clause 2), establishes that a state law is void if it conflicts with the US Constitution or if it is inconsistent with federal statutes enacted by Congress under a specific power enumerated in the Constitution. If Congress has the constitutional authority to pre-empt state law, pre-emption (total or partial) can be imposed either by specific provision in a statute or by judicial decision.

Partial pre-emption, often used for environmental laws affecting agricultural land, centralizes policy formulation, but shares implementation with state government. The federal government exercises its authority to set regulatory policy; state governments are then encouraged to adopt, administer and enforce national policy standards. States retain some control and can design programmes for individual problems (Grossman, 1987).

## II. Agricultural Land

### A. Real property

The term 'property' is used broadly to refer to anything that is the subject of ownership, that has exchangeable value, or that makes up wealth or an estate. Rights in property are classified according to the nature of the object with which they are connected. Modern American law distinguishes between real property (land with objects permanently attached) and personal property (chattels). This distinction corresponds closely with the civil law distinction between immovable and movable property. Rights and responsibilities of owners may depend on the classification of the property.

Real property encompasses land and (usually) whatever is erected, growing on, or affixed to that land. Thus, real property ordinarily includes buildings constructed on land, as well as unsevered minerals found on the land. Some things are so closely associated with land that for some purposes they are treated as realty. Fixtures (permanently affixed to realty), growing crops, and sometimes water fit into this category. The treatment or even the nature of property may change. For example, trees or growing crops may be considered real or personal property, depending on the stage of development and the intentions of the owner. Soil is part of the real estate, but severed topsoil or fill may become personalty.

## B. Agricultural land

These general distinctions between real and personal property also apply to agricultural property. Agrarian real property (land) constitutes a large part of the area of the United States. Only about 2% of the 2.3 billion acres is urban land. Indeed, of the 1.414 million acres of non-federal land, the majority is rural. Cropland makes up 421 million acres; pasture, 133 million; rangeland, 406 million; and forest, 394 million; other uses, 60 million (USDA, 1989a). Much of this land is privately owned.

The federal government owns approximately one-third of rural land in the United States. Much federal land is located in the West (in the Mountain and Pacific states) and in Alaska, and a large majority is forest and range land (USDA, 1989a). Management is assigned to several federal agencies; state or local governments have little input in management decisions. The Bureau of Land Management in the Department of the Interior manages over 60% of federal lands, much of which is tundra and sagebrush, used for rangeland and a number of non-agricultural uses. The Forest Service in the Department of Agriculture manages national forest land on a 'multiple use-sustained yield' basis, designed to provide returns continuously over many years. In recent years, the Forest Service has developed land-use plans to provide multiple uses in each national forest. Some federally-owned land forms part of the National Wilderness Preservation System, the National Wildlife Refuge System, and the National Parks (Daniels *et al.*, 1989).

## C. Land-use decision-making

Land-use decision-making in the United States involves a balance between private rights and the public interest. Compared to many other nations, governmental intervention in land-use has been rather minimal, reflecting the attitude that landowners should enjoy maximum discretion over the use of their land. The public interest has justified some regulation, and enhanced focus on environmental problems suggests that agricultural land will face more regulation in the future.

Local governments (municipalities and counties) have traditionally been land-use decision-makers in the United States. In recent years, however, their decision-making power has been shared with state organizations. In part, this trend reflects the fact that states are the only political entities capable of devising techniques and structures to solve land-use problems that go beyond the capacity of individual local governments (Bosselman and Callies, 1971, p. 3). Moreover, society has become increasingly aware of the vulnerability of natural resources and the importance of viewing land as a resource, not a commodity (Duncan, 1987, p. 409).

A number of political entities have the power of eminent domain, the right of the government to take property for public use without the owner's consent upon paying just compensation. States have this power as an attribute of their sovereignty, which is not prohibited by the federal Constitution. States may delegate their eminent domain power to counties, municipalities, and other public bodies or corporations. The federal government also enjoys the power of eminent domain, implicit in the fifth amendment's prohibition of taking private property for public use without just compensation.

Determining what types of acts constitute a taking of private property continues to be a controversial issue. Condemnation and physical intrusion, even of a limited portion of an individual's property, almost certainly constitute a taking. More problematic are so-called regulatory takings. The Supreme Court has adopted a balancing test, considering the economic impact of a regulation, its interference with investment-backed expectations, the character of the governmental action and whether the interference is an actual physical invasion. Recent cases indicate that a taking exists if the individual demonstrates a permanent or temporary physical invasion of property or an interference that nearly destroys the value of the property by leaving almost no reasonable use.

The proper exercise of eminent domain also requires that the property be taken for a public use. The current understanding of this requirement is quite broad, probably extending the right to use eminent domain as a means to achieve any objective within the scope of the legislature's authority.

Many challenges to eminent domain actions have raised the issue of just compensation for the taking of property. Generally, compensation is determined by the amount of the property owner's loss from the taking. The value of the property taken is set at the property's highest and best use in light of present and potential uses. Just compensation for agricultural land may pose particular difficulties. When only part of a farmer's tract is taken, the remaining parcels may be less valuable or even useless to farming. For example, when agricultural land is condemned for highway construction, isolated triangular or circular fields may result, which would be difficult or impossible to farm with large equipment. Similarly, condemnation may affect drainage patterns essential to productive agriculture. Thus, determination of just compensation for taking agricultural land is complex, requiring analysis beyond mere appraisal of the land actually taken (Grossman, 1985).

In the United States, no special courts exist for the disposition of cases involving agricultural land. State courts have general jurisdiction; most local land-use cases (e.g. zoning disputes) will be filed in state courts. Federal courts may also provide a forum when the controversy fits within federal jurisdictional guidelines (e.g. cases involving federal statutes or constitutional questions).

## III. Keeping Agricultural Land Rural

### A. Agricultural land conversion

Though the vast area of the United States seems to offer unlimited acres of agricultural land, demand for agricultural crops and conversion of farmland to other uses have made farmland an endangered resource. The National Agricultural Lands Study (NALS) concluded that by the year 2000 most of the nation's cropland base (540 million acres) was likely to be cultivated. Moreover, if the irreversible loss of farmland continued at its then-current rate (about 2.1 million acres, corrected from the original estimate of nearly 3 million acres, per year between 1967 and 1975), the nation's supply of cropland would be threatened (NALS, 1981a, pp. vi–vii, xvii; USDA, 1989a, p. 20).

Critics attacked both the data and the conclusions from the NALS study (e.g. Fischel, 1982), and asserted that the study did not prove that the United States faces a shortage of cropland. In fact, more recent statistics show an annual conversion rate of 1.5 million acres, including about 60% cropland (USDA, 1989a, pp. 4, 20). Nonetheless, pressure on prime farmland remains intense because much prime farmland is located near major urban centres with development needs. Despite some disagreement and recent improvements (and the current existence of surplus production), the serious consequences of a shortage of cropland for future generations mean that the issue cannot be dismissed.

### B. The federal role

Activities of the US government have long played a significant role in the loss of agricultural land. Numerous federal programmes directly or indirectly have provided 'financial support which leads to increased urbanized uses of land, inundation of agricultural land for water reservoirs, fragmentation and isolation of farm parcels by transportation corridors, and the idling of previously productive agricultural land' (NALS, 1981a, p. 48).

Since 1981, the federal Farmland Protection Policy Act (7 USCA, sections 4201–9) has directed federal agencies to evaluate the adverse effects of federal programmes on farmland preservation, consider alternatives to minimize adverse effects, and ensure that federal programmes are compatible with state, local, and private farmland protection programmes (section 4202(b)). The Act reflects federal recognition that farmlands are an endangered resource, but its operation is restricted to prime farmland, unique farmland (used for high-value specialty crops), and land of statewide or local importance. The law does not authorize the federal government to regulate the use of private or non-federal land or to affect the property rights of its owners (section 4208). Only limited enforcement provisions are available to ensure that federal agencies will comply with its provisions (section 4209). Some assert that a more aggressive federal programme to protect cropland is justifiable. This could include more effective implementation of the purposes of the Act, federal scrutiny of non-federal programmes to protect agricultural land, and improved consistency between farmland protection policy and other federal agricultural policy (Johnson and Fogleman, 1986, pp. 577–9). Indeed, the Farms for the Future Act of 1990 (Pub. L. no. 101–624, sections 1465–70), authorizes a pilot loan guarantee/subsidy programme to encourage states to acquire interests in land to protect important farmlands for future agricultural use.

### C. State and local efforts

Although laws preserving farmland are generally directed toward avoiding unnecessary conversion to non-agricultural uses, individual legislative schemes often demonstrate specific goals. These suggest that agricultural land protection has both long-term and short-term components. One objective is to avoid random farmland conversion and ensure orderly development in urban fringe areas. Another is to provide the scenic and aesthetic values of open space in urban areas. A third is to preserve farmland permanently as a scarce and valuable resource, so that it will be available to succeeding generations (see Grossman, 1985, pp. 104–6). These goals of orderly development, open space, and permanent preservation are reflected in various types of farmland preservation programmes.

States approach the legal protection of agricultural land in two major ways: regulatory programmes with mandatory controls and voluntary programmes with incentives to encourage participation.

### *1. Regulatory programmes*

#### a. Zoning

The most common form of land-use control in the US is zoning, 'a legally binding designation of the uses to which land may be put, including the type, amount, and location of development' (NALS, 1981a, p. 63). It can guide orderly development of land and avoid inconsistent adjacent land uses. Zoning is authorized by state police power and often delegated by an enabling act to local (e.g. county and municipal) governments. In some states, these jurisdictions must adopt a comprehensive land-use plan, and the zoning ordinance (normally a text creating districts with permitted uses and a map assigning uses to geographic districts) must be consistent with that plan. Apart from a few statewide programmes, most zoning occurs locally, primarily within municipal boundaries. Some counties also exercise their zoning power. (Unlike some other nations, rural land is not normally part of a municipality.) Zoning of rural land is usually voluntary, and in 1981 only about 300 jurisdictions had used agricultural zoning (NALS, 1981a, p. 72). The majority of US agricultural land is not zoned.

Because of the technical nature and unequal burden of zoning regulations, most municipalities have established special mechanisms for administering and enforcing zoning ordinances. In some municipalities, the building commissioner or inspector must determine whether a proposed building and use is consistent with the zoning regulations and any building code before issuing a building permit. Larger municipalities commonly have a zoning administrator who must issue a zoning certificate before a building permit may be issued. To ensure that subsequent use of the building conforms to zoning regulations, many municipalities require occupancy permits issued by the building commissioner or zoning administrator. In addition, most municipalities have boards of adjustment with power to review administrative rulings, allow exceptions and special permits, and grant variances (Anderson, 1986, sections 19.01–19.07, pp. 308–27).

When agricultural land is zoned, two approaches predominate. Exclusive agricultural zoning, unpopular with farmers and little used, generally prohibits most non-farm development on land zoned for agriculture. Non-exclusive agricultural zoning, used more frequently, discourages non-farm development by one of several different techniques. The most common approach permits non-farm development as of right on large lots (e.g. 10–640 acres). Another allows development of one small building lot for each land unit of a specified size (e.g. 1 acre for each 40 acres). Development may be clustered so that blocks of contiguous farmland remain. Sliding scale zoning allows a proportionately smaller number of lots as the land area increases (e.g. one lot per 5 acres, but only four lots for 60 acres). Conditional use zoning permits non-farm dwellings only under specific criteria (NALS, 1981b, pp. 110–21). Court decisions have upheld agricultural zoning in the face of constitutional attack, but unreasonable land-use restrictions may be challenged.

Although zoning is vulnerable to amendment and variance with shifts in political power, it is among the more effective ways of protecting agricultural land, particularly when accompanied by careful community, or state, land-use planning. Because the farmer bears the cost of agricultural zoning (primarily through lower land values), however, zoning is often unpopular politically and difficult to enact (Duncan, 1984, p. 112). Zoning alone will probably not preserve agricultural land, and some have suggested that state or regional controls should replace local land-use controls (e.g. Delogu, 1984).

### b. State-wide programmes

Serious development pressure has led several states, including Hawaii (1961), Vermont (1970), California (1972, 1976), and Oregon (1973), to enact comprehensive land-use planning statutes that encompass agricultural land. Although these programmes differ in design, long-range policies adopted at the state level protect agricultural land, which may be developed only with approval from the appropriate public body. Pressure for development continues to threaten farmland even under these comprehensive programmes, and their success is mixed. The more successful place equal value on agricultural protection and the enhancement of growth; they recognize that agricultural land can best be preserved by protecting the long-term viability of agriculture (Duncan, 1987, pp. 478–83).

Coastal Zone Management Acts affect some agricultural land. The federal law (16 USCA, sections 1451–61, amended and reauthorized by Pub. L. no. 101–508, sections 6201–17) provides financial incentives for states to develop and implement approved coastal management plans. All coastal and Great Lakes states control coastland land use to some extent, but the amount of rural land involved varies. In California, for example, mandatory county coastal programmes include land-use plans and zoning ordinances, and require permits for development within coastal areas. Agriculture is an important land use in coastal counties, and the California law works to ensure that the maximum amount of prime agricultural land remains in production and that justifiable development is concentrated to protect agriculture (Duncan, 1987).

### c. Transfer of development rights

Another type of mandatory programme, transfer of development rights (TDR), offers less promise for farmland, although it has been used in urban areas. Under TDR, a farmer whose land has been zoned as agricultural receives extra development rights for ‘receiving land’ elsewhere in the jurisdiction. TDR is rarely used in rural areas (Church, 1986).

### 2. *Choice-influencing programmes*

#### a. Tax relief

One state law incentive for keeping land in farm use involves reduced *ad valorem* real estate taxes through preferential assessment of farmland. Normally, real estate taxes are assessed annually on the value of property at its highest and best use; preferential assessment reduces the tax burden for farmers by assessing land in agricultural use on the basis of its (lower) value as farmland.

Although every state has a preferential assessment law, these state laws vary. Some include only farmland; others, forest land or open space. Each state's methods of determining eligibility (e.g. minimum acreage or years of farm use) and assessing value are established by statute. Some states have only preferential assessment laws; if property is later converted to a non-qualifying use, the owner will pay no penalty. A slight majority of states combine preferential assessment with deferred taxation. When land is converted to a non-qualifying use, a deferred tax (often the amount saved through preferential taxation for a specific rollback period) must be paid. A few other states combine preferential assessment with restrictive agreements. Under these laws, the landowner contracts with state or local government; the promise to limit land use to agriculture for a specific time period is tied to the preferential assessment. When the covenant is broken, a deferred tax will be imposed (Grillo and Seid, 1987).

Although these preferential assessment laws help to maintain farmers' property taxes at manageable levels, they do not keep farmland in agricultural use.

#### b. Agricultural districts

Agricultural districts are designed to prevent the premature cessation of farming on the urban fringe. Authorized in fifteen states, districts are formed voluntarily although prescribed procedures for a specific term (often 10 years). In exchange for a commitment to restrict land use to agriculture, district landowners receive statutory protection, including property tax relief, limits on local ordinances that restrict and regulate farming activities and structures, and relief from some *ad valorem* property taxes. Individual owners may withdraw from the district, which is dissolved or continued at the end of the term (Grossman, 1985). Because districts are temporary and voluntary, they do not prevent the ultimate conversion of farmland. Instead, they keep agriculture in place until farmland is needed for immediate urban growth; thus they foster orderly and efficient development.

#### c. Development restrictions

Development restrictions (conservation easements or purchase of development rights) separate the right to develop land from underlying ownership of land itself. They protect farmland over the long term, while the farmer maintains a property interest in the land and farms normally. Conservation easements may be sold or donated. Federal tax law allows a charitable contribution deduction for qualifying donations of perpetual conservation easements (IRC, section 170(h)).

At least eight states and six counties have programmes, under which over 200 000 acres are protected (Thompson, 1989b); private organizations also have purchased or accepted donations of development rights on many more acres. Public programmes are administered by an agency authorized to purchase development rights on vulnerable land at a price (often the difference between fair market value and agricultural value) governed by statute. The agency holds the development rights and enforces preservation restrictions[1]. The owner retains title to the land and uses the property for ordinary agricultural activity. Conservation easements are normally permanent and are therefore effective for preventing the development of farmland. Their use is limited by the high cost of purchasing development rights, especially on the most vulnerable land. In fact, development rights programmes may be more effective for providing open space preserves in urban areas than for protecting significant amounts of farmland (Grossman, 1985, 1988).

#### d. Right to farm laws

Right to farm laws have been enacted by nearly every state since the late 1970s. The influx of urban residents into rural areas often brings the threat of common law nuisance suits and a demand for local ordinances to restrict agricultural activities. Right to farm laws (and their predecessors, feedlot statutes) protect farmers from nuisance litigation resulting from changes in surrounding land-uses. Conditions for protection vary among state statutes. Typically, a farm that has operated for at least a year cannot become a nuisance because of changed circumstances, when that farm was not a nuisance when it began operation and when its operation is not negligent or improper. Other requirements sometimes exist. By discouraging nuisance suits, these laws promote continued agricultural activity in the face of urban encroachment, but do not actually preserve farmland. Moreover, limited experience with these laws makes their effectiveness uncertain (Grossman and Fischer, 1983).

## IV. Protecting the Quality of Agricultural Land

### A. Soil conservation

Soil erosion on US farmland has long been a problem, because of both damage to the fertility of the land itself and off-site impacts (e.g. air and water pollution). Federal efforts to control erosion began in the early 1930s. The USDA Soil Conservation Service (SCS), created in 1935, has taken an active role in conservation, e.g. developing the Land Evaluation and Site Assessment System (LESA) for ascertaining the agricultural importance of land sites, and conducting a national soil survey programme. Since its creation, it has provided technical assistance (primarily without cost-sharing) for soil conservation practices. The USDA Agricultural Stabilization and Conservation Service (ASCS), created in 1936, has also been involved in soil conservation, and has authority to provide cost-sharing incentives. Some conflict between SCS and ASCS developed. SCS has focused on public goals; ASCS (which also administers price and income support programmes) has had responsibility for private goals to benefit individual farmers. Perhaps in competition for farmers' loyalty, both agencies have focused to some extent on production, rather than conservation (Steiner, 1987; Malone, 1989a).

Although a number of programmes under different federal agencies attempt to control erosion, three are most significant. The Conservation Operations Program, administered by SCS, provides technical assistance to farmers and ranchers for application of conservation practices. The Great Plains Conservation Program, also administered by SCS, combines technical assistance and cost sharing with multi-year contracts for conservation plans. This programme is targeted to counties in the plains area with specific drought and erosion problems. The Agricultural Conservation Program, administered by ASCS, also involves contracts, coupled with cost sharing for conservation practices and technical advice from SCS. Federal programmes to control soil erosion have generally been voluntary, with few sanctions available to compel participation (Malone, 1989a, pp. 317–20). Federal tax law provides an incentive by allowing deduction (rather than capitalization) of certain conservation expenses implemented under an approved conservation plan (IRC, section 175).

With USDA encouragement, states have passed laws enabling voluntary creation of soil conservation districts. Most privately owned farmland is now part of one of the almost 3000 soil conservation districts, which normally have authority to develop conservation plans and provide cost-sharing funds. In some states, districts have regulatory authority (Malone, 1989a). Districts often receive federal cost-sharing funds and co-operate in implementation of federal conservation programmes.

Some states have effective soil conservation programmes. For example, Iowa has mandatory soil erosion control, with state cost-sharing for soil conservation practices and authority in soil conservation districts to enforce soil loss limits. A seminal court decision found the Iowa programme constitutional.

## B. Federal farm policy and agricultural land

Important federal statutes govern US agricultural policy. Federal farm programmes vary with the commodity, but three approaches predominate: price supports (loans, purchases); income supports (direct indemnity or disaster payments, target prices, deficiency payments, marketing loans); and production controls. Many of the federal farm programmes are administered by ASCS acting for the Commodity Credit corporation, which has no staff. At the local level, elected ASCS county committees administer the programmes.

Income and price supports are designed to raise farm incomes and still ensure reasonably priced food and fibre, and to stabilize prices in the agricultural economy. Producers' land-use decisions are often influenced by the existence of a price or income support programme. Production controls (for example, percentage setasides or acreage limitations) avoid excess commodity supplies by limiting the number of acres a farmer may produce as a condition for participating in other farm programmes. Acreage removed from production must be devoted to conservation uses; production controls also affect land use.

Although the majority of the US farm programmes were long directed toward production and marketing of farm commodities, the Food Security Act of 1985 (Pub. L. no. 99–198) enacted several programmes to protect fragile rural land. The Food, Agriculture, Conservation, and Trade Act of 1990 (Pub. L. no. 101–624) included major amendments to these programmes and further conservation initiatives. The central provisions are referred to as 'swampbuster', 'sodbuster', and the Agricultural Resources Conservation Program (ARCP). They are governed by statute and detailed USDA regulations and supported by tax law changes designed to encourage conservation (IRC, sections 175, 1252, 1256).

In part, these environmental programmes ensure cross compliance between federal price and income support programmes and conservation programmes (Malone, 1989b). A farmer must comply with conservation requirements or be ineligible for USDA price support, storage, insurance, disaster, and loan programmes for any commodity produced that year and for certain other federal conservation payments.

### *1. Swampbuster*

The swampbuster provisions (16 USCA, sections 3821–4) recognize the importance of wetlands for wildlife habitat, groundwater recharge, stream quality, flood control, and shoreline protection. Wetlands are defined as land with hydric soils, wetland hydrology, and hydrophytic vegetation, and will be identified on wetland delineation maps. Anyone who converts wetlands to make production possible or produces an agricultural commodity on drained wetlands cannot receive specified USDA farm programme benefits or certain conservation payments. Exemptions from loss of benefits apply to wetlands converted before 23 December 1985, conversion with minimal effects on wetland values, and conversion mitigated by restoration of previously converted wetlands; graduated partial loss of benefits may apply in cases of good faith violations of the swampbuster provisions.

### *2. Sodbuster*

The sodbuster provisions (16 USCA, sections 3811–13) focus on conservation of highly erodible land (as defined by law), which includes nearly a quarter (345.2 million acres) of US agricultural land. Farmers who produce agricultural commodities on fields in which highly erodible lands predominate, or who have setaside or diverted highly erodible lands, are not eligible for USDA farm programme payments and other benefits unless their land is operated according to an approved conservation compliance plan. Some exemptions (e.g. minor violations or variances) from sanctions exist, and violations committed in good faith can be subject to a graduated partial loss of benefits.

By January 1991, conservation plans had been developed on nearly 135 million of the nation's 140 million acres of highly erodible cropland for which plans were then required, and were fully implemented on nearly 40% of this land. Full implementation is required by 1 January 1995, but some areas are exempted temporarily until soil surveys are completed (USDA, 1990; 1991).

### *3. Environmental Conservation Acreage Reserve Program*

The 1985 Farm Bill established the Conservation Reserve Program (CRP), intended primarily to reduce damage and costs from soil erosion, but also to decrease productive capacity and support crop prices and farm income. The 1990 Farm Bill broadened this concept to create the Environmental Conservation Acreage Reserve Program (ECARP) (16 USCA, sections 3831–37E), part of ARCP, to protect highly erodible lands, other fragile lands, and wetlands through contracts and acquisition of easements. ECARP encompasses the CRP and a new wetland reserve programme, and will involve at least 40 million acres (with a maximum of 45 million acres – 18.225 million ha) by 1995.

The CRP applies to highly erodible cropland, certain marginal pasture, areas with identified water quality problems, and other fragile lands. Producers may submit bids to contract with the US government to retire eligible land from production for 10 (sometimes 15) years. Producers whose land is accepted in the CRP receive annual rental payments, technical assistance, and cost-share payments for establishing approved vegetative cover or trees on CRP land. Some long-term conservation easements are possible. A conservation plan approved by the state conservation district or by a representative of the SCS will prescribe the producer's land-use practices, particularly the obligation to plant permanent conservation cover on the land. Nearly 34 million acres have been placed in the CRP; tree cover has been planted on 2.2 million acres. Estimates suggest that CRP participation has reduced annual soil erosion by over 660 million tons (USDA, 1989b). In addition, it has encouraged some states to implement programmes to supplement the federal CRP.

The new wetland reserve programme will help owners to restore and protect wetlands. The government will purchase permanent or 30-year easements on eligible wetlands, which will be subject to a wetland easement conservation plan. In most cases, the plan will limit alteration of habitat, crop production, livestock grazing, and chemical application. Technical assistance and cost sharing for restoration expenses are available. During 1991–5, one million acres may be enrolled in the reserve, with priority for easements for habitat for migratory birds and other wildlife. A related programme (sections 3839–39D) authorizes environmental easements to ensure long-term protection of environmentally sensitive land.

### C. Surface mining on prime farmland

The federal Surface Mining Control and Reclamation Act of 1977 (30 USCA, sections 1201–1328) (SMCRA) regulates surface mining of coal. Enforced by the US Department of the Interior, SMCRA focuses on the environmental impacts of surface coal mining, with provisions that require operators to reclaim surface-mined land to its premined condition. A programme of 'co-operative federalism' combines federal performance standards and funds with state enforcement under an approved state programme meeting federal environmental protection standards and demonstrating enforcement ability. Surface mining operations require a permit (imposing environmental standards) under a state or federal programme, as well as a performance bond.

SMCRA includes provisions to ensure that after surface mining, prime farmland will be returned to productive capacity. When prime farmland is mined, the operator must demonstrate the technological capacity to restore the mined area to equivalent or higher yields compared with non-mined prime farmland in the locality. The operation must meet the soil reconstruction standards of SMCRA. Distinct soil layers must be removed, stockpiled, and protected from erosion or contamination; after mining the operator must replace, regrade, and revegetate. A performance bond ensures compliance with the prime farmland provisions. These requirements, challenged on constitutional grounds, were upheld by the US Supreme Court (*Hodel* v. *Indiana*, 452 US 315, 1981).

SMCRA imposes a federal solution for a national land-use problem, an approach perceived as a significant intrusion into an area traditionally reserved to state regulation. The constitutionality of these intrusive provisions confirms that the federal government has rather extensive power to regulate land-use without interfering with either state sovereign powers or individual property rights. Political realities may limit the use of federal power to regulate agricultural land use. Nonetheless, a federal programme of agricultural land-use guidelines, implemented by the states with federal technical assistance and financial incentives, is not inconceivable (Grossman, 1983–1984).

## V. Environmental Protection Laws and Agricultural Land

During the past several decades[2], Congress has enacted a series of environmental protection statutes implemented by the federal Environmental Protection Agency (EPA). States, too, have enacted environmental laws and regulations, often in response to federal legislation with provisions for state implementation of federal environmental standards. Albeit not directed specifically at rural land, these laws and their regulations have implications for agrarian land. Moreover, although some agricultural activities have been exempted from regulation, increasing degradation of the US environment may result in more intrusive environmental regulation on agrarian land, especially in connection with pollution of ground and surface waters.

### A. Air pollution

The federal Clean Air Act (32 USCA, sections 7401–626, substantially amended in 1990, Pub. L. no. 101–549) requires federal regulations to establish national ambient air quality standards, along with state implementation, maintenance, and enforcement of those standards. The law has had little impact on agricultural land. Its focus is major pollution sources (e.g. industry, motor vehicles), and it relies on objective measurement of pollutants. Thus, it has not been effective in controlling odours, which are an important source of air pollution from rural land (Brussaard and Grossman, 1990). Odours, traditionally abated through common-law nuisance litigation, are regulated as air pollution under some state environmental protection laws.

## B. Water pollution

Surface and groundwater sources in the United States are increasingly polluted, and agricultural activities are a serious cause of this pollution. Fertilizers, pesticides, and animal wastes find their way to surface and ground waters in significant quantities. Recent research indicates that an estimated 50 million people in the United States get drinking water from groundwater sources, often private wells, that may be contaminated by agricultural chemicals. The risk of pesticide contamination is greatest along the Eastern Seaboard, the Gulf Coast, and the Upper Midwest. The potential for nitrate pollution is highest in the Great Plains and portions of the Northwest, Southwest, and Corn Belt. Both pesticides and nitrates threaten groundwater in portions of the Corn Belt, and Lake States, and the Northeast (Nielsen and Lee, 1987). Until now, regulation has not been particularly effective in preventing water pollution from agricultural land. The Food, Agriculture, Conservation, and Trade Act of 1990 authorized a voluntary incentive programme, with an enrolment goal of 10 million eligible acres during 1991–5, to help farmers implement agricultural water-quality protection plans. The Act also requires more extensive record-keeping for pesticide application.

The Clean Water Act (33 USCA, sections 1251–387) treats ‘point’ and ‘non-point’ sources of pollution with different regulatory schemes. A point source is ‘any discernible, confined and discrete conveyance from which pollutants are or may be discharged’ (section 1362(14)). Point sources that discharge into navigable waters (broadly defined) often require permits through the National Pollutant Discharge Elimination System (NPDES), based on effluent limitations for pollutants and performance standards for new sources of pollution. State NPDES programmes implement and enforce federal law.

EPA regulations set effluent limitations and performance standards for feedlots, the most significant point source of pollution from agrarian land. ‘Concentrated animal feeding operations’ (large feedlots) are point sources subject to NPDES permits, which govern the discharge of pollutants, but only a small proportion of feedlots are actually subject to NPDES requirements. (State statutes and rules, however, often govern the storage and application of animal manure, to avoid water pollution.) Another point source of pollution, return flows from irrigated agriculture, is specifically exempted from NPDES permits.

Non-point source water pollution occurs from diffused land activities and includes soil erosion, run-off of fertilizers and chemicals, as well as livestock farms not subject to NPDES. ‘Section 208 planning’ (section 1288) and state water-quality planning (section 1313) are designed to control non-point pollution from agricultural land. Section 208 requires states to develop and implement state and area-wide waste treatment management plans to meet water quality standards established by each state. 'Best management practices' – soil conservation techniques to control erosion – are required for agricultural sources of non-point pollution. Most state plans for non-point pollution rely on voluntary programmes with cost-sharing. Thus, control of non-point water pollution has not been particularly effective (Brussaard and Grossman, 1990).

The Clean Water Act also affects the ability of private landowners to alter or eliminate small waters or wetlands, including many wetlands (sometimes called 'prairie potholes') on rural land. Increasingly strict regulation and broadened jurisdiction have made these restrictions on rural land critically important. Section 404 of the Act requires permits for the discharge of dredged or fill material into waters of the United States. The US Army Corps of Engineers (ACE) has primary authority to issue 'dredge and fill' permits, pursuant to Environmental Protection Agency (EPA) and ACE regulations. Permits can be denied if there are 'practicable alternatives' to the proposed discharge or if the proposed activity will have 'significantly adverse effects' on the wetland. Although some exceptions exist (e.g. certain areas smaller than 10 acres, minor drainage from ongoing farming activities), the section 404 permit requirement substantially limits a landowner's right to convert a wetland to farmland, unless that land had previously been used for farming. (See the swampbuster provisions discussed above.) In addition to federal law, a number of states also regulate to protect wetland areas.

### C. Hazardous and toxic wastes

Increasing focus on hazardous and toxic substances used or deposited on land has led to a number of regulatory schemes with applicability to agrarian land. In fact dumping in rural areas has been common, and both the land itself and groundwater supplies have been threatened. A number of statutes, in addition to the Clean Air and Clean Water Acts, are relevant. The Federal Insecticide, Fungicide, and Rodenticide Act governs registration and labelling of many agricultural chemicals, while the Toxic Substances Control Act regulates the manufacture of other hazardous chemicals. The Resource Conservation and Recovery Act governs disposal of hazardous wastes (but regulations exempt farmers who dispose of waste pesticides as prescribed) and large underground storage tanks. The Comprehensive Environmental Response, Compensation, and Liability Act (CERCLA) focuses on clean-up of hazardous waste disposal sites, and makes owners and others responsible for clean-up costs. The Emergency Planning and Community Right to Know Act requires specific information on hazardous chemicals to be provided to state and local authorities.

Agriculture involves use of numerous substances considered hazardous:

pesticides, fertilizers and petroleum products. Moreover, hazardous materials may have been deposited on rural land, either in the normal course of farming or in a past or present use of the land (e.g. as a landfill). Although numerous agricultural exemptions exist, these statutes and accompanying regulations impose significant obligations. Moreover, landowners, former owners, and even some lenders may face significant financial risk under CERCLA (Thorson, 1990).

## VI. Other Agrarian Land Issues

### A. Agricultural tenancy

A significant percentage of agricultural land in the United States is farmed by tenants. Landlord–tenant law is generally state law, and statutes govern some aspects of farm leasing, particularly issues involving termination of tenancies and remedies for breach of the lease. On most issues, landowners and their tenants enjoy considerable freedom of contract. No government agency supervises the process of lease formation, and disputes are handled like other cases in the state court systems.

Under a farm lease, the tenant is in possession and control of the land for the lease term, and the landlord's right to enter the property is limited. Unless the lease provides otherwise, the tenant is free to determine the cropping system. The tenant must farm in a 'husbandlike' manner, and may not commit waste (wilful or negligent destruction of the property) on the land. In practice, many farm lease relationships involve close co-operation between landlord and tenant in making important management decisions concerning both crop production and conservation practices. Rent is commonly paid in cash or as a share of crops, with the amount depending on custom in the area and quality of the land.

Short-term leases (e.g. 1 year) are common, and no automatic right of renewal exists. Many tenants operate under written leases with fixed termination dates. Others have only oral leases, often year-to-year contracts that continue automatically for another year, unless a party gives timely notice of termination as prescribed by statute or common law. A landlord who wants to terminate a lease at the end of the term needs no particular justification. When the tenant has breached the lease, termination during the term is also possible. When a lease for an 'uncertain' term ends through no fault of the tenant and before the crop is mature, the doctrine of emblements may apply to let the tenant return to the land to harvest the crop. Without a contrary agreement, a landlord who plans to sell the farm is under no obligation to give the tenant the first opportunity to buy.

The existence of a farm lease raises issues in connection with eligibility for payments under USDA farm programmes. If the lease is carefully drafted to comply with requirements, both a crop-share landlord and tenant may qualify separately for farm programme benefits, which are subject to a limit for each person actively engaged in farming (Looney *et al.*, 1990, p. 219).

A tenant's violation of sodbuster, swampbuster, and related conservation programmes may disqualify the landlord from farm programme benefits even on other land, if the landlord requires or acquiesces in the tenant's disqualifying activities (Looney *et al.*, 1990, p. 252). Regulations under the Conservation Reserve Program provide that the USDA may enter into contracts and make payments to eligible owners or operators of qualifying cropland. Payments are divided fairly and equitably among all those who enter into the contract. In addition, specific provisions require equitable treatment of tenants and sharecroppers in dividing payments (7 CFR, sections 704.6, 704.26, 1990).

### B. Water use

Adequate supplies of water and efficient drainage are essential to agricultural uses of rural land. Both common law and statutory rules govern these areas.

The diversion and distribution of water is governed primarily by state law. In the arid West, many states follow the principle of prior appropriation – a 'first in time, first in right' system initially developed to meet the needs of miners and farmers who settled the region. Prior appropriation normally requires notice of intent to appropriate, actual diversion, and application of the water to a beneficial use (Tarlock, 1990, section 5.10, p 5-46.1). At present, most western states have adopted water codes under which appropriation rights are quantified and memorialized in permits. Special procedures exist for adjudicating water rights. Prior appropriation offers substantial security for senior appropriators, because the most junior appropriator is first to lose his water supply in times of shortage. The system makes it difficult to establish new uses, however, and offers little incentive for senior appropriators to conserve (Goldfarb, 1988, pp. 40–1).

The more humid East follows the riparian rights doctrine, which limits diversion rights to persons owning land adjacent to natural watercourses for use within the watershed (Goldfarb, 1988, p. 21). Allocation of water among riparian owners is a difficult issue. Most riparian jurisdictions adopted a reasonable use standard, which applies a balancing test to determine whether one riparian should be permitted to interfere with another's use (Tarlock, 1990, section 3.12[4], pp. 3-62, 63). Today, many eastern states have modified common law riparian doctrine by statutes that determine priorities or require a permit for specific water uses.

About one-fifth of the fresh water supply in the United States consists of groundwater. Because there was initially little scientific understanding of groundwater, it was subject to a rule of absolute ownership: a landowner could use groundwater freely, without regard to the needs of others, as long as there was no malicious intent to injure. Most states now apply a reasonable use standard, either by statute or decisional law (Tarlock, 1990, section 4.04-5, pp. 4-6 to 4-11).

In some areas, agricultural production requires drainage of diffused surface water from rural land. Several different common law doctrines govern the upper landowner's right to drain water off land and the lower landowner's obligation to receive water. Some states follow the anti-development civil law rule that lower lands are under a servitude to receive water from higher lands only when it flows through natural drains. Others have the pro-development common enemy doctrine, which allows landowners to fight surface water as they choose, with little regard to its impact on neighbouring landowners. In recent years, a reasonable use standard has allowed owners to make reasonable changes in flow of diffused surface waters, even if some injury occurs to other landowners (Goldfarb, 1988, pp. 61–2; Tarlock, 1990, section 3.05, pp. 3-13 to 3-15).

In many states, a drainage code governs formation of drainage districts with power to construct drainage works for the benefit of land in the district. Some states permit county boards or local courts to hold proceedings to construct or repair drainage systems. Normally, landowners who benefit from drainage projects are assessed a proportionate share of the costs.

Although water allocation is primarily state-administered, some aspects are governed by federal law. The federal government has an implied reserved water right where it has held land for a public purpose (e.g. an Indian reservation, national forest, or national park) (Goldfarb, 1988, pp. 49–50). The federal government has also provided irrigation water in western states, based on the Reclamation Act of 1902, designed to promote family farming in the West through residency and acreage requirements. These limits were ineffective, and since 1982 the residency requirement has been abolished and acreage limits relaxed. Since 1987, reclamation activities have focused less on major irrigation projects, and more on water conservation and environmental protection (Goldfarb, 1988, pp. 76–8).

## C. Control of agricultural land ownership

US agricultural policy, structurally and philosophically, has retained many of the concerns of the nation's founders. The importance of land ownership by family farmers has influenced agricultural policy and law. Two types of legal restrictions continue to reflect this ideal of family farm ownership: restrictions on alien ownership and limits on corporate ownership.

The federal Agricultural Foreign Investment Disclosure Act (7 USCA, sections 3501–8) does not restrict alien ownership of farmland, but is a reporting law. Alien owners of farmland (including corporations with at least 10% foreign ownership) must report their holdings and transactions in agricultural land to the US Secretary of Agriculture. Statistics compiled pursuant to these reports indicate that in 1990, slightly more than 1% of privately-owned agricultural land (and much of this, forestland) was owned by foreign interests.

A majority of individual states actually restrict to some degree the ownership of agricultural (or all) real estate by aliens. Some states impose major restrictions.

To prevent concentration of farmland ownership by large corporations, a number of states (especially in the important midwest farming region) have constitutional provisions or statutes that prohibit certain corporations and sometimes limited partnerships from buying farmland or farming. Family farm corporations, in which the majority of the shareholders are family members and at least one family member operates the farm, are normally not restricted. Other states require only annual reports from corporations that own or operate farmland.

## D. Recreational use of rural land

The majority of US rural land is privately owned, and owners have no obligation to permit public access to their land. Some publicly-owned rural land (e.g. federal or state parks) is designed for recreation. Demand for recreational land (e.g. for fishing, hunting, hiking, camping, and other activities) is increasing, but potential liability and problems obtaining insurance have made owners reluctant to grant public access. The owner or other person (e.g. tenant) in possession and control of the land may be liable for injuries to entrants on the land under tort liability rules. In many states, liability exists if the possessor of land has failed to exercise reasonable care under the circumstances. Other states link the duty of care to the status of the person on the property; the highest duty is owed to the invitee; a lesser duty to the licensee; and the lowest duty to a trespasser.

To encourage recreational use of private land, most states have enacted 'recreational use' statutes. Under many of these, one who makes land available for recreational use without charge owes no duty of care to keep the property safe or to warn of dangerous conditions on the property. Liability results from wilful or malicious failure to guard or warn against dangerous conditions. These statutes do not protect one who charges a fee for recreational use of land. Moreover, they do not prevent lawsuits against landowners, but are raised in defence to limit liability. Questions exist about their applicability to specific owners, types of land, activities, and individual land users.

## Conclusion

The vast expanses of farmland in the United States are a critical source of food and fibre for the nation and the world. In addition, rural environments offer habitats for valuable species of wildlife, aesthetic pleasure, and opportunities for recreation. Farm enterprises located in these environments contribute significantly to the economic well-being of their communities and regions.

Because the United States is a large federalist nation with a history of minimal intervention in land use, the law governing agricultural land is both fragmented and relatively non-intrusive. Jurisdiction over various issues that affect rural land is divided among federal and state legislatures and administrative agencies; common law principles continue to govern many aspects. Local authorities sometimes exercise their power to regulate agricultural land use. Some federal laws provide opportunities for co-operation and co-ordination between the federal government and the states; others do not. Moreover, the goals of federal programmes are not always consistent, and state programmes and policies concerning agricultural land vary considerably from state to state.

Despite the large number of jurisdictions and the many laws involved, government interference with agricultural land in the United States has been relatively slight, compared to other nations. Many programmes involving soil conservation have been voluntary, for example, and environmental statutes have included significant exceptions for agriculture. Many state programmes to preserve agricultural land have offered incentives rather than land-use controls. On the local level, much rural land is not subject to any zoning regulation; when zoning does occur, the methods most effective for protecting farmland are often rejected in favour of more politically palatable zoning schemes.

Given this background, comprehensive federal regulation of agricultural land use seems rather unlikely. Indeed, efforts to enact national land-use laws in the 1970s failed, and the subject of federal land-use regulation evokes conflict (Grossman, 1983–1984). Nonetheless, if present trends continue, more intensive regulation of agricultural land and its use can be anticipated, both at federal and state levels. It is increasingly clear that agricultural activities affect surface water, groundwater, and air quality. Widespread concern about these environmental effects and their impact on society at large is likely to lead to more intrusive regulation of agricultural land-use practices. Moreover, the inclusion of significant conservation initiatives in recent federal agricultural legislation may point toward more thoughtful land-use policies in the future.

## Notes

1. The Farmers Home Administration (FmHA), the federal lender of last resort, also may take conservation easements for at least 50 years on fragile lands in exchange for cancelling a portion of certain delinquent borrowers' debts. FmHA may also convey conservation easements on property it has taken from borrowers. (7 USCA, sections 1981, 1997). Because of delay and rigid administration, the programme has failed (Thompson, 1989a).
2. The National Environmental Policy Act of 1969 (42 USCA, sections 4321–70), a statement of national environmental policy, requires increased focus on the environment in the planning process but prescribes no environmental protection standards. Under NEPA, 'major federal actions' affecting the environment require an Environmental Impact Statement prepared for public and peer review. Although NEPA affects federal agencies, in at least twenty-nine states, state agencies have similar obligations (Palmer, 1984, p. 30).

## References

Anderson, R. (1986 & Suppl. 1989) *American Law of Zoning 3d*, Vol. 3. Lawyers Cooperative Publishing Co., Rochester, New York.

Bosselman, F. and Callies, D. (1971) *The Quiet Revolution in Land Use Control.* Council on Environmental Quality, Washington, D.C.

Brussaard, W. and Grossman, M.R. (1990) Legislation to abate pollution from manure: the Dutch approach. *North Carolina Journal of International Law & Commercial Regulation* 15, 85–114.

Church, W.L. (1986) Farmland conversion: the view from 1986. *University of Illinois Law Review* 1986, 521–61.

Daniels, T.L., Lapping, M.B. and Keller, J.W. (1989) Rural planning in the United States: fragmentation, conflict and slow progress. In: Cloke, P.J. (ed.) *Rural Land-Use Planning in Developed Nations*, pp. 152–177. Unwin Hyman, London.

Davidson, J.H. (1989) Environmental analysis of the Federal farm programs. *Virginia Environmental Law Journal* 8, 235–70.

Delogu, O.E. (1984) Local land use controls: an idea whose time has passed. *Maine Law Review* 36, 261–310.

Duncan, M.L. (1984) Toward a theory of broad-based planning for the preservation of agricultural land. *Natural Resources Journal* 24, 61–135.

Duncan, M.L. (1987) Agriculture as a resource: statewide land use programs for the preservation of farmland. *Ecology Law Quarterly* 14, 401–83.

Fischel, W.A. (1982) The urbanization of agricultural land: a review of the national agricultural lands study. *Land Economics* 58, 236–58.

Freeman, H.A. (1972) Dynamic federalism and the concept of preemption. *DePaul Law Review* 21, 630–48.

Goldfarb, W. (1988) *Water Law*, 2nd edn. Lewis Publishers, Inc., Chelsea, Michigan.

Grillo, K.A. and Seid, D.A. (1987) *State Laws Relating to Preferential Assessment of Farmland.* Government Printing Office, Washington, D.C.

Grossman, M.R. (1983–84) Prime farmland and the Surface Mining Control and Reclamation Act: guidance for an enhanced federal role in farmland preservation. *Drake Law Review* 33, 209–301.

Grossman, M.R. (1985) Exercising eminent domain against protected agricultural lands: Taking a second look. *Villanova Law Review* 30, 701–66.

Grossman, M.R. (1987) The position of agricultural law in the United States. *Agrarisch recht* 47, 123–33.

Grossman, M.R. (1988) Agricultural districts and conservation easements: voluntary agreements to keep America's farmland in agricultural use. *Agrarisch recht* 48, 262–70.

Grossman, M.R. and Fischer, T.G. (1983) Protecting the right to farm: statutory limits on nuisance actions against the farmer. *Wisconsin Law Review* 1983, 95–165.

Johnson, C.W. and Fogleman, V.M. (1986) The Farmland Protection Policy Act: stillbirth of a policy? *University of Illinois Law Review* 1986, 563–79.

Looney, J.W., Wilder, J.R., Brownback, S. and Wadley, J.B. (1990) *Agricultural Law: A Lawyer's Guide to Representing Farm Clients.* Section of General Practice, American Bar Association, Chicago.

Malone, L.A. (1989a) The renewed concern over soil erosion: the current Federal programs and proposals. *Journal of Agricultural Taxation and Law* 10, 310–54.

Malone, L.A. (1989b) Conservation at the crossroads: Reauthorization of the 1985 Farm Bill conservation provisions. *Virginia Environmental Law Journal* 8, 215–33.

National Agricultural Lands Study (1981a) *Final Report.* Government Printing Office, Washington, D.C.

National Agricultural Lands Study (1981b) *The Protection of Farmland: A Reference Guidebook for State and Local Governments.* Government Printing Office, Washington, D.C.

Nielsen, E. and Lee, L. (1987) *The Magnitude and Costs of Groundwater Contamination From Agricultural Chemicals: A National Perspective.* Economic Research Service, Department of Agriculture, government Printing Office, Washington, D.C.

Palmer, A.E. (1984) Environmentally based land use planning and regulation. *Pace Environmental Law Review* 2, 25–65.

Steiner, F. (1987) Soil conservation policy in the United States. *Environmental Management* 11, 209–23.

Tarlock, A. (1990) *Law of Water Rights and Resources.* Clark Boardman Co. Ltd., New York.

Thompson, E. (1989a) FmHA conservation easements-for-credit program fails to save any farmers or land *Journal of Soil and Water Conservation* 44, 462–5.

Thompson, E. (1989b) Purchase of development rights: ultimate tool for farmland preservation? *Zoning and Planning Law Report* 12, 153–9.

Thorson, N.W. (1989) *Hazardous and Toxic Substances on Agricultural Lands: Problems for Buyers and Lenders.* American Agricultural Law Association, Convention Handbook, Tenth Annual Meeting and Educational Conference, San Francisco, California, November 1989, ch. 39.

United States Department of Agriculture (1989a) *The Second RCA Appraisal: Soil, Water, and Related Resources on Nonfederal Land in the United States – Analysis of Condition and Trends.*

United States Department of Agriculture (1989b) *Conservation Reserve Program Enrolment Almost 34 Million Acres. Selected Speeches and News Releases,* 15–22 December, 1989, pp. 13–15.

United States Department of Agriculture (1990) *Conservation Planning Complete on 135 Million Acres of Highly Erodible Land. Selected Speeches and News Releases,* 15–22 February, 1990, pp. 9–11.

United States Department of Agriculture (1991) *Conservation Work Completed on 40 Percent of Highly Erodible Land. Selected Speeches and News Releases,* 7–13 February, 1991, pp. 11–14.

# 11

# AGRARIAN LAND LAW IN CANADA

Carl F. Dombek and Cynthia Button

## I. General

Canada, with its own unique way of developing a flexible federalism[1], has developed a structured approach to land law issues. The Constitution Act, 1982 (Canada Gazette Part III, 21) consists of a number of statutes which together make up the Canadian constitution. One of these statutes is the Constitution Act, 1867 (formerly the British North America Act, 1867), which divides legislative power in Canada between the provinces and the federal government (Ince and Pereboom, 1984, p. 7). While the Parliament of Canada has some ability to make laws in the area of land use (Troop, 1974), the general authority for land laws and agrarian land law lies with the provinces. Section 92.13 of the Constitution Act, 1867 provides:

> In each Province, the legislature may exclusively make laws in relation to matters coming within the classes of subjects hereinafter enumerated . . .
>
> 13. Property and Civil Rights in the Province

The Constitution Act, 1867 also gives the provinces power over 'municipal institutions in the province' (Ince and Pereboom, 1984, p. 8). Thus, the provinces make laws regarding land-use, and not the federal government. Using this provision, each province has transferred the authority for land planning to local governments through some form of planning legislation (Planning Act, RSO 1980, c. 379). In Canada the local government may pass subordinate legislation, usually referred to as a by-law, to deal with planning matters. The provincial government retains overall control to ensure uniformity.

In addition to land planning legislation, provinces may pass statutes that deal with a myriad of agrarian issues. Laws relating to water drainage and use, topsoil use, pollution, farm ownership and even the 'right to farm' exist in many of the ten provinces. This chapter will focus on a variety of agrarian land laws throughout the ten provinces. It will not present a fully detailed account of agrarian land law in each province, but will only mention provincial agrarian laws where they are substantially different or unique. Because federal laws are less significant, they will not be discussed.

To understand the wide scope of agrarian laws in Canada one must first understand the importance of agriculture to Canada. The most recent census (1986) found that there are 930 000 people living on farms in Canada.[2] This figure represents 3% of Canada's population. The province of Ontario has the largest farm population in Canada with 239 000 people (3% of the population) living on farms; in the province of Saskatchewan, 17% of the population lives on farms.

A great deal of diversity also exists among Canada's farms. In the province of Quebec and in parts of Eastern Ontario, dairy farms produce the major product for many census divisions. In the prairies grains are the dominant product. Fruit farms abound in some regions of British Columbia and Ontario. Ontario's agricultural sector is a good example of the diversity found in Canadian agriculture as indicated in Table 11.1.[3] In 1985, a small number of large farms had a relatively high percentage of total sales of agricultural products. For example, in Ontario approximately 75% of the value of agricultural products is produced by 25% of the farms.

Agriculture in Canada generates and consumes large amounts of money. Ontario, with the highest sales of agricultural products in Canada, demonstrates the importance of agriculture. Ontario sold $5.5 billion worth of agricultural products in 1985. Ontario ranked first among the ten provinces in cash receipts for the following crops: grain corn, vegetables (including

**Table 11.1** Farm diversification in Ontario

| Commodity | Number of farmers | Commodity | Number of farmers |
|---|---|---|---|
| Beef cattle | 20 000 | Tomatoes | 2 100 |
| Dairy | 11 400 | Potatoes | 350 |
| Hogs | 13 000 | Apples | 1 050 |
| Chickens | 780 | Sweet corn | 2 150 |
| Eggs | 740 | Peaches | 650 |
| Sheep/lambs | 3 000 | Grain corn | 22 300 |
| Turkeys | 160 | Tobacco | 1 800 |
| Hay | 44 000 | Soyabeans | 12 700 |

potatoes), soyabeans, tobacco, floriculture, nursery, and fruit. In livestock production, Ontario ranked first in hogs, poultry, and eggs. The sale of cattle, calves, and dairy products were ranked second on a national basis. In 1988 Ontario exported agricultural and food goods worth approximately \$2.2 billion, which represented about 22% of Canada's total exports of agricultural and food products. Almost two-thirds were sales to the United States. Also, in 1987 net government programme payments to Ontario producers amounted to about \$490 million. In 1987 the agri-food sector provided direct employment for about 12% of the employed labour force in Ontario; in 1985, the sector accounted for \$11.1 billion or 7% of Ontario's Gross Domestic Product.

## II. Relevant Legislation

With such a diverse and important agricultural economy, many pieces of legislation in Canada are devoted to agriculture. For instance, the Ontario Ministry of Agriculture and Food has responsibility for administering over fifty pieces of legislation. In addition, other government departments or ministeries also administer statutes that may affect agricultural land[4]. This legal diversity is not unique to Ontario; other provinces are in similar situations. Needless to say, when different government agencies attempt to resolve an agrarian land-use problem tensions develop. In some ways it may be compared to a spider web: if the web is pulled at one end, the other components of the web feel the strain.

It is fair to state that all of the Canadian provinces experience problems regarding land use. These concerns range from the preservation of farmland to environmental issues. The purpose of this section of the chapter will be to discuss legislation that is currently in place to deal with these problems.

### A. Non-resident ownership of land

In several Canadian provinces, the subject of non-resident ownership of land has become significant. Increasingly, provinces are passing legislation that restricts the amount of land non-residents can own. The reasons for this phenomenon are the problems associated with the acquisition of land by foreigners. First, non-resident ownership often forces land prices to rise, making it difficult for new farmers to acquire land. Second, it leads to more farm tenants and thus causes changes in the farm structure. Third, non-residents often contribute to changes in land use by either developing or overworking the land to the detriment of conservation efforts. Last, absentee foreign landownership contributes to changes in rural communities by altering the decision-making forces in a community (Mage and Lapping, 1982, pp. 3–5).

Prince Edward Island – Canada's smallest province and an island of 5660 square kilometres – is currently debating the issue of non-resident ownership of land (Redmond, 1990). The issue of foreign land ownership on Prince Edward Island has been a major topic for at least a hundred years. The island's fear of non-resident ownership of land originates from its early settlement. When the British settled in Canada, the province's lands were distributed by the Crown with the result that much of the land remained in the hands of residents in Britain, and island residents became farm tenants. After the Second World War, the province attracted many Canadian and American tourists, reviving the old debate over foreign land ownership (Mage and Lapping, 1982). Consequently, Prince Edward Island has enacted many laws regarding land ownership over the years. The Real Property Tax Act (RSPEI, 1974, c. R–4), passed in 1959, restricted landowners to a maximum of 200 acres. The act has often been amended; an amendment in 1972 extended landownership restrictions to all non-residents, including all Canadians not resident on the island (RSPEI, 1979, c. R–4). Another law to restrict foreign ownership of land, introduced by the government in 1982, is the Prince Edward Island Lands Protection Act (SPEI, 1982, c. 16). This act controls all land holdings in excess of 405 ha (1000 acres) by an individual and 1214.5 ha (3000 acres) by a corporation (Mage and Lapping, 1982). Also non-residents wanting to buy land in excess of 5 acres or 165 ft of shorefront must first get approval from cabinet under the Real Property Tax Act (Audet and Le Henaff, 1983, p. 105).

Despite the fact that some of these acts have existed for years, the landownership debate has heated up again in Prince Edward Island. Although non-residents must first get approval for land purchases, few applications have been turned down by the provincial government. The province's Royal Commission on the Land 'called for strict control of land ownership by non-residents and corporations' (Redmond, 1990). The Commission was also concerned about large holders of farm land, stating that 'unlimited farm size would very likely lead to enhanced pressures for corporate control of agriculture through vertically-integrated operations'. Thus, it is probable that further legislation will be forthcoming in Prince Edward Island.

Saskatchewan is another province concerned with non-resident ownership of land. The concern here arose from beliefs that the control of the land should be left in the hands of those involved in the day-to-day agricultural operations and that farmers in the province should not be forced to compete with capital from outside Canada (Ward, 1978, p. 98). Under the Saskatchewan Farm Ownership Act (RSS, 1978, c. s-17) the Saskatchewan Farm Ownership Board monitored all sales of farm land in the province and restricted the sale of land to non-residents. The act created some of the strictest regulations regarding non-resident ownership of land in Canada (Ward, 1978, p. 14). During the Canada–US Free Trade debate, this act received some attention from the legislature. Members of the Opposition were concerned that American investment in Canadian farmland would be allowed once Free Trade was in place, and the Farm Ownership Act was cited to defeat this argument (Debates of the Legislature, 8 October 1987, p. 3196). This act was repealed, however, when the Conservative Party took power, replacing the New Democratic Party (NDP).

The Land Bank Act (RSS, 1978, c. L-2) helped to regulate the non-resident ownership of land in Saskatchewan. This act established a corporate entity that purchased farm land as an agent for the Crown and then leased the land to farmers who were most deserving (Young, 1974, p. 1). This policy allowed the establishment and survival of family farms and allowed Saskatchewan farmers to sell their land for a fair price. It helped to stop non-residents from buying up farm land and also helped young farmers without large amounts of capital to get started in farming (Ward, 1978, p. 93).

This act has now been replaced by the Farm Purchase Program Act (RSS, 1982–1983, c. F-8.1), under which qualified farmers receive interest rebates on loans they obtain to buy farm land. Qualifications for participation are established by regulations to be issued from time to time.

Similarly, the provinces of Alberta and Manitoba have specific legislation to limit the ownership of land by non-residents. In Manitoba, the Agricultural Land Protection Act (SM, 1977, c. 44) limits non-residents to 20 acres of land. In addition, Alberta's Agricultural and Recreational Ownership Act (RSA, 1980, c. A-9), passed in 1979, limits non-residents ownership to 20 acres.

Many of the other provinces simply control non-resident ownership of land through the existing land-use controls. Non-resident ownership of land can be controlled indirectly through provincial planning acts, which establish criteria for development. For instance, Ontario, British Columbia, and Quebec use these types of laws to control, although minimally, foreign ownership of land. On the other hand, provinces like Newfoundland and New Brunswick are more concerned with attracting investment and consequently have not enacted legislation to control foreign land ownership.

### B. Land-use regulation

In the past few decades Canada has experienced a reduction in the number of farms; the 1986 Census of Agriculture showed 7.9% fewer farms than in 1981. Except for Newfoundland, the percentage decrease in the number of farms has been largest east of Manitoba. For example, in Nova Scotia the number of farms declined by 15% between 1981 and 1986. With the decrease in the number of farms, the farm population in Canada has also dropped significantly. In 1956, the farm population was 17% of the total population of Canada, compared to the 1986 figure of 3.6%.

Urbanization of the Canadian countryside is one factor in the loss of farmland, especially in Eastern Ontario. Because the problem of loss of farmland is acute in Ontario, this section will largely deal with Ontario policies to prevent loss of farmland. In 1976 more than 55% of Canada's total good agricultural land lay within 161 km of Canada's 23 Census Metropolitan Areas. As one report explains:

> The existence of good agricultural lands around the CMAs is a consequence of Canada's settlement history. Initially, settlement was oriented towards areas of fertile soils which could supply agricultural products. The success of initial settlement, often related to the area's agricultural productivity, which then formed a solid basis for subsequent growth. The result has been a conflict between urban areas and agricultural resource lands; both urban and agricultural uses are competing for the same land resource
>
> (Neimanis, 1979, p. 3)

For instance, the Niagara Fruit Belt, which extends east from Hamilton, Ontario along the south shore of Lake Ontario, suffers from the encroachment of urbanization on farmland. This area produces 67% of the value of tender fruit (peaches, pears, cherries) and grapes. Despite the existence of excellent agricultural land and conditions, between 1961 and 1976 this region lost 23% of its farms, and agricultural land declined by 16%. Between 1966 and 1976, 84% of the land converted to urban use in the Hamilton and St Catharines–Niagara urban areas was class 1–3 soils suitable for agriculture (McCuaig and Manning, 1982, p. 29). Similarly, most of the cities in the Windsor–Quebec City axis are situated on high capability agricultural land (Yeates, 1985, p. 83).

Ontario's rapid urbanization around the city of Toronto has caused the Provincial Government to establish an Office for the Greater Toronto Area (GTA), responsible for co-ordinating the Government's policies, programmes and projects in this region. The area includes not only all provincial government departments but also about thirty local municipalities and five regional governments in the GTA. Because the GTA incorporates some of Ontario's best farmland, it will be of interest to monitor the progress of this body; initial impressions suggest that it may have a pro-development approach.

Unlike some provinces, Ontario has no strict agrarian land-use laws. In 1978, after extensive consultation, the government of Ontario released the Food Land Guidelines (Canadian Press Report no. 1157ED, 25 January 1990).

The Guidelines were:

> designed to assist at all levels in planning for agriculture within the land-use planning process in Ontario. They outline a methodology for accommodating agricultural land needs in the planning process, and their implementation will ensure an adequate land base for agricultural needs in the future.
>
> (Minister of Agriculture & Food, 1978)

If the Guidelines are followed by local governments, there should be some central control over development in agricultural areas. Municipalities are only encouraged to take the Guidelines into account, however, and there is little 'legal' authority to strengthen their use in planning.

The guidelines have been influential. The quasi-judicial tribunal established to hear appeals about planning matters, the Ontario Muncipal Board, has adapted the Guidelines as reflecting the philosophy of the Provincial Government:

> Second, s. 4.4.1 of the official plan (of the local government) generally reflects the philosophy of the Government of Ontario as expressed in their 1978 Food Land Guidelines . . . and the board (Ontario Municipal Board) is unable to find any special circumstances in this case which would allow it to conclude that the philosophy and policy of the guidelines do not apply here
>
> *(Leerentveld* v. *County of Wellington Land Division Committee)*

This situation in Ontario could deteriorate substantially because the Ontario Municipal Board is not bound by the concept of *stare decisis.* Moreover, individual panel members could interpret the Guidelines differently. For example, to develop good agricultural land, a prospective developer must demonstrate need for the land use (Minister of Agriculture & Food, 1978, p. 12). Individual interpretations have meant that different hearing boards have interpreted the meaning of 'need' differently (Marshall, unpublished).

This problem could be resolved by a provincial government Policy Statement under the Planning Act 1983 (Leerentveld, 1990). Section 3 of this Act permits the Minister of Municipal Affairs together with any other Minister to issue policy statements on planning issues. These policy statements were intended to encourage implementation of provincial policies in local land-use plans and in the hearing process before the Ontario Municipal Board. After local and provincial consultation, the policy statements are to be approved by the Lieutenant Governor in Council (i.e. the Cabinet). This section does have weaknesses. Section 3(5) of the Planning

Act provides only that all planning agencies must have regard for any policy statements issued under the act. Thus, while the agencies mentioned must consider the policy statements, they do not need to follow them.

Moreover, although a number of policy statements have been proposed, only three have been issued: Mineral Aggregate Resource Policy, Wetlands Policy and Flood Plain Policy. The Ontario Ministry of Agriculture and Food has been working on an agricultural land-use policy for a number of years, but it cannot obtain the final consents to issue the statement with the Minister of Municipal Affairs.

The difficulty with any type of land-use preservation legislation is that those favouring development will attempt to create ingenious methods to circumvent the statute. For example, the Planning Act in Ontario does not prohibit the use of a testamentary device to sever property, nor do such severances have to be approved by any planning committee of the local government. Therefore, it is possible to circumvent the Foodland Guidelines by paying farmers to bequeath parcels of their farm to the developers or their company. In one area of extremely good farmland (the Niagara Peninsula), developers were convincing terminally ill or elderly owners of farmland to enter into these types of arrangements.

Prior to the September 1990 provincial election, all candidates for Premier of the Province agreed that a change in the Planning Act was needed, but there was little focus on the exact means of prohibiting the practice, while still allowing the legitimate testamentary bequest. One proposal would permit severances only in favour of a farmer's sons or daughters who are also actively engaged in farming.

Another unique piece of agricultural legislation in Ontario is an Act respecting the Protection of Farm Practices (SO, 1988, c. 62). Under this act farmers cannot be found liable in nuisance to any person for an interference resulting from the operation of their farm (e.g., noise or dust), nor can an injunction be issued to prevent them from continuing with the operation of their farm because of an interference. However, it appears that this act has seldom been used. Constitutionally, this act may be *ultra vires* as it may infringe on the legislative jurisdiction of the federal government by establishing a court of law under section 96 of the Constitution Act. It has not yet been challenged.

Like Ontario, British Columbia has a significant problem with agricultural land loss. Unlike Ontario, however, British Columbia has enacted specific legislation to deal with the problem of loss of farmland and was in fact the first province in Canada to do so. Much of British Columbia's terrain is mountainous with narrow valleys. As a consequence of its landscape, little land is suitable for agriculture and unfortunately, this same land is highly populated. The resulting lack of land has made preservation of farmland a top priority in British Columbia (Wilson and Pierce, 1984, p. 272). The Agricultural Land Commission Act (RSBC, 1979, c. 9) establishes specific provisions to protect farmland (Audet and Le Henaff, 1983, p. 3); its enactment immediately froze the development of all farmland in British Columbia. This act establishes the Provincial Agricultural Land Commission, which acts as an agricultural land zoning authority. Under this act agricultural land may be designated as an agricultural land reserve, with activity within the reserve regulated by the act (Ince and Pereboom, 1984, p. 197). The procedure for desigating an area as an agricultural land reserve is complex, and allows for a public hearing if so requested by a private owner. The designation must be approved by a Regional Board, the Commission, and the provincial Cabinet. Once an area is designated as a reserve, all land can only be used for agricultural purposes, and all other activities are prohibited (Ince and Pereboom, 1984, pp. 200–3). Regulations include fish farms, harvesting of trees, and dwelling units necessary for farm use as acceptable uses of designated land. The act also contains provisions to have land removed from the reserve.

Criticism of this British Columbia law is mounting. Recently the refusal of the Provincial Agricultural Land Commission to remove 1618 ha of prime fruitland in the Okanagan Valley was appealed to the Provincial Cabinet by a 160 member group calling itself the Kelowna Land Rights Association. This body complained that the decision was flawed because the long-term outlook for agriculture in the Okanagan Valley was poor. The Association also argued that policy changes were needed to take into consideration changing economic and technical forces, which would then create a smaller but healthier farm sector (Canadian Press Report, no. 1157, 25-10-90). The conflict has not yet been resolved.

Similar legislative schemes exist in both Quebec and Newfoundland. In Quebec, farmland is protected under An Act to Preserve Agricultural Land (LRQ, 1977, c. P-41.1).

> Under this Act, the Government of Quebec identified the arable lands and designated certain protected agricultural zones. The Act prohibits in these zones all activity that is incompatible with agriculture and controls subdivision and parcelling in order to preserve existing productions units and help maintain the viability of farming operations
>
> (Audet and Le Henaff, 1983, p. 126)

The Development Areas (Land) Act (RSN, 1970, c. 95) protects agricultural land in Newfoundland. Agricultural reserves are identified in municipal zoning plans (Audet and Le Henaff, 1983, p. 4).

Other provinces control the development of agricultural land by the use of provincial planning acts. In Alberta, the Planning Act (RSA, 1980, c. P-9) contains criteria and standards that must be met for development or redevelopment of land. On the other hand, the Planning Act (SM, 1975, c.

29) of Manitoba controls development of agricultural land by dictating that a development plan that contains proposals for management as well as for preservation of agricultural land and related activities must be submitted. The Planning Act (SNS, 1969, c. 16) of Nova Scotia restricts urban expansion and prohibits development on class 2 and 3 agricultural land (under the Canada Land Inventory) (Audet and Le Henaff, 1983, p. 4).

## C. Environmental land planning

In recent years environmental concerns have become a high priority in Canada and throughout the world. In response to this concern a debate has arisen over the need for governments to pass legislation that forces people to act in an environmentally conscious way. Although '[t]raditionally, farmers have been subjected to a minimum of legislative controls on land use in Canada' (Stress on Land, 1983, p. 253), some provisions in Canadian law restrict farming practices.

In Alberta, a clause in the Soil Conservation Act (RSA, 1980, c. S-19) requires farmers to carry out emergency measures to stop soil drifting if so requested. Although action has seldom been taken under this statute it seems that the threat has been sufficient to make farmers themselves respond during times when wind erosion is severe. The Lieutenant Governor-in-Council also has authority over the environment:

> [H]e may enact regulations that establish any area as a special planning area where he can prohibit and control demolition, removal of buildings, land-uses, development, and occupation of land and buildings
>
> (Audet and Le Henaff, 1983, p. 33)

Specially designated environmental areas can be established under the Planning Act. Alberta also has an Environment Control Act (RSA, 1980, c. E-13) that prevents environmental degradation and protects natural or man-made environments by directing land use and development in the area so designated.

Saskatchewan has the Soil Drifting Control Act (RSS, 1978, c. S-54) that allows a rural municipality to pass bylaws to establish tillage practices. Under this act the council can, for example, require the growing of cover crops or prohibit the burning of stubble.

Under the Fires Prevention Act (1970), Manitoba can prevent farmers from burning organic soils. However, this act is more to prevent forest fires and traffic accidents than to preserve the soil (Stress on Land, 1983, p. 253). Manitoba's Planning Act addresses environmental concerns through provisions for the use of development plans, special planning areas, and zoning to regulate flood or other dangerous areas.

In British Columbia, the Environment and Land Use Act (RSBC, 1979, c. 110) gives the government extensive powers involving environmental control. This act establishes the Environment and Land Use Committee comprised of members of the provincial Cabinet; its duties include establishing programmes to develop public awareness of the environment, promoting policies that will minimize the harm to the environment caused by land development, and reporting its findings to the Cabinet (Ince and Pereboom, 1984, p. 86). The act basically gives the Cabinet unlimited powers:

> to make orders and regulations to deal with any matter involving the environment or land use, as long as its actions are within the constitutional jurisdiction of the province
>
> (Ince and Pereboom, 1984, p. 87)

The act has been used in a wide variety of situations, from land-use to water pollution control. Environmental concerns can also be addressed under the Land Commission Act by protecting agricultural land from other development. The Municipal Act (RSBC, 1979, c. 290) requires that the preservation of the environment be taken into account by municipal councils when establishing zoning by-laws. Lastly, the Local Service Act allows for the refusal of subdivision applications if the land is subject to flooding, has poor drainage or erodes easily (Audet and Le Henaff, 1983, p. 12).

## D. Expropriation law

The law of expropriation is not a controversial issue in Canada. Each province has an Expropriations Act that allows various bodies to expropriate land for highways, and public utilities. The Expropriations Act (RSO, 1980, c. 148) of Ontario is representative. Under this act owners are compensated for the fair market value of their land when it is expropriated. It also establishes a system of notice required before expropriation can occur.

## E. Tenancy law

Like expropriation law, tenancy is not considered a problem in Canada. Largely as a result of land settlement patterns, there are not many areas in Canada with a lot of farm tenants. Farm leases are covered under each provinces' Landlord and Tenant Act. In Alberta, for example, the Landlord and Tenant Act (RSA, 1980, c. L-6) sets out the obligations of both parties and the remedies each is entitled to when problems occur.

## III. Administration of Agrarian Land Law and Policy

Just as the laws regarding land use vary between provinces so do the land-planning frameworks of each province. As mentioned earlier, the provinces have transferred much of their authority to regulate land use to municipal and local governments. However, the provinces still retain central control over the implementation of the acts. In the context of this section, local governments refer to the municipal governments that exist in each town. On the other hand, regional areas refer to larger areas that have common development and planning problems. For instance, it is sometimes beneficial for a region to plan water, sewer, and other public services (Ince and Pereboom, 1984, pp. 30–2).

The Planning Act in Alberta establishes a framework in which planning and development decisions are made in the province. The act:

> defines the nature of relations between municipalities and the provincial government and sets forth planning methods and tools as part of an administrative structure (regional plans, general municipal plans, and land use by-laws)
>
> (Audet and Le Henaff, 1983, p. 28)

The role of the provincial government is to set the policies to be followed and to approve regional plans. The Department of Municipal Affairs has the responsibility for implementing and enforcing the Planning Act. Connected to the Department of Municipal Affairs is the Alberta Planning Board, a quasi-judicial body. The responsibilities of this board are to review the plans received from the regional planning commissions, and to act as a court to resolve inter-municipal disputes and as an appeal body on land subdivision decisions (Audet and Le Henaff, 1983, p. 34). Between the provincial and local governments exists the regional planning commission, which has authority to approve subdivisions and prepare regional plans:

> The commissions can prepare municipal statutory plans, and/or land use by-laws at the request of a municipality within their region, advise local municipalities on planning related matters, and encourage public participation in the planning process
>
> (Audet and Le Henaff, 1983, p. 35)

Local governments have the responsibility of determining municipal plans and land-use by-laws.

British Columbia has established a planning framework similar to

Alberta's, but there are numerous government agencies involved in implementing provincial legislation. The Agricultural Land Commission, an administrative tribunal, is one such body. Although it has no specific mandate for planning, its powers over zoning affect planning powers of other provincial bodies. The Municipal Act (RSBC, 1979, c. 290) gives the province broad supervisory powers over regional governments:

> Where a Council (except the Vancouver City Council) or Regional Board has enacted any zoning, subdivision or master plan by-law, the Minister of Municipal Affairs may, if he is 'of the opinion that all or part of the by-law is contrary to the public interest of the province' notify the Council or Board of his objections to the by-law
>
> (Ince and Pereboom, 1984, p. 24)

The Minister can require that the by-laws be changed, and if they are not so changed then he may unilaterally amend them himself.

Manitoba has established a somewhat different system of land planning. The Provincial Land Use Committee is composed of ministers from several government departments that deal with land planning, for example, the Departments of Highways and Transportation, Municipal Affairs, Natural Resources, Energy and Mines, Agricultural and Northern Affairs, Government Services, and Environment. This group has the responsibility to recommend provincial land-use policies to the Cabinet, to co-ordinate governmental programmes involving land, to approve municipal development plans, and to review land-use and environmental impacts. Local governments prepare zoning by-laws, make development plans, and enforce both by-laws and plans. If they so desire municipalities can join together to form a District Planning Board, which hear appeals regarding zoning by-laws (Audet and Le Henaff, 1983, pp. 59–60).

## IV. Evaluation of Agrarian Land Law in Canada

As outlined above, a wide range of laws across Canada address agrarian law issues, and they have met with varied success across Canada. For example, a survey of British Columbia's legislative scheme showed that the development of agricultural land had been slowed. There also appears to be renewed confidence in the future of farming along with an increased investment in farming. However, although the rate of loss has been reduced, the rate of good land being lost has increased. Moreover, the rate of loss was still 18 square miles per year (Wilson and Pierce, 1984, pp. 282–3). In contrast, the Food Land Guidelines under Ontario's legislative scheme need only be *considered* by the local municipalities when making their zoning by-laws. Thus, the voluntariness of this programme may be a problem.

Notwithstanding specific flaws in each statute, the primary problem in Canadian land law is its diversity. Although each province is unique and has particular problems, provincial governments have exacerbated the diversity by delegating much of their planning authority to local governments. These local municipalities, whose only income stems from real property taxes, then compete with one another to develop their tax base. As industrial, commercial, and even residential zones command a higher tax base than agricultural land, it is tempting to rezone agricultural areas to permit other development. Farmers, who have been struggling financially, are not adverse to this strategy as the value of their land has increased dramatically. In some regions such as Ontario's fruitbelt area (the Niagara Peninsula) the results have been phenomenal. Tracts of land have been subdivided for residential purposes and taken out of agricultural production. It has probably reached the stage where any rehabilitation is impossible.

Governments, farmers and farm lobby groups have unwittingly aided in this demise. Adherence to the belief in the viability of the 'family farm' has led to laws and programmes that encourage the inefficient operations of small farms. Limitations on non-resident ownership of farm land prevent larger corporations from efficiently operating a farm. While not espousing a 'bigger is better' attitude, provincial laws should be encouraging the consolidation (and hence the vertical integration) of farming operations. A family farm of 25 acres in the Niagara Peninsula will not become a viable operation unless it is encouraged to expand. Unfortunately the present agrarian land laws do not always permit this type of expansion.

The other difficulty of Canadian land laws is that they do not have the flexibility to deal with new government policies. When the Canadian federal government entered into a free trade agreement with the United States, farmers in some provinces quickly sounded the death knell of Canadian farming and sold their land to developers. If the legislation had required a cooling off period before the disposal of these valuable assets, it is likely that much farmland would still be in operation.

The future does not look totally bleak. Provincial governments must develop long-term strategies for preserving farm land and allowing for orderly development. The governments need to centralize and consolidate their agrarian land laws in order to facilitate this goal. Once that has been accomplished, farming can regain the position it once held in Canada.

## Notes

1. The recent failure by the federal government (June 1990) to get all ten provinces to agree to an accord (Meech Lake Accord) that would officially bring the province of Quebec under the constitution led to a political crisis of such magnitude that many Quebec citizens demanded a political secession from the rest of Canada and many non-Quebecers seemed prepared to accept this alternative. The interesting point is that the crisis probably could have been avoided entirely had proper consultation taken place between the ten provinces, two territories and the federal government prior to a last-minute attempt to save the Accord.
2. The following data have been taken from the 1986 Agriculture Census data compiled by Statistics Canada.
3. The following data and table have been taken from an Ontario Ministry of Agriculture and Food document entitled '*Facts and Figures on the Agri-Food Sector Ontario*', Issue 3, January 1989, compiled by the Economics & Policy Co-ordination Branch from data provided by Statistics Canada and Agriculture Canada.
4. For example, the *Ontario Water Resources Act*, RSO 1980, c. 361 is generally administered by the Ministry of the Environment, and in some respects by the Ministry of Housing (plumbing provisions).

## References

Audet, R. and Le Henaff, A. (1983) *Land Planning Framework of Canada; An Overview.* Environment Canada, Land Use Policy and Research Branch, Lands Directorate.

Cox, K. (1990) PEI's lack of land policy decried. *Toronto Globe & Mail,* 24 October p. A6.

Edwards, G.M. and Ince, J.G. (1984) *Environmental Law British Columbia Handbook.* Butterworth, Vancouver.

Environment Canada (1983) *Stress on Land.* Lands Directorate, Policy, Research and Development Branch, Ottawa, Folio 6.

Ince, J.G. and Pereboom, Z.M. (1984) *Land Use Law British Columbia Handbook.* Butterworth, Vancouver.

*Leerentveld* v. *County of Wellington Land Division Committee* (1990), 23 OMBR 183.

McCuaig, J.D. and Manning, E.W. (1982) *Agricultural Land Use Change in Canada Processes and Consequences,* Land Use in Canada Series No. 21. Environment Canada, Lands Directorate, Ottawa.

Mage, J.A. and Lapping, M.B. (1982) Legislation related to absentee foreign land ownership in Canada. *Agricultural Law Journal* 4(3), 3–5. (Reprint)

Minister of Agriculture & Food (1978) *Food Land Guidelines.* Queen's Printer, Toronto.

Neimanis, V.P. (1979) *The Canada Land Inventory Canada's Cities and Their*

*Surrounding Land Reserve.* Environment Canada, Lands Directorate, The Canada Land Inventory Report No. 15.

Redmond, M. (1990) Emotions run deep as PEI maps out its land strategy. *Financial Post,* 8 August, p. 10.

Statistics Canada, 1986 Census, *Profile on Agriculture.*

Troop, P.M. (1974) Federal land-use control. *Law Society of Upper Canada, Special Lectures.* De Boo, Toronto.

Ward, E.N. (1978) *Land Use Programs in Canada.* Environment Canada, Lands Directorate, Ottawa.

Wilson, J.W. and Pierce, J.T. (1984) The agricultural land commission of British Columbia. In: Bunce, M.J. and Troughton, M.J. (eds), *The Pressures of Change in Rural Canada,* Geographical Monographs. Downsview, Ontario.

Yeates, M. (1985) *Land in Canada's Urban Heartland,* No. 27. Environment Canada, Lands Directorate, Ottawa.

Young, Kim (1974) The Saskatchewan Land Bank. *Saskatchewan Law Review,* 40, 1–24.

Young, Kim (1975) The Saskatchewan Farm Ownership Act. *Saskatchewan Law Review* 40, 117–22.

# 12

# AGRARIAN LAND LAW IN AUSTRALIA

Ben Boer and Ian Hannam

## I. Introduction

In Australia, it is not possible to think of the agricultural use of land without thinking of the problem of land degradation. The Australian land mass is geologically very old and weathered; it has very fragile soils due to low levels of organic matter and poor aggregation (Charman, 1983, p. 1). Until 200 years ago, the continent was inhabited at a sustainable rate by its aboriginal population, which was low in numbers in keeping with the carrying capacity of the land. Unlike European Australians, Aboriginals did not practise any form of gardening or animal husbandry (Broome, 1982). Since then:

> Agriculture in Australia has been dominated by European attitudes which sought to recreate open, park-like landscapes, and were exploitative, viewing the continent as a source of apparently unlimited cheap land, where 'development' was socially justified. Similar attitudes have prevailed in the use of forests and fisheries. Sustainability has not been a feature of the use of natural resources until very recently
>
> (Hamblin, 1991, p. 21)

Eighty percent of Australian people live along the fertile eastern seaboard. Some 7.6 million square kilometres of the Australian land mass now need soil conservation treatment. Approximately 1.5 million square kilometres are so badly damaged by agriculture that repair work is urgently needed. Three-quarters of New South Wales, Australia's largest and most populous state, is degraded, with some 4 of every 10 ha being rated as severely damaged (Beale and Fray, 1990, p. ix). Australia's land degradation problems have been known for at least half a century. Specific soil conservation legislation has been in place in New South Wales since 1938, with other States following suit in the years thereafter. Although the problem is of national dimensions, and despite the fact that since 1972 there have been some sixteen federal government-sponsored inquiries into land degradation, there is as yet no uniform approach to combat the difficulties. One of the reasons for this is the tortuous history of Federal/State politics. However, an important facet of this is the perceived limitation that the Australian Constitution, introduced in 1901, does not give the federal parliament any particular power over resource use and environment protection within the six States. This has been the basis for the assumption that the Federal government does not and should not have any direct influence on environmental policies in the States. This assumption has been shaken in the past few years by virtue of a number of major environmental cases, particularly in the area of world heritage, that have been heard in the High Court of Australia in the 1980s (see Boer, 1989). Thus, although the value of primary industries to the Australian economy is very high, agricultural practices continue to erode, in more ways than one, the ecological basis for continued agricultural productivity in the country. It is recognized that, particularly for Australian conditions, the effect of soil erosion on productivity was irregular. This is because erosion patterns reflect the spasmodic nature of Australia's erosive rainfall events. Major soil losses occur on a very irregular basis, and this means that a particular management system may not necessarily be a safe one even though soil erosion has not occurred for a number of years (Aveyard and Charman, 1991, p. 317).

Specific problems relating to the European-style development of land in Australia include soil erosion, watercourse sedimentation, dryland salinity over vast stretches of the country, and a very high rate of extinction of native species of fauna and flora. The cause of land degradation is largely related to inappropriate agricultural practices. As a result of the low natural fertility of the soil, vast areas have had to be cleared or heavily grazed to maintain an adequate economic output (see Prately and Rowell, 1987). No exact data exist concerning the extent of modification of tree cover in Australia since European settlement, but it is now generally believed that some two-thirds of the original cover has been removed to make way for agricultural crops and for urban and industrial activities (Firth *et al.*, 1984, p. 2).

> Tree loss has been at the core of almost every aspect of land degradation in Australia. Tree replacement will be essential if we are to redevelop the fertility of many of our degraded soils and maintain sustainable systems of agriculture
>
> (Australia, 1989a, p. 155 and see Beale and Fray, 1990)

The recent introduction of the 'one billion trees programme' (Hawke,

1989, p. 48) is hardly likely to address the problems of tree loss on the Australian continent in the next decade.

The practice of large-scale irrigation, which has been carried out for over a century, has also contributed to these difficulties (Beale and Fray, 1990, p. 78), a factor most evident in the Murray-Darling Basin (see case study below).

## A. Land tenure

The Australian land tenure system is much the same as the British system, on which it is based. In Australia, land cannot be absolutely owned. The Crown is the fundamental owner of all land, and all so-called 'fee simple' owners hold from the Crown (many Aboriginal people would probably have a different view of this account of ownership of the continent). Fee simple ownership is the equivalent of freehold. For all practical purposes, land that is granted or bought from the Crown is privately owned. This is more likely to be the case in areas where the farms are relatively small and more intensively managed.

Although many farms are privately owned, in the Northern Territory and the States of Western Australia, South Australia and New South Wales, large tracts of semi-arid land are used for grazing purposes, and a high percentage of these lands are held under leasehold title. These leases are subject to a wide variety of conditions, including minimum stocking rates, obligation to maintain improvements, maintenance of fencing and roads, fire control, the level of rent and so on. These leases are very often for long periods of time. In some States, there is a category of 'perpetual leasehold', which in effect means indefinitely unless the grazier commits serious breaches of the conditions of the lease. It is possible in some circumstances for these leaseholds to be converted to private ownership. This extent of leasehold may have important bearing on the way in which the land is treated. Although various Land Acts include provisions for the reversion of the land to the Crown if it is not adequately or appropriately exploited, many of these provisions are not well enforced. The result is that leasehold tenure can continue indefinitely without sufficient responsibility being placed on landholders; this apples particularly to graziers.

It is possible for either the State or Federal governments to expropriate land compulsorily, subject to compensation being satisfactorily arranged. At State level this would occur most often in relation to acquisition of land for national parks and for public forestry purposes (for example, for plantation forestry).

## B. Ecological sustainability

Aboriginal land-management practices, developed over many thousands of years on the Australian continent, have been largely ignored by European colonizers in the last two centuries. This ignorance seems to have been at the peril of exploitation of soil and land resources to the extent that major areas are now used beyond their physical capacity for intensive agriculture. The emphasis in this chapter is on how the legal and policy mechanisms available in the States, the Northern Territory (which for the purposes of this chapter will be regarded as a State) and at Commonwealth level can be used to protect and conserve Australian agricultural lands rather than how to further extend and almost inevitably degrade them. The most significant element of the environmental debate in Australia in the 1990s is the notion of 'ecologically sustainable development'.

Ecologically sustainable development in Australia has been defined to mean 'using, conserving and enhancing the community's resources so that ecological processes, on which life depends, are maintained and the total quality of life, now and in the future can be increased' (Australia, 1990a). In the specific agrarian context, Bradsen (1991, pp. 17–18) has pointed out that the definition of 'capability' as it applies to land, found in the recent South Australian Soil Conservation and Land Care Act, 1989, comes closest to a definition of sustainability: 'the ability of the land to sustain particular uses without suffering permanent damage or reduction in future productivity'. Sustainability has become a familiar, although abused, concept in recent times, particularly in Australia, which came into the sustainable development debate rather late in the piece, several years after the term had been popularized in the report *Our Common Future* (World Commission on Environment and Development, 1987; for further critique, see Boer, 1992). Bradsen maintains that sustainability:

> must refer to the maintenance, and where possible the restoration of the natural resources of the land and the focus must be truly long term. Its meaning must ultimately be governed by scientific–factual truth about the state of the land, not by shorter-term profitability nor by theoretical or ideological postulates
>
> (Bradsen, 1991, p. 18)

Importantly, Bradsen also makes the point that in defining sustainable *use*, not only long-term productivity must be addressed, but also the conservation of other natural resources not obviously related to productivity, such as genetic diversity.

One of the features of this debate which has not as yet received sufficient attention, is the question of how many people the Australian land mass can support in an ecologically sustainable way. Without specifically addressing the fundamental issue of population, any national or State land-use strategy would be seriously deficient. The issue of population by migration has been subject to debate in recent years both within government and among conservationists. Paul Erhlich of Stanford University has argued that Australia's population of 17 million should be decreased to about 10 million over the next few decades, in order to combat the problems of land degradation (in Beale and Fray, 1990, p. 164).

## II. Use of Land for Agrarian Purposes

There is no broad legislative scheme at Federal or State level to protect the continuation in use of agricultural land. Apart from one Bill, the Right to Farm Bill of 1989 in Western Australia (see below), much of the modern legislation relates to more general resource allocation and environment protection systems.

Nevertheless, a very strong developmental ethic of agricultural exploitation exists, with powerful lobby groups such as the National Farmers' Federation being able to influence governments in such a way that legislative endeavours are not necessarily effective. This ethic is emphasized by the fact that soil conservation organizations in the Australian States have traditionally been either part of a department of agriculture or ministerially tied to them, and that the legislation is largely directed to matters of agricultural productivity.

In June 1991, however, the New South Wales soil conservation agency was abolished and its functions incorporated within a new Department of Conservation and Land Management. Although this decision took the agency out from under the Minister for Agriculture, it could prove to be a detrimental move because in effect it means the disintegration of the largest specialist soil conservation institution in the southern hemisphere. There are now three States (Western Australia, South Australia and New South Wales) where soil conversation is less identified with the agriculture portfolio.

An ethic contrary to the developmental one, embracing the idea that soil and vegetation might be regarded as common property of a community or, more broadly, as part of the common heritage of humankind (see Farrier, 1990, p. 98; Boer, 1990) would be a notion unknown to most farmers anywhere. The idea that environmental law is in itself a restriction of the rights of private property is one that could see more popular acceptance in the near future (see further Boer, 1990).

Although many of the soil conservation Acts have express powers to intervene in land use (in effect restricting the rights of the user), the quality of the legislation varies greatly from one State to the other (Bradsen, 1988, c. 2;). Some States have amended their legislation to broaden its scope from one of control and prevention of soil erosion and land degradation to include provision for the management of various conservation values. For example, the New South Wales Soil Conservation Act under its 'Protected Land' provisions exercises a control over the destruction of trees on special parts of the landscape where trees are considered vital to land stability and the control of land degradation. The protected land concept was expanded in 1986 to control the destruction of trees that are rare or endangered, contain certain significant habitat, or have other sensitive ecological values. This concept could certainly be expanded even further to import a holistic approach to rural land management. However, the effectiveness of tree and vegetation controls in New South Wales and South Australia in particular has been limited by legal problems and administrative structures (Bradsen, 1987; Farrier, 1990).

## III. Special Government Policies for Rural Land Use

Rural land use in Australia generally comes under the environmental planning system in each State. As Farrier notes (1990, p. 99), there is no significant historical tradition of vigorous land-use regulation in rural areas. Although each system differs, the general picture is that a zoning system applies, whereby land is divided into a broad range of uses from residential through industrial to rural uses. There is no separate rural planning legislation as such, although in New South Wales there is special legislation relating to the entire western half of the State, a sparsely populated area that has experienced severe land degradation through the effects of overgrazing on native perennial species. This legislation, which covers the area known as the Western Lands Division, purports to govern rural land use through a range of strategies (see Western Lands Act, 1901 (New South Wales); Farrier, 1990, p. 109).

Particular government policies protect rural land in specific instances. Various eradication programmes, in relation to rabbits (Hamblin, 1991, p. 22), kangaroos, foxes, and dingoes have been instituted over the years. Australia is famous for its incredibly long (several thousand kilometres), but spectacularly ineffective 'rabbit fences', built to keep rabbits out of wheat and other crops. The prickly pear was a problem for many years, and the Commonwealth Prickly Pear Board was established by the Federal Government in 1920. The prickly pear was brought under control by the importation of a South American moth, which was responsible for the virtual eradication of the two species of prickly pear over an area of some 24.3 million ha in New South Wales and Queensland.

Drought has, until recently, also been regarded as an aberration in weather patterns in the Australian farming community. In 1990, with the downturn in the world wool market and the drought conditions then prevailing in the country, there was an official authorization and compensation to farmers for the culling of some millions of sheep that were virtually worthless on the market, either for meat or for their potential wool-growing capacities.

However, the attitude of the Federal government changed in 1991. Special relief programmes were cut, and farmers were urged to cope with drought as part of the normal ecological and economic cycle.

## IV. Agrarian Land Law and Policy

### A. The connection between planning and development in rural areas

One of the reasons why land degradation problems occur widely throughout Australia has been the lack of uniform regulatory control over agricultural land-use management. This has arisen through the ineffective implementation of specific laws covering various agricultural activities. Many of these laws have acted against the environmental requirements of agricultural land by encouraging development and through the absence of adequate, or any, planning and land-use control provisions in some areas.

Although the activity of town planning has existed in Australian urban environments since about the turn of the century, where it was primarily associated with local government health and surveying responsibilities, planning in rural areas has only been implemented since the late 1970s. The historical development of planning law in Australia shows that it is substantially a 20th century exercise, and early legislation imitated the first English statutes on the topic (Fogg, 1982, p. 10). As the Australian Federal Government has no direct constitutional power to legislate for environmental planning apart from the federal Territories, it has largely been left up to each State to develop its own planning regimes.

Until the 1970s, ‘planning’ in relation to rural land was virtually nonexistent. Rural land comprised all the land not being used (or not wanted) for urban purposes (i.e. commercial, industrial, residential uses, and in some cases, open space or recreational use). There was thus no control over most rural activities through planning law. The major consequence of not having development control was the reinforcement of an attitude among rural land-users that their activities could not be interfered with.

Agricultural and rural uses have been specifically contemplated within the zoning provisions and development control of the Planning and Environment Act 1987 of Victoria; the State Planning Commission Act 1985 of Western Australia; the Planning Act 1982 of South Australia; and the Environmental Planning and Assessment Act 1979 of New South Wales. The legislation of Victoria and New South Wales incorporates an extended conception of planning that moves toward a system of natural resource management (Fisher, 1980, p. 278; Fisher, 1987).

The plans found in most Australian jurisdictions are binding on both government and private persons, although government can change zonings and other details of plans, generally subject to public participation processes and ministerial approval. There are also local council 'codes', which are generally binding on people applying for development approval. These codes generally conform to the plan approved for the particular area in question.

Building and construction permits are required for the development of land in each jurisdiction. These permits can normally be issued only if the use is allowed by the zoning for those particular areas. Each Australian State has a somewhat different system.

### B. Vegetation clearance controls

The question of regulation of private lands for agricultural purposes is just as problematic as that of leasehold lands. This has to do with the ethic of largely unbridled development that existed in Australia from the first settlement of European colonists, not helped by the lack of perceived need for specific rural planning regimes in the individual States. The emphasis in recent years has been on the control of clearance of vegetation on private land through a variety of mechanisms in the planning system (see Hannam, 1990a). South Australia and New South Wales will be used as examples here.

A significant limitation on the regulation of land use, both rural and urban, is the mechanism of the 'existing use', found in the legislation of most Australian jurisdictions. 'Existing use' provisions mean that where the land has been approved for use for a particular purpose under a zoning scheme, the power on the part of a local authority to change or restrict this use is limited in most circumstances. These provisions have a particularly limiting effect in relation to vegetation clearance controls, as a consequence of a High Court challenge to the validity of South Australia's vegetation clearance control legislation. The South Australian provision reads:

> Notwithstanding any other provision in this Act, no provision of the Development Plan shall–
>
> (a) prevent the continued use, subject to and in accordance with the conditions (if any) attached to the use of that land, for the purposes for which that land was lawfully being used at the time the provision took effect
>
> (section 56(1)(a), Planning Act 1982, South Australia)

In opposing this provision it was argued that 'land forming part of an overall farm unit but which had not been cleared was the subject of an existing use for farming purposes' (Fowler, 1986, p. 51). Therefore, no planning permit was needed to clear the land of vegetation. In an enforcement proceeding, the State Planning Commission sought to stop a farmer from further clearing his land. In acceding to this argument, the High Court of Australia held that the defendant did not need consent because the activity was part of an existing use for which he already had permission; i.e. it was part of the continuing farming activity (see *South Australian Planning Commission* v. *Dorrestijn* (1984), 59 *Australian Law Journal Reports*, 105; for a critique of this case see Farrier, 1991). Subsequent legislation overturned the effect of this decision (Native Vegetation Management Act 1985; see Bradsen, 1991, p. 17).

The Environmental Planning and Assessment Act 1979 of New South Wales has perhaps the broadest provisions for the protection of private lands in Australia. This is not to say that it is necessarily the most successful in preventing land abuse. The State has embraced explicitly the concept of environmental planning, moving away at least in a formal sense, from the old town and country planning model derived from the United Kingdom in the 1930s. The New South Wales system of statutory planning has three levels: State Environmental Planning Policies, Regional Environmental Plans and Local Environmental Plans. These instruments may include specific provisions for 'protecting, improving or utilising to the best advantage, the environment', as well as providing for the protection or preservation of important natural resources like trees or other vegetation (Environmental Planning and Assessment Act 1979, section 26). As Farrier notes, these provisions 'clearly envisage the possibility of broadacre clearing controls being introduced through planning instruments, not simply the traditional tree preservation order' (Farrier, 1991).

New South Wales applies its Environmental Planning and Assessment Act 1979 to the planning of rural land. Under this Act, planning can regulate rural land use through the development of State, regional, or local plans with development control provisions (Farrier, 1988, p. 213). Specific guidelines direct planners to allocate land to various rural zones, and to prepare development control provisions to cover vegetation clearing, water catchment management, protection of environmentally sensitive areas, and for the management of multiple occupancy developments. A special *Rural Land Evaluation Manual* prepared by the State government is used to assess environmental and social values of rural land, and sets out guidelines for zoning the land (Department of Planning, New South Wales, 1988).

Under the New South Wales planning system, there is scope to control land degradation, first by applying an appropriate land-use zone based on physiographical features, and second by using statutory land-use control provisions to prohibit activities that can degrade the land. Development consent can detail specifically the method of land use.

The use of the these powers by local government planning departments is being resisted strongly by rural land-user groups who in some cases have sought to have the planning legislation and the planning department abolished (Bond, 1986, p. 66).

In addition, in New South Wales, local councils, when considering development applications, are obliged to take into account the question of soil conservation, both in relation to rural and urban land, before any approval can be given (Environmental Planning and Assessment Act 1979, section 90(1)(m)). The difficulty with this is the definition of the word 'development', which does not normally include soil disturbance. Under these circumstances, the Regional or Local Environmental Plan should to specify clearly, for various types of land-use activity, the soil, landform, and vegetation characteristics that need to be investigated prior to a council granting a consent.

In the interests of a uniform approach to plan preparation and development control, the New South Wales Department of Planning recently issued a Sample Draft Rural Local Environmental Plan for local councils to use as a model when making a new Local Environmental Plan in rural areas.

## C. The right to farm

Western Australia recently attempted to counteract any interference of land planning law with agricultural activities by introducing specific legislation to give a right to farm. In Western Australia, a proposed Right to Farm Act, was put forward in 1989 as a counter-measure to public intervention in agriculture. It sought to establish the principle that a farmer who follows generally accepted practices and who acts within the land-use regulations of the relevant local government area cannot be stopped from carrying on farming operations on the grounds of causing nuisance. The legislation sought to extend the protection of the right to farm even where there is a change in land-use regulations, where the farm is sold to another farmer, or most importantly, where there is a change in the classification of land adjacent to the farm. The Bill placed the onus of proof on the complainant to establish that the farm was being operated outside generally accepted practices (Western Australian *Hansard*, 20 September 1989). This Bill has not yet proceeded, largely for political reasons.

## D. Application of government policy

Under the Australian system of government, responsibility for agrarian land policy is shared between the State and Territory governments and the

Federal government (see Crawford, 1991). All six State governments have ministers responsible for agriculture, primary industry, Crown (government-owned) land, conservation, and environmental protection, supported by an array of departments and agencies. Each jurisdiction has different administrative arrangements, a consequence of political and historical factors (see Fowler, 1984). Government land policy has been an important determinant of the level and nature of rural development. An important aspect of land policy is the leasing of Crown land to individuals, for farming, government ownership and use, for forestry, and for direct investments, as in land-development schemes and water-resource projects (Sinden and Kingma, 1972, p. 273). Land-use planning and management in the past has not generally ensured that the economic benefit derived from the use of land has been consistent with the maintenance of environmental quality. This has occurred for a range of reasons including insufficient understanding of the Australian environment, ecology and the characteristics of land, the lack of a national land-use policy, and fragmented administration. There has also been inadequate public knowledge of Australian environmental limitations, which has contributed to inappropriate community attitudes (see e.g. *Land Use in Australia*, Australia, 1975).

At the national level, rural land-use policy has traditionally been associated with primary industry. Various Standing Committees and Advisory Councils have been used to co-ordinate State policy-making. In 1990 there were 1594 bodies listed as associated with agriculture, covering Commonwealth Government organizations, State government organizations, general agricultural groups, agricultural education groups, animal industry groups, field crop groups, and horticultural crop groups. There were a further 168 government bodies with natural resource management responsibilities (*Rural Industry Directory*, Australia, 1990b). On any reckoning, such a proliferation of bodies is unlikely to produce nationally consistent and effective agricultural policies.

Although the constitutional division of powers means that the Commonwealth and the States share legal responsibility for agricultural matters, the legal position is modified by the financial arrangements between the Commonwealth and the States, especially by the Commonwealth's revenue-raising powers. There is clearly a continuing need for contact, co-operation and oversight between Commonwealth and State governments in the formulation and application of agricultural and natural resource policy. The Commonwealth is often required to provide financial incentives to the States to achieve a national policy on matters where the States are perceived to have primary constitutional responsibility. The National Soil Conservation Program is an example where the Commonwealth provides finance for the States to undertake special soil conservation projects within a standard set of guidelines for all the States. This programme complements State government activities in soil conservation. Finance is provided under the Commonwealth Soil Conservation (Financial Assistance) Act, 1985, and grants are made available for plans, demonstrations, investigation, provision of technical advice, extension, education, training and resource assessment (Australia, 1989, p. 65).

Not all policies have acted in the interest of wise rural land management. For example, many drought-assistance policies have contributed to a deterioration of the agricultural resource base. In fact, some forms of land degradation are related to drought measures taken by landholders. The Australian Soil Conservation Council convened a special working party to report on the effects of drought-assistance measures and policies on land degradation (Australia, 1988). The working party found that there are a number of relief measures that minimize land degradation, including general purpose loans, specific purpose loans, subsidies, incentives to accumulate financial reserves, incentives for soil-conservation, loans for encouraging drought fodder reserves, and taxation concessions. It also recognized that soil-conservation agencies should be given more resources to encourage or require land users to use their land within its physical capability and to adopt conservation farming techniques. Drought-related research needs were seen as a priority (Australia, 1988, pp. 27–41).

The national recognition of land-degradation problems during the period 1980–90 has instigated many policy investigations and reforms in an attempt to gain greater co-operation between the Commonwealth and the States, and greater responsibility by the States to manage the deterioration of the natural resource base. In 1984 the document *Land Use Policy in Australia* (Australia, 1984), developed over several years, recognized that a national land-use policy was essential to facilitate co-ordination of existing land-use agencies; provide a nationally consistent land-use database; undertake and disseminate research on land-use issues; and negotiate relevant national targets for various land uses. It was also suggested that the general policy statement should be supported by individual policy statements by the Commonwealth and each of the State and Territory governments appropriate to their own areas of jurisdiction.

In addition, various groups have prepared special policies and strategies to address specific problems on rural land. The Australian Soil Conservation Council, which comprises the Commonwealth, State and Northern Territory Ministers responsible for soil-conservation matters, prepared a National Soil Conservation Strategy as a statement of the way in which land degradation will be tackled in Australia (Australia, 1989b). It is not a Federal Government strategy but a combined strategy based on the roles of the Commonwealth, State, and Territory Governments in regard to land management. It is left up to each party to determine the way in which the strategy will be implemented within its own particular jurisdiction. Like most policies relating to rural land management in Australia, it does not stem from legislation and has no direct legislative backing.

While the National Soil Conservation Program has been the major programme at the Commonwealth level, other programmes include a National Tree Program, a National Afforestation Program, a Natural Resources Management Policy, and a Federal Water Resources Assistance Program. Many of these policies are the direct outcome of joint Commonwealth–State co-operation (see Australia, 1990c).

## E. Case study: the Murray-Darling Basin

The Murray-Darling Basin covers one-seventh the area of Australia and accounts for about one-third of the national output from rural industries (see Fig. 12.1). It is vital to Australia's balance of trade and to the welfare of almost 3 million people who depend directly on its natural resources. The Basin supports 25% of the nation's cattle and dairy farms, some 50% of its sheep, lamb and cropping land, and almost 75% of its irrigated pasture and crops. It is referred to as Australia's food bowl, without which the country might literally starve (Beale and Fray, 1990, p. 75). Major land-degradation problems occur throughout the Basin. These include rising salinity levels in soils and streams (salinity was recognized as a problem in the early 1900s), deteriorating quality of water supplies, soil erosion and acidification, decline and loss of native vegetation, loss of natural habitats, over-commitment of, and competing demands for, water supplies and cultural losses.

In 1987 it was estimated that losses to agriculture alone amounted to \$260 million a year, and costs due to river salinity were \$35 million a year (see Beale and Fray, 1990, c. 3). A Murray-Darling Basin Ministerial Council was established in 1985 pursuant to the River Murray Act, 1983 (Commonwealth) to guide planning and management for the Basin's natural resources, based on sustainable land-use practices. The Council is concerned with policy issues requiring common action by member governments, i.e. the Commonwealth, Queensland, New South Wales, Victoria, and South Australia. The Council aims to promote 'effective planning and management for the fair, efficient and sustainable use of water, land and environmental resources in the basin' (Beale and Fray, 1990, p. 84). In 1987 the Ministerial Council published a major study on the status of the Basin's environmental resources, which detailed the extent and severity of their degradation. The Environmental Resources Study (Murray-Darling Basin Ministerial Council, 1987), became the base document for a further *Natural Resources Management Strategy* (Murray-Darling Basin Ministerial Council, 1990).

The strategy sets out policies for community and government involvement, where the specific role of government is to provide policy and an

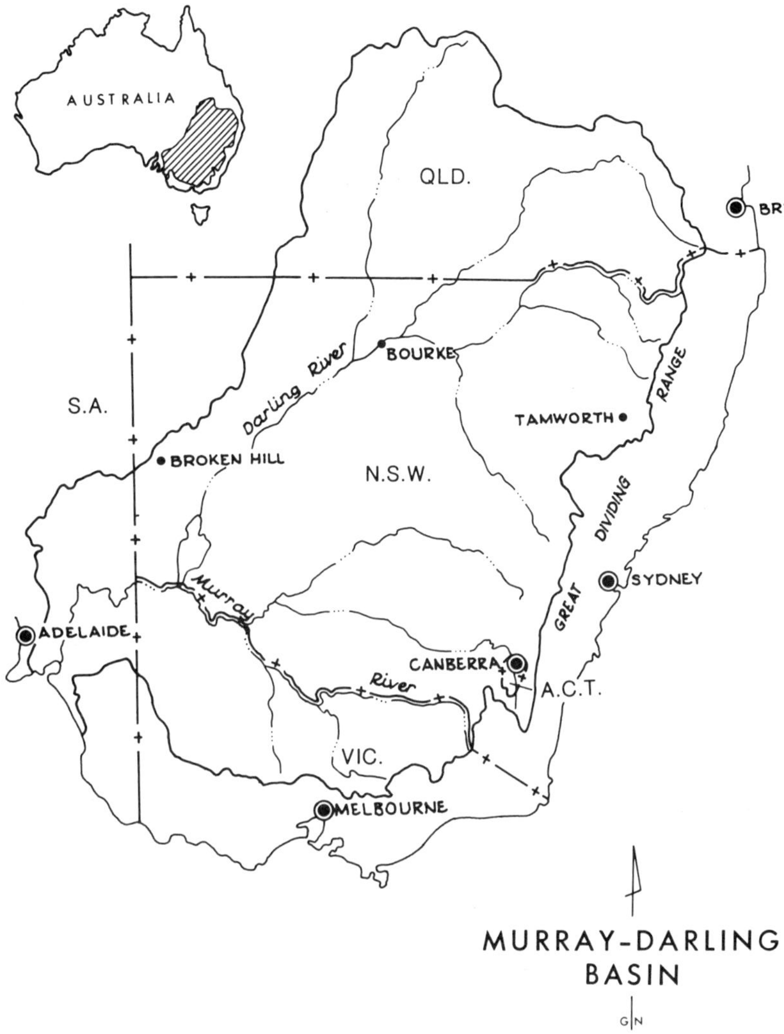


**Fig. 12.1.** The Murray-Darling Basin in Eastern Australia. (Figure reproduced with the permission of the Department of Conservation and Land Management, Sydney.)

institutional and legislative basis for land management. This includes review of existing policy, institutional arrangements, and legislation. Despite the best of intentions there is no guarantee that this process will be more effective than previous efforts:

> The administration of the Murray-Darling Basin's resources has long been a confusion of overlapping and conflicting State and Federal

> powers and responsibilities. The 1980s saw some improvement on that score. Until a streamlined, synchronized legal and political framework is established to deal with the region's overwhelming environmental problems, however, little progress will be made, and the basin's precious soil and water will continue to be squandered
>
> (Beale and Fray, 1990, p. 87)

## V. A Sustainable Land-use Policy

The past decade in Australia has seen an increase in use of sustainable land-use objectives in conservation, resource management and land-use policies, and environmental laws. However, the implementation of this concept is subject to the same restraints and limitations as other types of rural land-use policies.

The *National Conservation Strategy for Australia* (Australia, 1983) was the first major policy document to use the concept, but the strategy was largely tied to objectives for the development of major natural resources. The strategy proposed that sustainable land-use objectives be adopted by all States in the development of environmental land-use policies and laws.

Various forms of the sustainability concept are being used in the objects of environmental laws, to promote the sustainable use of natural resources (see, e.g. section 5 of New South Wales Catchment Management Act, 1989). Even a special journal has been created to promote the adoption of sustainable land-use practices on rural land (*Acres Australia*; *Journal of Sustainable Agriculture*, 1988). Since regulatory legislation that applies over rural land, such as soil-conservation legislation, was developed before the adoption of sustainable land-use policies in Australia, these laws are clearly inadequate to enforce the type of land-use practices and standards required to achieve practical sustainability. On the other hand, planning legislation contains provisions that could require sustainable land-use practices. The use of the legislation for this purpose will only come about with a change in attitude, because it is best implemented in conjunction with much wider land-management provisions (see Hannam, 1990b).

At the Federal level, a joint policy has been developed between the Government, major conservation organizations and the National Farmers' Federation, to outline the responsibilities of each party for the achievement of sustainable land-use goals specifically for rural land (Toyne and Farley, 1989). This policy is directed toward a co-operative relationship between farming and conservation interests and avoids the use of legal regulation to achieve sustainable land use.

Although the Commonwealth Government has attempted to achieve uniformity among the States by proposing that a national strategy for ecologically sustainable development objectives be adopted (Australia, 1990a), its success depends on the ability of a number of working groups to reach agreement on its implementation. The Ecologically Sustainable Development working groups, formed in 1990, cover the areas of agriculture, energy use and energy production, fisheries, forestry, manufacturing, mining, tourism, and transport (see Australia, 1991).

The principal means for the adoption of sustainable land use are the joint Commonwealth–State funded projects under the National Soil Conservation Program, the Murray-Darling Basin Natural Resources Management Strategy and Landcare Australia (Australia, 1990c). A National Association of Sustainable Agriculture was formed in 1984 to establish guidelines for standards for organic agriculture and to create a national information base on this topic.

The ability to achieve sustainable land-use practices rests primarily with a change in attitude by land users as well as the development of workable sustainable land-use policies and laws that contain a wide suite of land planning and enforcement powers. Difficulties associated with the successful adoption of sustainable land-use practices include the ability of the Federal and State governments to conduct long-term research and monitoring.

## A. Environmental Law and the Use of Agrarian Land

The current state of land degradation in Australia is testimony to the ineffectiveness of the environmental policy and law that has applied to rural land. Farrier (1988, p. 17) points out that environmental law does not necessarily guarantee the protection of the natural environment. This has been the case, in particular, with the soil-conservation legislation that currently exists in most Australian States and the Northern Territory (see Bradsen, 1987, 1988). Four soil-conservation regimes (outlined by Bradsen, 1987; i.e. leasehold supervision, optional soil-conservation legislation, the common law, and self-interest) have not been successful, even though the legislation comprises a variety of provisions to regulate the activities that create or worsen existing soil erosion (i.e. cultivation practices, over-grazing, and in some cases, tree removal). It is generally recognized that direct legislative land-use controls and more stringent soil-conservation orders will not be appropriate unless the exploitative private property rights attitude is replaced by a new ecological ethic based on care and respect for land. The development of such an ethic, let alone its implementation, is likely to be some time in being achieved (see Boer, 1984, 1989, 1990; Bradsen, 1991).

There is no single piece of legislation in any Australian State that details legal obligations over rural land. Rural land is generally zoned to permit development for most agricultural purposes without the need to obtain development consent. Plans prepared by local government may require development consent for those agricultural activities with a high pollution potential, such as piggeries, poultry farms, and cattle feedlots. These may also require an environmental impact assessment prior to development consent (see Bates, 1987; Farrier, 1988, p. 213).

State governments have retained long-term control over land by leasing and licensing activities, rather than selling off or granting freehold rights. Regulatory conditions can be placed over land use, including cultivation and grazing activities, vegetation retention and management, weed control, fencing, water supply, vermin control, and fire control (Western Lands Act 1901 (New South Wales); Crown Lands Consolidation Act 1913 (New South Wales); Lands Act 1958 (Victoria) 1962; Queensland 1933 (Western Australia); and Crown Lands Act 1929 (South Australia); (Fisher, 1987; Farrier, 1988, c. 11).

Specific regulations apply in some States for tree-clearing control (New South Wales, Soil Conservation Act 1938; South Australian Native Vegetation Management Act 1985; Victoria Flora and Fauna Guarantee Act 1988) and other forms of weeds and plants (New South Wales Noxious Insects Act 1934; New South Wales Pastures Protection Act 1934). These forms of legislation, which have applied to Crown land and freehold title land, have had limited effect in controlling land degradation because they have either covered limited areas or have been managed with insufficient human resources.

Also of interest in New South Wales are provisions for the assessment of the capability of land in terms of use for a variety of purposes. These include grazing, agriculture, commerce, community or public purposes, forestry industry, mining, nature conservation, recreation, residential purposes, environmental protection and tourism (Crown Lands Act 1989, Part 3: Land Assessment).

### B. Land courts and tribunals

Each Australian State and Territory has some form of tribunal or court to deal with land-use matters. The jurisdiction and power of these bodies vary considerably, with some being directed only to the regulation of private use of land, while others cover both the public and the private sector. One of the better known bodies is the Land and Environment Court in New South Wales, which has broad jurisdiction dealing with all aspects of environmental protection and planning, including the enforcement of environmental impact legislation, pollution control, heritage, and Aboriginal land-rights matters. It employs specialist judges and assessors who, for most matters relating to the planning and use of land, have final decision-making power.

The Federal government, having little direct legislation relating to environmental planning and land-use issues, has no special tribunal dealing with these matters. However, if the 1991 proposal to establish a Federal Environment Protection Authority is carried through, it may well be that the Federal government will need to set up a tribunal to deal with at least a limited range of environment protection, resource allocation and planning matters generally.

An interesting development at Federal level has been the setting up of the Resource Assessment Commission in 1989 (Resource Assessment Commission Act 1989). The Commission is a permanent inquiry body that deals with references from the Federal government relating to resource allocation and land-use matters both under its direct jurisdiction and within the States. In the formulation of its terms of reference for various inquiries, the Federal government ensures that each State and Territory government is in agreement with the subject matter and scope of the inquiry. This Commission could look into land-use matters generally within the States, and in particular, use of land for agricultural purposes.

Other Federal bodies that have dealt with agricultural lands have been the Senate Standing Committees on environmental protection as well as specific inquiries established under special legislation at Federal level.

## C. The evaluation of existing strategies

In assessing the statutes and policies governing the regulation of the agricultural use of land in Australia, the only general conclusion that might be drawn is that the various statutory planning systems have generally failed to control the continuing degradation of Australia's farming lands. The inconsistencies between the various jurisdictions, the lack of co-operation between States and relevant agencies within States, the relative weakness of protective regimes in the hierarchy of legislative enactments, and the lack of tight enforcement regimes contribute to this failure. However, the reasons for the failure do not lie with the inadequacy of the legislative and policy mechanisms alone, but with their lack of appropriate implementation. This comes down to a question of Federal and State politics in some cases, as well as the attitudinal differences among land-users and land-managers.

Fortunately, there is now a good deal occurring to ensure that these problems are addressed. The Decade of Landcare announced by the Federal Government has increased awareness and indicated the need to act decisively at State level (see e.g. *Decade of Landcare, Draft Plan for New South Wales*, 1991) with innovative suggestions being made by a variety of analysts (see e.g. Gardner, 1990; Bradsen, 1991). Further, in New South Wales the introduction of the Catchment Management Act 1989, is an effort to achieve co-operation between the natural resource management departments in the State in policy development and land-use decision-making, particularly in relation to large rural catchments. The Act also makes provision for the formation of trusts to manage urban catchment water quality problems. The implementation of this Act is co-ordinated by a multidisciplinary committee.

## Conclusion

This chapter has concentrated on the environmental problems relating to the use of land for agricultural purposes in Australia. The coming of the Europeans in 1788 meant not only the destruction of much of Australia's Aboriginal culture but also the continuing degradation of its natural ecosystems and in particular its soil. The chapter has indicated that Federal and State governments have floundered over the years in trying to cope with the issue of rural land use and have largely failed to come up with appropriate strategies. The Ecologically Sustainable Development process that the Federal government is presently undertaking may turn the tide of those agricultural practices resulting in general environmental degradation. The question, however, will be whether any ecologically sustainable development strategies will be able to do more than ameliorate the present situation. Additionally, the enormous cost involved in the rehabilitation measures required to restore the tens of thousands of hectares of land affected by land degradation may be the barrier to improving the land's productive capacity. Even if these lands can be restored to something approaching a reasonable condition, many would argue that their continued use for intensive agriculture may be quite unwise. There is even a case for suggesting that considerable areas of land used for commercial agriculture should be removed from any sort of agriculture and allowed to revert to a natural state. The Australian community can no longer tolerate the fact that a kilogram or more of soil may be lost for every bottle of Australian wine consumed and that each loaf of bread produced costs some 7 kg of top soil (Beale and Fray, 1990, p. x).

The Australian Decade of Landcare ending in the year 2000 is consistent with the warning given by the Worldwatch Institute in 1989 that we have little more than 10 years to address the world's environmental problems (Worldwatch Institute, 1989, p. 194). As Gordon and Suzuki say in their book *It's a Matter of Survival*:

> More than any other time in history, the 1990s will be a turning point for human civilization. Not only are we facing ecological disasters that could affect our ability to survive, but the crisis is forcing us to

re-examine the value system that has governed our lives for at least the past 2000 years.

(Gordon and Suzuki, 1990, p. 1)

While this statement applies to all countries, it is particularly apposite in this old and fragile continent, where the impact of intensive agricultural land-use practices seems to have taken a heavier environmental toll than in most other 'western' countries.

## References


Acres Australia (1988) *Journal of Sustainable Agriculture.*

Australia (1975) Department of Environment and Conservation, *Land Use in Australia,* Australian Advisory Committee on the Environment, Report No. 4. Australian Government Publishing Service, Canberra.

Australia (1983) *National Conservation Strategy for Australia.* Australian Government Publishing Service, Canberra.

Australia (1984) The Parliament of the Commonwealth of Australia, *Land Use Policy in Australia,* Senate Standing Committee on Science, Technology and the Environment. Australian Government Publishing Service, Canberra.

Australia (1988) Department of Primary Industries and Energy and Australian Soil Conservation Council, *Report of the Working Party on the Effects of Drought Assistance Measures and Policies on Land Degradation.* Australian Government Publishing Service, Canberra.

Australia (1989a) *National Soil Conservation Strategy.* Australian Soil Conservation Council, Canberra.

Australia (1989b) Parliament of the Commonwealth of Australia, *The Effectiveness of Land Degradation Policies and Programs,* Report of the House of Representatives Standing Committee on Environment, Recreation and the Arts. Australian Government Publishing Service, Canberra.

Australia (1990a) *Ecologically Sustainable Development,* A Commonwealth Discussion Paper. Australian Government Publishing Service, Canberra.

Australia (1990b) Department of Primary Industries and Energy, *Rural Industry Directory.* Australian Government Publishing Service, Canberra.

Australia (1990c) *Landcare Information: Land, Water and Vegetation Programs 1990–1991.* Australian Government Publishing Service, Canberra.

Australia (1991) *Ecologically Sustainable Development Working Groups.* Reports on Agriculture, Energy Use and Energy Production, Fisheries, Forestry, Manufacturing, Mining, Tourism, Transport. Australian Government Publishing Service, Canberra.

Aveyard, J.M. and Charman, P.E.V. (1991) Soil degradation and productivity – A concluding perspective. In: Charman, P.E.V. and Murphy, B.W. (eds), *Soils, Their Properties and Management, A Soil Conservation Handbook for New South Wales.* Sydney University Press.

Bates, G.M. (1987) *Environmental Law in Australia.* Butterworths, Sydney.

Beale, B. and Fray, P. (1990) *The Vanishing Continent.* Hodder and Stoughton, Sydney.

Boer, B.W. (1984) Social ecology and environmental law. *Environmental and Planning Law Journal* 1, 233.

Boer, B.W. (1989) Natural resources and the national estate. *Environmental and Planning Law Journal* 6, 134.

Boer, B.W. (1990) Some legal and ethical issues. In Boer, B.W. and James, D.E. (eds), *Property Rights and Environmental Protection.* Environmental Institute of Australia.

Boer, B.W. (1992) Implementing sustainability. *Delphi Law review* (forthcoming).

Bond, G. (1986) The farmers' view of New South Wales rural planning policy. *Review of Marketing and Agricultural Economics* 54:3.

Bradsen, J. (1987) Land degradation: Current and proposed legal controls. *Environmental and Planning Law Journal* 4, 113–33.

Bradsen, J. (1988) *Soil Conservation Legislation in Australia,* Report for the National Soil Conservation Programme. University of Adelaide, p. 263.

Bradsen, J. (1991) Perspectives on land conservation. *Environmental and Planning Law Journal* 8, 16.

Broome, R. (1982) *Aboriginal Australians: Black Response to White Dominance 1788–1980.* Allen and Unwin, Sydney.

Charman, P.E.V. (1983) *Australian Soils in Crisis.* Soil Conservation Service of New South Wales.

Crawford, J. (1991) The environment and the constitution. *Sydney Law Review* 13, 11.

Farrier, D. (1988) *Environmental Law Handbook, Planning and Land Use in New South Wales.* Redfern Legal Centre Publishing, Sydney.

Farrier, D. (1990) Regulation of rural land use: coercion or consensus? *Current Issues in Criminal Justice* 2, 95.

Farrier, D. (1991) Vegetation conservation: the planning system as a vehicle for the regulation of broadacre agricultural clearing. *Melbourne University Law Review* 18, 26.

Firth, D., Wells, K., Wood, N. and Walker, P. (1984) *Priorities for Tree Establishment: Areas of High Tree Loss, Salinity and Soil Erosion.* Environment Division, Department of Home Affairs and Environment, Canberra.

Fisher, D.E. (1980) *Environmental Law in Australia: An Introduction.* University of Queensland Press, St. Lucia, Queensland.

Fisher, D.E. (1987) *Natural Resources Law in Australia: A Macro-Legal System in Operation.* The Law Book Company.

Fogg, A.S. (1982) *Australian Town Planning Law: Uniformity and Change* (rev. edn). University of Queensland Press, St. Lucia, Queensland.

Fowler, R.J. (1984) Environmental law and administration in Australia. *Environmental and Planning Law Journal* 1, 1.

Fowler, R.J. (1986) Vegetation clearance controls in South Australia – a change of course. *Environmental and Planning Law Journal* 3, 48.

Gardner, A. (1989) A consensus system of planning and management for land conservation: a grassroots solution to a national problem. *Environmental and Planning Law Journal* 6, 249.

Gordon, A. and Suzuki, D. (1990) *It's a Matter of Survival.* Allen and Unwin, Sydney.

Hamblin, A. (1991) *Sustainability: Physical and biological considerations for Australian environments.* Working paper No WP 19/89 (rev edn). Bureau of Rural Resources, Department of Primary Industries and Energy, Canberra.

Hannam, I.D. (1990a) Laws for trees: Regulation or co-operation? *Australian and New Zealand Association for the Advancement of Science* Vol. 22, No. 2. Blackwell Scientific Publications, Melbourne.

Hannam, I.D. (1990b) Pursuing sustainable development: soil conservation in New South Wales. *Australian Journal of Soil and Water Conservation* 3: 2, 13.

Hawke, R.J.L. (1989) *Our Country, Our Future.* Australian Government Publishing Service, Canberra.

Murray-Darling Basin Ministerial Council (1987) *Murray-Darling Basin Environmental Resources Study.* New South Wales State Pollution Control Commission, Sydney.

Murray-Darling Basin Ministerial Council (1990) *Natural Resources Management Strategy: Towards a Sustainable Future.*

New South Wales (1988) *Department of Planning Rural Land Evaluation: A Manual for Conducting a Rural Land Evaluation Exercise at the Local Planning Level* (rev. edn).

Prately, R.E. and Rowell, D.L. (1987) From the first fleet – evolution of Australian farming systems. In: Cornish, P.S. and Prately, J.E. (eds), *Tillage: New Directions in Agriculture.* Inkata Press, Sydney.

Sinden, J.A. and Kingma, O.T. (1972) Land policy, land use and rural development. In: Sinden, J.A. (ed.), *The Natural Resources of Australia; Prospects and Problems for Development.* Angus and Robertson (in association with the Australian and New Zealand Association for the Advancement of Science).

Soil Conservation Service, New South Wales, (1991) 'Decade of Landcare, draft plan for New South Wales'.

Toyne, P. and Farley, R. (1989) A national land management program. *Australian Journal of Soil and Water Conservation* 2: 2.

World Commission on Environment and Development (1987) *Our Common Future.* Oxford.

Worldwatch Institute (1989) *State of the World.* Washington DC.

# 13

# The Agrarian Land Law of New Zealand

Michele Slatter and David Round

## I. The Importance of Agriculture

New Zealand comprises 26.90 million ha of land, in three principal islands. Since European settlement it has been a primarily agricultural nation. Today, 53.5% of its land is used for arable or pastoral purposes, and agricultural products account for 54% of the country's overseas exports. At the time of writing, the country is accommodating significant policy shifts implemented by successive governments since 1984, each designed to deregulate the economy and to encourage a market driven efficiency. Two particular aspects of these policies have impacted directly on agriculture.

First, economic deregulation has resulted in the lifting of tariff barriers, the removal of import licensing, the abolition of agricultural subsidies, the introduction of charges for advisory and information services and the conclusion of a trans-Tasman Closer Economic Relationship with Australia. All these developments have affected agriculturalists.

Secondly, the restructuring of the state sector, heralded by the State Owned Enterprises Act 1986, makes a clear distinction between the public service and trading functions of government. The latter are now carried out through state-owned enterprises, corporatized departments whose primary objective is 'to operate as a successful business' (State Owned Enterprises Act 1986, section 4(1)). One SOE, the Land Corporation of New Zealand Limited (Landcorp), has a significant role as landowner and land-agent of agricultural and pastoral land held by tenants and former tenants of the Crown.

New Zealand is a constitutional monarchy, ruled by Elizabeth II, and in her absence by a Governor-General. There is no written constitution, and parliament has unlimited powers of legislation. Cabinet Ministers are chosen from the single house of parliament, and, in practice, government is largely by the Cabinet. Elections are by the first-past-the-post system, and both of the main political parties have evinced great reluctance to introduce any system of proportional representation. Since 1876, when the provinces were abolished, central control has been a striking feature of New Zealand government. However, Regional Councils now have many functions concerning transport, planning and environmental regulation, and District and City Councils are the units of local administration.

This chapter describes the agrarian land law of New Zealand and indicates actual and expected changes consequent on the far-reaching reforms mentioned above.

## II. The Historical Context

### A. Land tenures

European settlement of New Zealand began in a small way in the late 18th century, by which time the whole of the country had been long settled by Maori. By the 1830s an appreciable number of settlers were established around the coasts and more were eager to set out from Britain. In February 1840 the Treaty of Waitangi was signed between the British Crown and numerous Maori chiefs. Article 2 of the Treaty secured for the Crown a right of pre-emption over all land: Maori owners were entitled to keep their land and their rights were to be respected. If they wished to sell, however, they were to sell to the Crown, not to the settlers. The declaration of British Sovereignty over New Zealand in May 1840 was thought to bring all title to the Crown, by virtue of sovereignty, subject to the Maori title of possession and occupancy of their lands (Hinde *et al.*, 1986). The Crown subsequently acquired much land by purchase, although in many cases the consideration paid was negligible. In later decades, as pressure from settlers for more land increased, lands were confiscated from their Maori owners by the Crown in the wake of the Land Wars of the 1860s and were then available for regrant (Sorrenson, 1989).

The legacy of this history is that today there are three distinct land-holding regimes in New Zealand. Land may be:

**1.** freehold, sometimes called 'general' land, having been granted by the Crown to a private owner at some date since 1840. This accounts for the vast majority of the land;
**2.** Crown land, retained by the Crown, or held subject to one of the tenures described in the Land Act 1948;
**3.** Maori land, held under Maori traditional title or held by Maori owners under freehold title and recognized as Maori land by the Maori Land Court, as defined by the Maori Affairs Act 1953.

### B. Land settlement policies

It has been said that 20th-century land settlement policy in New Zealand has been dominated by the promotion of closer settlement (Fairweather, 1985). 'Closer settlement' is used here to describe land policies designed to increase the number of farmers, whether by subdividing and intensifying use of existing farm land or by increasing through development the acreage of land available for occupation. The principal purposes of closer settlement in New Zealand have always been to improve export production and to provide farming opportunities for 'landless' farmers.

In the early years of European settlement the Crown alienated much high-quality land to immigrants, either as freehold or Crown leasehold. However, this resulted not in the settlement of the country in owner-operated farms but in the establishment of large-scale estates employing agricultural labourers. In the 1890s legislation was introduced to reverse this pattern and to actively promote the policy of closer settlement. Statutes facilitated land purchase, including compulsory purchase, by the Crown for subdivision and alienation, on freehold or Crown leasehold tenures. Provision was later made to enable most Crown tenants to obtain a simple interest loan for purchase of their holdings if they desired. Specific concern for the undue aggregation of farmland was expressed in the Land Laws Amendment Act 1912, which provided for the compulsory purchase of aggregated farmland if the aggregation was found to be 'contrary to the public interest'. The statutes included an upper limit on any individual grantee's holding from the Crown.

These measures vigorously promoted closer settlement of the land for agriculture. Current legislation ostensibly continues the same policy. In New Zealand agriculture today, the ideas of family farming, one-man one-farm, and striving to improve productivity are important and intimately related policies. However, as discussed below, the Land Act 1948 and the Land Settlement Promotion and Acquisition Act 1952 are designed to emphasize restrictive policies rather than positive incentives to closer settlement, and their practical effectiveness is very limited.

## III. Restraints on the Ownership of Agricultural Land

### A. General land

Freehold land is subject to the provisions of the Town and Country planning legislation discussed below. Two other statutory restrictions are relevant to freehold land used for agriculture.

### 1. Anti-aggregation provisions

Since 1890 it has been the 'policy of the Legislature to foster the ownership of land by the greatest number of independent farmers rather then the development of larger farming projects in the hands of those with special ability and efficiency' (*Maginess to Munday* (1955) *NZLR* 764,767). This policy continues to be expressed in statute law, the primary Act being the Land Settlement Promotion and Acquisition Act 1952.

The Act purports to control the undue aggregation of farmland in the hands of individual purchasers or lessees. This is achieved by requiring any contract for the purchase or lease of more than 2 ha of farm land to be submitted for consent to the Land Valuation Tribunal, unless the prospective purchaser or lessee is in a position to lodge a sworn declaration evidencing his or her 'landless' state or the lease is for a period of less than 3 years. Where a contract is subject to the consent of the Tribunal, the Crown may object to consent on the grounds that it would result in undue aggregation of farmland. The onus is then on the contracting parties to satisfy the Tribunal that it is appropriate for consent to be given. If no objection is raised on behalf of the Crown, consent will be granted to the transaction as no one other than the Crown has the *locus standi* to object to a transaction. If consent is not obtained, the transaction is illegal and is thus unenforceable by either party. However, such contracts may sometimes be validated under section 7 of the Illegal Contracts Act 1970.

'Farmland' is defined in section 2 of the Act as land that is or should be used exclusively for the cultivation of the soil for the production of food products and other useful products of the soil, including the use of land for horticultural and pastoral purposes or for keeping pigs, bees, or poultry.

In considering any contract, the Tribunal is concerned to see whether the applicant purchasers or lessees already control an economic unit of farm land. Section 31 of the Act directs the Tribunal specifically to have regard to the applicants' standard of living, their existing land holdings, the uses they intend for the land and their ability to achieve them, and whether the acquisition would be in the public interest. In this last respect, the Tribunal is directed that it is in the public interest:

**1.** to ensure and preserve the diversification of the ownership of farm land;
**2.** that underdeveloped or depreciated farm land be acquired by persons competent and able to bring the land into production;
**3.** that the acquisition of land by any person will result in substantially increased production thereon;
**4.** that the intended use of the land will be in the interests of the community generally.

The Tribunal is also to consider whether a refusal of consent would result in unavoidable and substantial hardship to the owner of the land.

In determining whether an applicant is eligible to make a 'landless' declaration, the Act provides that farmland held by a company with fewer than ten shareholders will be treated as held by each of the shareholders; farmland held by the spouse of any person is treated as held by that person; farmland in which any person has an interest under a will or intestacy is treated as being held by him or her; farmland held by the parent of a child under 17 years of age is considered as being held by the child also.

The Land Settlement Promotion and Acquisition Act 1952, thus provides a detailed scheme to ensure the scrutiny of transfers of farmland and to prevent undue aggregation of farmland by individuals or small companies. In reality, its effect is minimal. In 1982 the operation of the Act was reviewed by a Committee of the New Zealand Law Society. Their conclusion was that the anti-aggregation provisions have 'never controlled the acquisition of farmland, because those who have doubts about their eligibility to purchase more farmland have almost invariably formed ten-man companies and bought the land anyway' (Bradley, 1984). The Act was thus said to provide:

> an expensive bureaucratic obstacle course, the avoidance of which has caused a proliferation of farming companies, which are often totally inappropriate structures to operate farms and unnecessarily increase the legal and other costs of farm purchase . . . and it can safely be assumed that applications have only been proceeded with when the outcome has been a foregone conclusion.

However, a consideration of the Act remains a necessary prerequisite for all farmland transactions. Despite its ineffectiveness, there is no evidence of any substantial movement away from family farming concerns (Fairweather, 1989).

### *2. Purchase of agricultural land by overseas interests*

Part IIA of the Land Settlement Promotion and Acquisition Act 1952, controls the acquisition of land in New Zealand by overseas corporations and by people who are not New Zealand citizens. It is primarily directed against absentee owners.

The Act applies to every contract or agreement for the sale or transfer of a freehold estate or interest or a lease for 3 years or more or an option to purchase relating to any land of 2 ha or more which is zoned for rural purposes, or is so zoned that farming of any kind is a predominant or conditional use in that zone. Where the prospective purchaser or lessee is not a New Zealand citizen or is an overseas body corporate, then the consent of the Land Valuation Tribunal must be obtained for the transaction before the dealing may be registered as a completed transaction. Any contract for a transfer to which Part IIA relates will be illegal unless it is entered into subject to the consent of the Tribunal and an application for such consent is made within 1 month from the date of the contract.

Where a transaction requires consent, section 35H indicates the criteria. The Tribunal 'shall grant its consent' when it is satisfied that the applicant is a person who is ordinarily resident in New Zealand. If the Tribunal is considering an application on behalf of a non-resident or on behalf of an overseas corporation, then section 35H(3)(c) provides that the Tribunal must be satisfied that the purchaser intends:

**1.** to conduct experimental or research work on the land that will be of benefit to the development of agricultural industries in New Zealand and be in the interests of the community generally; or
**2.** to use the land for other than agricultural purposes with greater advantage to the community generally; or
**3.** in the case of individuals, to reside permanently in New Zealand and farm the land exclusively for their own use and benefit.

and that the purchaser or lessee has the ability and the means to achieve those purposes.

Two exceptions to these provisions may be noted. First, given the traditionally high proportion of British immigrants into New Zealand, it is relevant to note that the consent of the Tribunal will not be necessary if the purchaser is a British subject who has resided in New Zealand for not less than 2½ years during the 3 years immediately preceding the transaction and who intends to continue to reside permanently in New Zealand. A statutory declaration to this effect will remove the transaction formally from the Tribunal's jurisdiction. Secondly, section 35C(d) provides that transactions to which the Minister of Lands has consented, with the concurrence of the Minister of Finance, do not require Tribunal consent. However, if a Tribunal has already refused consent on the merits of an application, this decision cannot be overturned by the Ministers. There are no criteria in the Act to govern the exercise of Ministerial discretion in these matters, nor is there any formal procedure indicated for applicants to follow. In practice the Minister usually applies criteria similar to those used by the Tribunal, although he or she retains a broad residual discretion.

A further mechanism for supervising and controlling overseas investment in New Zealand is the operation of the Overseas Investment Commission, established under section 3 of the Overseas Investment Act 1973. The Commission's functions are essentially to consider applications for investment in New Zealand made by non-resident individuals or non-New Zealand companies and to keep under review the level and extent of overseas investment in the country, including, for example, investment in agricultural concerns.

Recently, the Minister of Lands has suggested that the various avenues for consent should be unified.

### B. Crown land

'Crown land' is a term used for the land retained by the Crown without permanent alienation. Under the Land Act 1948, Crown land may be classified as urban, commercial, farm, or pastoral land. With the restructuring of the public service in 1986–7 a clear distinction was drawn between Crown land with productive value and Crown land retained essentially for its conservation interest or its public utility. In general, productive lands were transferred to Landcorp. Included in this transfer were farm lands held on 33-year perpetually renewable leases with a right to acquire the 'fee simple' granted under section 52 of the Land Act. Landcorp has a primary duty to operate as a successful business (State Owned Enterprises Act 1986, section 4(1)). Therefore these erstwhile Crown lands are now subjected to a fully commercial management regime, including increased rents. Crown lands retained because of their conservation or public importance have mostly been committed to the Department of Conservation.

One anomalous category of Crown land has fallen outside this neat division. Lands held on pastoral leases or pastoral occupation licences under the Land Act 1948, have been retained by the Crown under the supervision of the Office of Crown Lands. They are managed on a day-to-day basis under contract by Landcorp Management Services who act as the Crown's land agents. Although the Crown receives a rent for these lands, the return is outweighed by the cost of administration. The Crown pastoral lease lands are mainly located in the High Country of the South Island. They are areas of fragile ecology in which there is a relatively restricted pastoral use potential, a significant conservation importance, and an increasing public interest in access for recreational uses such as tramping, hunting, and skiing. Pastoral leases, although perpetually renewable, do not include any right to the soil nor any right to acquire the fee simple. Like all agricultural leases granted by the Crown, they include covenants of good husbandry, residence and pest control, and may be forfeited for breach of covenant. They are also subject to restrictions against burning, cultivation, and afforestation designed to conserve the land, consent of the Commissioner of Crown lands being required for any projected operations. Recreation permits are available over Crown lands for the use or occupation of the land for commercial undertakings including 'any recreational, tourist, accommodations, safari or other purposes'. These have most frequently been granted in respect of the operation of skifields. The administration of these Crown lands was governed by policies developed before 1987 by the Land Settlement Board, with the aim of preserving a balance between the conservation and development uses of the lands. Although the Board has now been abolished, the management contract between the Crown and Landcorp relating to the pastoral lease lands requires observation of these earlier management policies and consultation with the Department of Conservation as appropriate. The role of the Crown/ Landcorp in relation to these lands is seen variously as guarantor of the public interest, preserver of the ecological balance and helpful co-developer. Although the occupiers enjoy only the 'exclusive right of pasturage' in perpetuity, it has been accepted that they control access through 'their' lands and thus may regulate the ingress of trampers, hunters, fishermen, and any other third parties.

Crown land and land transferred to Landcorp is subject to the provisions of the Town and Country Planning legislation described below. In addition, these lands may be affected by two other developments.

### *1. Reform of the Land Act 1948*

Reform of the Land Act has been projected since 1987, in the wake of the restructuring of the public service. The most significant aspect of the proposals is the categorization (reclassification) of Crown pastoral lease lands into farm land (which could be freeholded), restricted-use land (held subject to tenures less than freehold and used subject to consent for a range of pastoral/recreational/conservation purposes) and conservation land. Under the new regime it is proposed that the various possible uses of the lands be more overtly recognized and public participation be integral to decisions as to classification and use decisions. At the time of writing no timetable for reform has been published, nor have the terms of new legislation been finalized (Robertson, 1989).

### *2. Maori claims in the Waitangi Tribunal*

In recent years steps have been taken in New Zealand to begin to address claims by the Maori people that since 1840 the Crown has ignored its obligations towards them as expressed in the Treaty of Waitangi. In 1975 the Treaty of Waitangi Act established the Waitangi Tribunal. The function of the Tribunal is to investigate Maori grievances. Claims may now be brought before the Tribunal by any Maori or group of Maoris where the fundamental allegation is that they have been, or will be, prejudicially affected by an act, omission, policy, or practice of the Crown, dating from any time since 1840, which was contrary to the Treaty of Waitangi. The jurisdiction is thus potentially very wide. In the present context, its importance is that the Tribunal can be called upon to investigate claims relating to land: for example, that original land purchases by the Crown were improperly conducted or that confiscations of land were in conflict with the Treaty. Land has an inestimable cultural importance to the Maori people and the wrongful taking of land since 1840 has been a source of deep grievance to them (Temm, 1990).

The Tribunal usually acts as a fact-finding body only. However, it has power under the 1975 Act to make recommendations to the Crown regarding compensation or any constructive response. Recommendations may be in general or specific terms. In appropriate cases, they may include a recommendation that Crown land be transferred back to its Maori owners. The position of land granted to State-owned enterprises is governed by the Treaty of Waitangi (State Owned Enterprises) Act 1988, and the State Owned Enterprises Act 1986. The Tribunal, exceptionally, may make an imperative recommendation that SOE land be returned to Maori ownership. If land is returned in this way from a SOE, the Crown is liable to compensate the SOE for such loss. With this one exception, land in private hands is not treated as vulnerable to such recommendation from the Tribunal; only Crown land is seen as available for transfer. There is no obligation on the Crown to adopt the Tribunal's recommendations apart from those relating to the return of SOE land.

Land retained by the Crown and land transferred to Landcorp may therefore be the subject-matter of an application to the Tribunal. Ultimately it may also be the subject-matter of a Tribunal recommendation. It was planned to transfer to Landcorp approximately 2655000 ha of Crown farmland held under leases and licences. The Crown has, to date, retained an additional 2.5 million ha of pastoral leaselands, administered on its behalf by Landcorp. In 1986 a major series of claims concerning the South Island was lodged before the Waitangi Tribunal on behalf of the Ngai Tahu Maori, including a number of grievances affecting Crown pastoral lease lands (O'Regan, 1989).

The Tribunal's Report on the Ngai Tahu claim sustained many of these grievances but, as requested both by Ngai Tahu and the Crown, it 'deferred the important question of recommending the principal remedial measures until the parties have had an opportunity to study the determinations of the Tribunal'. The Tribunal expressed the hope that the parties, in the light of the findings, 'will negotiate and conclude a final settlement' (Waitangi, 1991), but it indicated quite strongly that a transfer of the pastoral lease reversions to Ngai Tahu would be an appropriate response by the Crown. Concern has been expressed by pastoral lessees and licensees as to their own position within this changing scenario. At the time of writing there is no indication as to how these claims will ultimately be resolved.

### C. Maori land

Only a tiny proportion of the land of New Zealand is now held as 'Maori land', technically understood. This land is subject to the provisions of the Maori Affairs Act 1953, and transfers or alienations are subject to scrutiny or record by the Maori Land Court. Although anti-aggregation provisions may apply to transfers of land used for agriculture, the impact of these provisions, as with 'general' land and Crown land, is minimal. Where Maori land is used for agricultural purposes, it is generally held by an incorporation or a trust. Otherwise, no special characteristics of tenure apply.

## IV. Access to Land

There is no general right of public access onto rural land in New Zealand. Usually access is controlled by the owner or occupier and may be prevented by reasonable force or an action for trespass.

Statutory rights of entry to inspect and do work are enjoyed by officials under the Agricultural Pests Destruction Act 1967, Wild Animal Control Act 1977, and The Noxious Plants Act 1978. Currently, rabbits, possums, and hawkweed are so widespread locally that they are not realistically controllable by individual farmers.

In addition, there is much pressure from recreational groups for access to rural land. Roads, both developed and 'paper' only, are public rights of way, as are the few walkways established under the New Zealand Walkways Act 1990, the national parks, and areas of public access established under the Queen Elizabeth the Second National Trust Act 1977. Otherwise, the admission of hunters, trampers, game shooters, mountaineers, skiers, and recreational users lies with the occupier of the land – a situation that can lead to friction when, for example, the farmer anticipates disturbance of stock or crops by entrants.

## V. Environmental Regulation

The Maori, a Polynesian people, gradually colonized New Zealand from about the 9th century. After some centuries of forest destruction and extinctions they gradually developed delicate and sophisticated laws regulating the use of the natural world they depended on. Particular areas were reserved from hunting or gathering at particular times, or only creatures of a certain size or age might be gathered. Maori agriculture, although significant in northern areas, where the kumara could grow, was never nearly adequate to support the population, and hunting, fishing, and food-gathering were vital parts of daily life.

None of these laws of wise resource husbandry was adopted by British settlers. As Peter Hooper observed in *Our Forests Ourselves* (1981):

> The nineteenth century was [perhaps] the worst in which to send Europeans into new lands. A working class that had ... been uprooted from the land to become machine slaves, a ruling class that used its power largely to aggregate private wealth, were ill partners to treat a new environment with respect.

New Zealanders are now, however, very conscious of environmental issues, and the country has, per capita, the world's highest citizen membership of environmental organizations.

Europeans brought their agriculture with them, and the 'untamed' country could not be used until cleared, drained, and made suitable for sheep and cattle. The history of European settlement is that of pioneers battling against Nature to carve out the farms that have brought the country its prosperity. Native forests, although valuable timber resources, were also impediments to civilization. In the words of New Zealand Prime Minister, Sir Julius Vogel, 'a swagger would burn down a forest to light his pipe.' The gradual realization that the pioneering era is over, and that we require a new ethic of wise sustainable husbandry, is being reflected in our laws about natural resources.

The pioneers possessed little statute law about what we might categorize as 'resource management'. The existing law was part of the common law and part of the law of private property. Early statutes aimed to aid the 'development' and exploitation of natural resources. The Mining Act, 1971, for example, a consolidation of older statutes, still has the facilitating of mining as its chief purpose, granting it preference even over other land uses such as agriculture. Some later statutes protected specific aspects of the environment (such as national parks and native plants). Yet later laws gradually brought environmental considerations into legislation – as matters to be considered in particular cases or as part of a wider policy or plan. The Environment Act 1986 (which finally gave a statutory basis to the Ministry for the Environment and created a Commissioner for the Environment responsible to Parliament) and the Conservation Act 1987 (which removed the Crown's remaining wild lands – forest, wetland, native grassland, and mountain – from departments with conflicting functions of preservation and development – departments 'schizophrenic by statute' – and gave them to a department dedicated unequivocally to their protection) mark the end of the pioneering stage of New Zealand's history. The Resource Management Bill, if it becomes law in its present form, will set all resource laws on a consistent and ecologically sound footing.

Present laws concerning natural resources display all these earlier attitudes. They have been criticised not only for inconsistency and contradiction but also for the duplication that may occur when some proposed development or change in land use requires, e.g. numerous permits under different statutes, involving different hearings before different tribunals, with different procedures. The same activity might be allowed by one county council's planning scheme, but not another's. The chief statutes affecting agrarian land users are listed below. Since 1987, however, there has been an immense and thorough process of public consultation directed towards replacing all these statutes, and many others, with one comprehensive statute dealing with urban and rural planning and land use, water use and preservation, air and noise pollution – procedures for assessing environmental impacts, marine farming, mining, and many other things. All such activities would have to be consistent with environmentally sound and sustainable principles. There would be one procedure before one tribunal before a 'resource consent' would be granted or refused. The Resource Management Bill, which embodied these changes, almost became law before the 1990 general election. At the time of writing it is still before the present parliament. Despite earlier promises of its passage, it seems at least possible that the Treasury 'new right' opponents of planning, and a combination of certain vested interests, may prevent its passing. It is however briefly described below.

## VI. The Town and Country Planning Act 1977

This statute governs all land use. It imposes on every local body (city and county councils) and regional government (the fourteen regional councils) a duty to prepare district schemes and regional schemes. These must be reviewed periodically. In both formation and review there is opportunity for public comment and participation. District schemes are a species of delegated legislation binding landholders and, in certain circumstances, the Crown. District schemes designate land for residential, commercial, industrial, rural, or certain other special purposes. In each zone certain activities are permitted (predominant uses are permitted as of right, subject to compliance with the Code of Ordinances contained in the district scheme; conditional uses require public notification and are open for public objection), and others prohibited. One may obtain a 'specified departure' from a district scheme, if such a departure is not contrary to the public interest and is of little planning significance. These are open to public notification and objection. Against local bodies' decisions there lies an appeal to the Planning Tribunal and thence to the courts.

Two sections of the Act are worthy of quotation here.

**Section 3(1)** – In the preparation, implementation and administration of regional, district and maritime schemes ... the following matters which are declared to be of national importance shall in particular be recognised and provided for:

**(a)** the conservation, protection and enhancement of the physical, cultural and social environment:
**(b)** the wise use and management of New Zealand's resources:
**(c)** the preservation of the natural character of the coastal environment and the margins of lakes and rivers and the protection of them from unnecessary subdivision and development:
**(d)** the avoidance of encroachment of urban development on, and the protection of, land having a high actual or potential for the production of food:
**(e)** the prevention of sporadic subdivision and urban development in rural areas:
**(f)** the avoidance of unnecessary expansion of urban areas into rural areas in or adjoining cities:
**(g)** the relationship of the Maori people and their culture and traditions with their ancestral land.

**Section 4(1)** – Subject to section 3 ... regional, district and maritime planning ... shall have for their general purposes the wise use and management of the resources, and the direction and control of the development of a region, district or area in such a way as will most effectively promote and safeguard the health, safety, convenience and the economic, cultural, social and general welfare of the people, and the amenities, of every part of the region, district or area.

It would be difficult to disagree with these commendable sentiments. Their application, needless to say, can lead to differences of opinion; much ink has been spilt and much money spent on the question of what exactly 'wise use' may be. Many aspects of plans and schemes depend on the nature of public involvement in their formulation, and even more on the quality and sympathies of local government councillors and their advisers. Local government has often been criticized as being unrepresentative, tied to local business interests, and not always particularly competent. Especially outside large cities, those with the time and income to involve themselves in local government are often those likely to gain financially from new developments (which are therefore unlikely to be assessed adequately). There has recently been a far-reaching reform of local government boundaries, and members of regional councils are now directly elected, instead of (as was the case with the United Councils they replace) being nominated by the various local councils – which often led to unpopular or incompetent local councillors being 'kicked upstairs.'

Unless a farmer wishes to subdivide his property (as mentioned below), the Town and Country Planning Act may well have less impact on his farm's management than the Water and Soil Conservation Act 1967. A district scheme's restrictions on forestry schemes may be the most significant in their impact. These are imposed because of concerns about landscape changes, effects of vehicles on roads and bridges, possible soil erosion after logging, and, should forests be extensive, possible population loss of farming families and, consequently, the loss of schools, hospitals, public offices and service industries, and service town population; for between tree-planting and felling little labour is required.

Several aspects of section 3 deserve comment. Its matters of national importance have a 'degree of primacy' over other planning aspects, and it is not proper merely to balance them against other purely local interests. This was the Court of Appeal's opinion in *Environmental Defence Society and Tai Tokerau District Maori Council* v. *Mangonui County Council* (1989) 13 NZTPA 197. That case concerned a proposed 'destination tourist resort' on the sea-coast in a remote and unspoilt area. There was no evidence of a developer prepared to undertake the project, and the Court of Appeal therefore found it 'unnecessary' within the meaning of paragraph (c). Two dissenting judges objected that any scheme must '... engage in some forward thinking. If schemes can take account of only those developments that are shown to be certain, planning will be restricted.... Planning is about looking forward more than looking behind.'

The same case affirmed that Maori 'ancestral land' (paragraph (g)) did not mean merely land still in Maori ownership, but rather lands with which Maoris have some close spiritual or cultural connection, regardless of its tenure, e.g. sites of historic significance, or where *urupa* (graves) are, or where some plant has traditionally been gathered.

Practically all district schemes contain provisions preventing subdivision and urban development in rural areas and the loss of cities' 'green belts', mentioned in paragraphs (d), (e), and (f). Some schemes allow as of right the subdivision and sale of farm houses surplus to requirements; others do not. Concerning farmland subdivision generally, many schemes forbid cutting off an area smaller than a certain size – often 100 acres – or certainly building a dwellinghouse thereon – unless that smaller area is an 'economic unit'. This elusive concept is certainly unattainable on 100 acres by ordinary sheep or cattle farming, but possible with more intensive land-uses. Some councils impose bond conditions to ensure that promises made on subdivisions are kept. As ordinary pastoral farming becomes less profitable, and therefore requires ever larger farm areas, and as mechanization renders casual labour less necessary, populations inevitably diminish, and local councils are torn between the law (and their natural wishes) not to allow suburban intrusion and rate increases, and its necessity in order to maintain population and rural services.

## VII. The Soil Conservation and Rivers Control Act 1941

This legislation followed widespread concern over soil erosion and floods following clearance of native vegetation cover. (During the 1938 East Coast floods, for example, small streams rose by as much as 58 ft and one whose normal flow was 0.6 $m^3$ per second peaked at 950 $m^3$ per second. Whole catchments' soil and subsoil collapsed.) The problem was publicized, and jealousies between government departments that prevented a proper response were exposed.

The Act's objects are to promote soil conservation, and prevent or mitigate soil erosion and damage by flood. A national authority (recently abolished) was empowered to investigate soil erosion, carry out hydrological research, instruct and supervise landholders, assist persons whose land has been affected by erosion and floods, and co-ordinate the policies and activities of government departments, local authorities, and other public bodies. The Act established Catchment Boards (whose functions have now been assumed by the new Regional councils), which designed and implemented river, flood and erosion control, soil conservation, and drainage works. A 1959 amendment imposed a general duty on land occupiers to carry out every operation affecting the land in a manner conforming to prudent land-use practice – a practice that, so far as economically practicable, will prevent or mitigate soil erosion, deposits in water courses and floods. Catchment authorities can issue public notices that require all owners and occupiers to obtain permission before carrying out certain activities (e.g. forestry or pastoral operations). Individual owners can also be required to adopt certain safeguards (e.g. changing numbers or kinds of stock, planting or sowing trees, shrubs, or grasses, or improving land-management practices). These 1959 powers were less often used than the powers to build flood-protection works, and catchment boards were therefore sometimes accused of being farmers' clubs for spending public money to improve their own properties. Nevertheless, they did much vitally important work.

## VIII. The Water and Soil Conservation Act 1967

This statute, now administered by Regional Councils, governs the use of all 'natural water' in New Zealand – which includes all freshwater, groundwater, artesian water, sea water, water vapour, geothermal water, snow, and ice (section 2). By section 21, the sole right to dam any river or stream, or to divert or take natural water, or to discharge natural water containing waste onto land or into the ground in circumstances that result in that waste, or any other waste emanating as a result of natural processes from that waste, entering natural water, or to use natural water, is vested in the Crown. Certain exceptions exist – for lawful uses of water existing in 1966, and registered with the regional water board, and also the taking or using of 'any natural water ... reasonably required for ... domestic needs and the needs of animals for which [the taker] has any responsibility and for ... fire-fighting purposes'. The 'needs of animals' seem to extend to animals raised in feed lots or buildings, but not to wild animals; a farmer's dam to create a pond for wildlife has been held unlawful. The 'needs of animals' extend only to watering, not to irrigating pasture for them to feed on. These exceptions apart, any use of natural water requires a 'water right', which is granted (or refused) by a Regional Council, which can impose conditions on its use. Such rights are for limited periods of time, and there is no automatic right of renewal. A farmer who is granted a water right has a right to that water use; not a licence revocable at will, or one whose terms may be modified at the grantor's discretion. (An authority does exist, however, to set 'minimum flow levels' in watercourses; these override any rights of water extraction for, say, irrigation.)

Rather surprisingly, the Act gives no list of matters to be considered before a water right is granted or refused. This has led to much judicial policy-making. Treadwell complained in *Annan* v. *NWASCA* (No.1) (1981) 7 NZTPA 417 of being:

> faced with trying to extract law from a statute that is lamentably lacking in any special direction ... It would be safe to say that never in the history of legislation in New Zealand has the long title to an Act been used so frequently in an attempt to find guidelines.

The usual test is to balance the various matters listed in the long title, which describes itself as:

> an Act to promote a national policy in respect of natural water, and to make better provision for the conservation, allocation, use and quality of natural water, and for promoting soil conservation and preventing damage by flood and erosion, and for promoting and controlling multiple uses of natural water and the drainage of land and for ensuring that adequate account is taken of the needs of primary and secondary industry, community water supplies, all forms of water-based recreation, fisheries and wildlife habitats, and of the preservation and protection of the wild, scenic and other natural characteristics of rivers, streams and lakes.

This balancing of interests, of benefit and detriment, obviously implies that no priority is accorded to any one of these interests. The balancing of these different considerations – electricity against lost farmland, or against wildlife habitat – is, if not impossible, at least a delicate art.

The Court of Appeal affirmed the test in *Auckland Acclimatisation Society* v. *Sutton Holdings Ltd* (1985) 2 NZLR 94, where a farmer applied for a right to drain part of an important wetland, valuable habitat for many rare fish and birds, which was part of his farm. The test was held to involve a contest between the economic benefit obtainable from additional grazing and the desirability of the wetland's preservation. Although farmers and landowners had the right to use their land *in its natural state*, they were held to have no *right to* a water right. This was a privilege to which a landowner was not entitled; there was no legitimate expectation of one. The onus of proof, accordingly, is on the applicant for a water right, not his opponents. The swamp's drainage was consistent with the Town & Country Planning Act; under the local district scheme the land was zoned for rural purposes, but this was held immaterial. One Act controlled water use, the other land-use. Neither Act had pre-eminence; compliance with one did not dictate a certain action under the other.

Regional Councils are now preparing Water Resource Management Plans, setting out the major water issues of each region and their policies on them. Considerable public participation is possible in their formulation. At present they have no statutory authority, and to that extent cannot be appealed against to the Planning Tribunal. Presumably they will be a relevant consideration in deciding water-right applications in future.

The Act originally provided for the nationwide classification of waters. The classification system is not sophisticated or flexible, and in any case has been virtually a dead letter since *Water Resources Council* v. *Southland Skindivers Club Inc* (1976) 1 NZLR 1 declared invalid the use of hold-all residual classifications. The Resource Management Bill contains a more sophisticated classification system, and would also allow Regional Councils to establish special standards and classes of their own.

The Act nowhere mentions Maori considerations. Yet in the daring and possibly far-reaching case of *Huakina Development Trust* v. *Waikato Valley Authority* (1987) 12 NZTPA 129, where a farmer sought a right to discharge treated cowshed waste into a tributary of the Waikato River (a discharge that met the river's classification standards), the Act's public rights of objection were held wide enough to encompass Maori spiritual, cultural, and traditional relationships with bodies of natural water.

A 1981 amendment established procedures for granting local water-conservation notices or national water-conservation orders over lakes, rivers, or streams (but not wetlands). Apart from the minimum flow levels (often insufficient, for they regulate only flow) these are the only mechanisms for ensuring permanent protection of a water body. They need not forbid all human uses of the water concerned, but they do allow extensive conditions to be set. The amending Act's object is 'to recognise and sustain the amenity afforded by waters in their natural state'. Section 20B requires that, in making the order, consideration had to be given to, *inter alia*, 'the needs of primary and secondary industry and of the community,' but in *Ashburton Acclimatisation Society* v. *Federated Farmers of N.Z.* (1987) 12 NZTPA 289 it was held that the object of the Act, although not necessarily overwhelming, had primacy; there was, in the amendment, not the usual balancing test, but a strong presumption in favour of conservation. The interest of farmers in water extraction for irrigation was therefore less important.

## IX. Further and Future Considerations

Numerous other statutes, needless to say, form part of the subject of agrarian land. The Historic Places Act 1980, deals not only with buildings but also with archaeological sites, which may not be damaged or altered without the Historic Places Trust's authority. The Mining Act 1971 may, depending on when land was alienated from the Crown, allow it to be mined without the landowner's consent; even in other cases, however, a procedure exists whereby, if it is 'in the national interest' to do so, land may still be declared open for mining despite the owner's refusal to consent. Conditions imposed on mining licences concerning tailings, leaching, water discharges, etc. may well also affect landowner's rights. The mining of coal, ironsands, and petroleum are governed by separate statutes. At the time of writing it seems likely that, even if the Resource Management Bill becomes law, its provisions concerning minerals will be removed and placed in a distinct statute which might possibly continue to grant mining its present privileged position. The Noxious Plants Act 1978, grants Regional Councils wide powers to contain the spread of noxious plants and to oblige landholders to control or eradicate noxious plants on their land. The Environmental Protection and Enhancement Procedures, at present without statutory authority, are required by the Crown to be applied to the works and management policies of all government departments and all statutory boards, corporations and commissions that may affect the environment and are subject to government programming; all actions funded even partly by money appropriated by parliament, and all licences, authorizations, permits, and privileges with environmental implications issued pursuant to various Acts, including the Mining Act 1971, Coal Mines Act 1979, Forests Act 1949, Land Act 1948 and Wild Animal Control Act 1977. Documented information on environmental implications may also be required where consents are sought under the Town and Country Planning Act, Soil Conservation and Rivers Control Act, and Water and Soil Conservation Act. The Ministry for the Environment administers the procedures. The proposer of the development prepares an Environmental

Impact Report, then audited by the Commissioner for the Environment. These procedures are not alternatives to any statutory procedures but are in addition to them, a duplication already criticized.

Space permits only the briefest mention of the Resource Management Bill. Its purpose (section 4) would be 'to promote the sustainable management of natural and physical resources'. 'Sustainable management' means

> managing the use, development and protection of natural and physical resources in a way ... which enables people to meet their needs without unduly compromising the ability of future generations to meet [theirs] and includes these considerations:
>
> **(a)** the maintenance and enhancement of the quality of the environment, including its life-supporting capacity and intrinsic values:
> **(b)** the use, development or protection of natural and physical resources in a way which provides for the social, economic and cultural needs and opportunities of people and communities:
> **(c)** where the environment is modified by human action, the full recognition of the adverse effects of irreversible change and their avoidance or mitigation to the extent practicable:
> **(d)** the use, development or protection of renewable natural and physical resources so that their ability to yield long-term benefits is not endangered:
> **(e)** the use or development of non-renewable natural and physical resources in a way that sees an orderly and practical transition to adequate substitutes including renewable resources:
> **(f)** the exercise of *kaitiatikanga* which includes an ethic of stewardship.

Section 5 lists many important matters to be considered in achieving the Act's purpose – a list similar to that in the Town and Country Planning Act, but fuller, and more ecologically-oriented. The Bill requires national, regional, and local government to prepare policy statements and plans. Replacing the various rights, licences and permits granted under various Acts are 'resource consents' of various types and a single simplified procedure to obtain them. Environmental Impact Procedures are incorporated into the new legislation, which would (as previously mentioned) replace nearly all the present resource-management statutes. Provisions also exist for various designations, heritage orders and water-conservation orders.

## Afterword

After 150 years of European settlement, New Zealand's prosperity still depends on a thin layer of topsoil. The new environmental awareness builds on pioneers' and farmers' older awareness of the land's importance. The land's preservation and wise and effective utilization is ever a matter of public concern. To this end laws still attempt to prevent undue aggregation of farmland and foreign ownership. Since the Second World War, statutes have slowly grappled with the tangled and related issues of resource planning, regulation, preservation, and enhancement. The heroic age of agricultural expansion is over. Present laws attempt to reconcile agricultural interests with social, economic, and environmental considerations. Future legislation looks set to do so more effectively and harmoniously.

## References

Bradley, J.J.G. (1984) Aggregation of land. *New Zealand Law Journal* 58–60.

Fairweather, J.R. (1985). *Land Policy and Land Settlement in New Zealand*, Research Report No. 165. Agricultural Economics Research Unit, Lincoln University, New Zealand.

Fairweather, J.R. (1989) *Some Recent Changes in Rural Society in New Zealand*, Discussion Paper No. 124. Agribusiness and Economics Research Unit, Lincoln University, New Zealand.

Hinde, G.W., McMorland, D.W. and Sim, P.B.A. (1986) *An Introduction to Land Law*, 2nd edn. Butterworth, Auckland.

Hooper, P. (1981) *Our Forests Ourselves.* John McIndoe, Dunedin.

O'Regan, T. (1989) 'The Ngai Tahu Claim'. In: Kawharu, I.H. (ed.), *Waitangi*, Oxford University Press, Auckland.

Robertson, B.T. (ed.) (1989) *Proceedings of the 1989 Hill and High Country Seminar*: New Zealand Mountain Lands Institute, Lincoln University, New Zealand.

Sorrenson, M.P.K. (1989) Towards a radical interpretation of New Zealand history: the role of the Waitangi Tribunal. In: Kawharu, I.H. (ed.), *Waitangi*, Oxford University Press, Auckland.

Temm, P. (1990) *The Waitangi Tribunal: The Conscience of the Nation.* Random Century New Zealand Ltd, Auckland.

Waitangi Tribunal (1991) *Ngai Tahu Report 1991* (3 vols) (Wai 27). Brooker & Friend Ltd, Wellington.

## NOTE IN PROOF

*Since this chapter was submitted, the Resource Management Bill has become law, and the Town and Country Planning Act and the Water and Soil Conservation Act have been repealed.*

# 14

# Agrarian Land Law in the Western World: Some Reflections

Wim Brussaard and Margaret Rosso Grossman

The agricultural law of a nation is often a reflection of the problems that farmers and the agriculture industry confront in that nation. Among other things, the quantity and quality of agrarian land, along with the pressures facing that land, help to shape the law. The material presented in the various chapters in this book has indicated that a great variety of laws, regulations, and policies affect agrarian land in different nations. As might be expected, some important agrarian law issues have been addressed in the majority, or even all, of the countries under consideration here. Other issues are more unique and arise from special political, social, or geographic features in a particular country. In this chapter, some of the more significant issues in agrarian land law are addressed, with the intention of indicating some of the comparisons that can be made and the trends that can be identified in agrarian land law.

As the laws described in the foregoing chapters indicate, the right to own farmland and the freedom to direct the use of that land are privileges granted and protected by law. In some countries, these privileges exist with little restriction; in others, potential farmland owners or users face substantial limitations. Indeed, a spectrum of approaches exists, with extremes of relative freedom to use land as the owner (or sometimes the tenant) prefers and rather stringent limitations on land use in agricultural areas. Countries vary, too, in the care with which agrarian land laws are implemented; laws are more effective in achieving their purpose when landowners know that implementation of the laws will be consistent and reliable.

Among the significant agrarian land law issues are physical planning laws and regulations; land consolidation; limitations on purchase, subdivision, or agglomeration of land; mandatory use of agricultural land; provisions for governmental (or quasi-governmental) pre-emption or expropriation of farmland; access to privately-owned land by members of the general public; and regulation of agricultural tenancy.

Each nation has developed its own system of regulating land ownership and use to ensure the most beneficial allocation of its unique agricultural land. These systems seem to be influenced by (or to reflect) both the legal–administrative structure and the scarcity of agricultural land. For example, more intra-country variety in regulatory approaches seems to be evident in federally organized countries, where both the national and state governments exercise authority over aspects of agrarian land. This variety is particularly evident when some land-use questions may be viewed as regional or local (rather than national) matters and regulatory authority is delegated to those levels of government. And, as expected, nations with a limited agrarian land-base tend to enact stricter regulatory systems to protect that land. Moreover, while the existence of special administrative bodies with competence in land-use matters is relatively common, some nations (or individual states) also have special courts with broad, or more limited, jurisdiction over issues related to agricultural land.

The discussion that follows is intended to indicate the types of regulation (or lack of regulation) that exist, without an attempt to mention the legal position of each country on every issue. Indeed, not all of the land-use issues have been addressed by the authors of the various chapters, either because no such regulation exists in the author's country or because, in the author's judgement, other issues are more significant.

## I. Physical Planning and Related Provisions

### A. Physical planning

In most countries, the protection of agrarian land has a connection with physical planning or zoning legislation. In the countries where this connection exists, physical planning provides guidelines for policy at different levels of government; these guidelines have influence as long as government officials are committed to them. Thus, the designation of land as agrarian land in the course of physical planning procedures can be important to protect that land, but it does not always guarantee that protection.

In some countries, however, the influence of physical planning is more significant, when physical planning regulations have binding effect. In the Netherlands, for instance, the local land-use plan is binding on every citizen and for all levels of government (even the higher levels) through a system of building and construction permits, and even with a possibility of expropriation to further planning purposes. The local land-use plan in fact has the force of law, and the protection of agrarian land depends on physical planning. Even so, physical planning regulation cannot be an absolute guarantee of protection in the long run, because the land-use plan can be changed as a result of new circumstances and after reconsideration in the course of the land-use planning procedure.

Other countries, too, have systems of binding physical planning legislation, although perhaps less far-reaching than in the Dutch situation. In the German legislation, land-use planning is a responsibility of each level of government. On the federal level, principles (for example, the guarantee for the maintenance of a rustic agriculture, characterized by family farms dependent on the cultivation of the soil) are formulated by the Federal Act on Physical Planning. These principles have a binding effect on the authorities of the Federal Republic and the *Länder.* They are implemented by the *Länder* in their land-use planning for the *Land* and the different regions of the *Land.* On the local level, the zoning plan, designating areas for different purposes, is the basis for the alignment plan, which contains provisions that are binding for private persons. In both plans, plots can be designated for agricultural use, guaranteeing that they are excluded from non-agricultural development. The construction of buildings in an undeveloped area is prohibited, with some exemptions especially for buildings that serve a farm.

Belgium, too, has a system of binding spatial plans. The sector plans indicate zones for different purposes. In agricultural zones, only buildings belonging to farms are allowed. The plans are legally binding for the citizens as well as for the public authorities of cities and municipalities. In Denmark, the Urban and Rural Zones Act, whose purpose is to prevent urban sprawl, divides the whole country in urban zones, summer house zones, and rural zones. Rural zones are protected against residential, industrial, and recreational development. Developing or building, as well as altering the use of existing buildings and land without buildings, needs approval of the county council and is permitted only if the building on the land is intended for agricultural purposes.

The Town and Country Planning legislation of New Zealand imposes on local bodies and regional governments a duty to prepare district schemes and regional schemes. District schemes designate land for different purposes. In each zone, certain activities are permitted and others prohibited. The schemes in particular have to provide for some matters of national importance, such as the protection of land with a high value for food production and the protection of rural areas against urban development.

Physical planning is not always focused directly on protection of agrarian land. In France, for example, the protection of farmland occurs only indirectly through urban zoning policy, intended to avoid scattered residential development. Half of the 36000 French municipalities have adopted a zoning map, on which the territory is divided into urban and natural districts. Natural districts with agricultural uses are protected according to the agricultural value of the land; in these zones, only buildings necessary for the farm holding are permitted. On the level of the 94 French *départements*, zoning ordinances may define special agricultural districts where all tree and timber plantations are prohibited.

In the United Kingdom, the use of land for agriculture is normally outside the control of the planning legislation. Nevertheless, certain kinds of agricultural development (such as the erection of buildings) need planning permission from the local planning authority. Some developments are permitted automatically through a General Development Order, with restrictions on large-scale developments and especially those constituting potential nuisances.

Even where legal authority to zone exists, zoning is not always used effectively to protect farmland. In the United States, zoning is a responsibility of the states, but is often delegated to local governments. Since local governments are not normally required to zone rural land, the majority of US agricultural land is not zoned. Where zoning exists, a variety of approaches has been used. On land zoned for agriculture, non-farm development can generally be prohibited or (more often) discouraged. Although zoning does not effectively protect most agricultural land from conversion to non-agricultural uses, other state laws are designed to discourage conversion. Often these take the form of financial or other incentives to continued farm use of rural land.

Programmes to preserve agricultural land seem to be more stringent when land is relatively scarce and under pressure from development. Some Canadian provinces have responded to the threat of farmland loss through special farmland protection acts; others rely on ordinary provincial planning controls. In British Columbia, legislation authorizes establishment of agricultural land reserves, in which all non-agricultural land use is prohibited.

As the above summary indicates, the influence of physical planning or zoning legislation in most cases limits the possibility of building in rural areas and thus helps to preserve land for agrarian uses. Moreover, in the countries that have a well-developed system of physical planning, the system offers an administrative and procedural framework within which conflicting claims on rural areas can be weighed. Once a planning decision is made, the (spatial) plan gives a certain guarantee of the continued existence of agriculture in the areas indicated in the plan. It is to be expected that this significance of physical planning, together with the increasing significance of environmental policy (see section IIH) will gain influence in the coming years.

## B. Land consolidation

Physical planning is not the only legal scheme intended, at least in part, to preserve and protect farmland. Several European nations have rather complicated laws that authorize and regulate the process of land consolidation (sometimes called land development or land reallocation). Although unimportant in some nations (e.g. Denmark, Italy), in others land consolidation has for decades formed a relatively significant part of agricultural land policy and has affected thousands of hectares of agrarian land (e.g. Netherlands, Belgium, Germany, France).

The process promotes agricultural use of rural land by restructuring sections of the countryside to improve agricultural productivity and working conditions. Landownership patterns are reorganized to consolidate scattered farm plots into larger parcels located near the farm buildings; roads and waterways are improved. In recent years, land consolidation has also been directed towards environmental, nature conservation, and other purposes (e.g. France, Netherlands, Germany). A complex process, land consolidation can take as long as a generation to complete (Netherlands).

Although the details of land consolidation vary under the different national laws, the general approach seems to be similar in a number of countries. Normally, the process is guided by a public administrative body. In some instances (e.g. Netherlands, France), both national and local administrative bodies exist. A land-consolidation project may be initiated by interested landowners as well as by the government (e.g. Norway, Netherlands). After investigation and perhaps public hearings, the decision to proceed with the project is made. A vote of landowners and/or land users may be taken (e.g. Netherlands, Italy), but under some laws a governmental authority must make the decision to proceed (e.g. Germany, some procedures in the Netherlands). Some type of cost/benefit analysis may be required to demonstrate that the project will be effective (e.g. Netherlands, Norway).

An early step in most countries' procedures is the evaluation of agricultural holdings within the boundaries of the project. One goal of the reallocation is to assign landowners new parcels with the same agricultural value (if possible) as those they brought into the project. Planning procedures focus on both the new public structures (roads, waterways, natural areas) and the new allocation of privately-owned land parcels. The various steps of the planning process normally provide opportunities for public notice and comment and chances for administrative or judicial appeals. Moreover, some laws (e.g. France, Netherlands) require close coordination between land consolidation and physical planning. Under some laws, too, the land-consolidation authority may have a pre-emptive right to purchase land within the project area (e.g. Belgium, Netherlands).

After final plans have been established, public works will be constructed and owners will take title to their reallocated land parcels. Cost may be shared between government organizations and landowners who benefit from the consolidation (e.g. France, Germany, Netherlands).

In some nations, land consolidation may be complicated by the existence of a number of types of procedures intended for different circumstances. In the Netherlands, four types of land consolidation exist; in Germany, five; in France, seven, though only three are commonly used.

## II. Restrictions on Freedom to Own and Use Agricultural Land

### A. Limits on acquisition

A number of countries impose administrative barriers to the acquisition of agricultural land (or even all real property). These barriers range from restrictions on purchase to more structural regulations that may discourage the subdivision or agglomeration of parcels of farmland. Acquisition or subdivision, for example, may not be carried out without the proper governmental license, and when the prospective land acquisition or use is undesirable (from the policy of the nation involved), that licence can be denied.

In Norway, for example, in most instances one needs concession of the king to purchase any realty, a restriction that controls sales of agricultural land and ensures beneficial use. Subdivisions of agricultural land are controlled on a more local level, through required approval from the County Agricultural Board. In Denmark, too, the law regulates the acquisition and ownership, as well as the size, of farms. Normally, a size limit of 125 ha applies; subdivision needs special licence to avoid undesirable fragmentation of farms. Similarly, in Germany, prior authorization is required for most land transfers. Authorization can be denied if the transfer would result in undesirable land distribution, loss of farm viability or harmful fragmentation, or if the price is distorted.

In some nations, regulation seems to focus especially on the size of the agricultural holding. In France, with only limited governmental control of land ownership, enlargements and subdivisions of farms must be authorized by an administrative committee. Size is governed by the minimum settlement acreage (SMI), an optimum farm size defined both nationally and locally and adjusted for specific types of operation. A similar approach in Italy, a minimum size farm unit connected with the Civil Code obligation of indivisibility, has been ineffective because no procedures exist for establishing that minimum size.

National agrarian policy may well direct the laws concerning farmland acquisition. New Zealand, with a policy to foster wide ownership of farmland, tries to avoid aggregation of farmland by requiring many purchases or leases involving over 2 ha of land to be submitted to a Land Valuation Tribunal. Subdivision of farmland, on the other hand, can be restricted in physical planning laws. And New Zealand also attempts to limit overseas interests in farmland by requiring consent to certain land purchases by non-citizens or overseas corporations.

A similar concern for alien (or non-resident) land ownership is reflected in North America. The United States has enacted a federal law requiring reports of farmland ownership by alien individuals or corporations with foreign ownership. Some individual states have gone farther, to prohibit alien ownership of farmland. In some states, farmland cannot be owned by corporations either, unless they are small family farm corporations. In Canada, provisions to discourage or prohibit non-resident ownership of farmland have been enacted in several provinces. Under some provincial laws, non-residents may own only 20 acres of land. In other provinces, provisions to facilitate farmland purchase by owner–operators can help to keep land from non-resident purchasers. Scarcity of farmland (e.g. on Prince Edward Island) results in particularly strict controls.

In some countries, special inheritance laws help to avoid undesirable subdivision of farm property. Normal patterns of heirship (that is, equal distribution of property to all heirs) are disrupted to keep an economic-sized unit of land in the ownership of the farming heir. Some federal and some *Länder* laws in Germany give the farm to a single heir; in France, too, the system of preferential allotment gives the farm to one heir, who is already farming. In both countries, other heirs receive monetary compensation. In Germany, monetary compensation is calculated on the basis of the value of the turnover or the taxable value of the farm, while in France the compensation is based on the commercial value of the farm. The family farm is protected in Italy, too, through a right of pre-emption for the members of the family actually farming the land; this right applies during estate distribution. Although not exactly analogous, allodial rights in Norway give certain family members preference to acquire land, when that land would otherwise be transferred outside the family.

## B. Farming requirements

Government control on the use of agricultural land sometimes goes beyond control of acquisition or size of land parcels to require that agricultural land actually be farmed or that the person farming the land have a licence to farm. In France, some farmers must have a licence to farm, which is related to the minimum settlement acreage. Land laying fallow may be reallocated – that is, leased to a tenant – unless the owner agrees to improve cultivation techniques. In Norway, with a limited amount of good farmland, agricultural land must be used for farming. If the land lays fallow or is farmed improperly, the owner must improve farming or lease the land; alternatively, under certain conditions, the State can take the land. Farmers in Denmark, too, are obliged to farm and to farm properly; registered 'agricultural holdings' are to be used for agriculture, horticulture, or forestry, unless the land is marginal. In Italy, some laws allocating farmland to new owners (e.g. peasant allocation) carry an obligation to farm.

Recent agricultural surplus production in Europe, however, has led to some changes in aproach. In Germany, for example, both farming and good husbandry were required under prior law. Now, surplus production has made this requirement unnecessary, and in general there is no longer an obligation to cultivate agricultural land. The absence of a legal obligation to cultivate farmland is not likely to mean that the land can be converted at will to non-agricultural uses. Other laws – physical planning or setaside, for example – are likely to govern changes in land use.

The obligation to farm, it might be added, is different from the 'right to farm', a limited protection against certain nuisance suits that some laws give to farmers whose operations existed before changes in surrounding land use (e.g. United States, France; a bill introduced in Western Australia; broader protection in Ontario, Canada).

## C. Pre-emptive rights and expropriation

The government, a quasi-governmental organization, or even private individuals may have the pre-emptive right to buy farmland, in certain (often limited) circumstances. This right is often for structural purposes, that is, to ensure that the land is owned by a farmer. Pre-emption is commonly authorized in land-consolidation procedures, but it occurs in other contexts as well. Pre-emptive rights, unlike expropriation, often apply to land that the owner has already decided to sell.

So, for example, in Norway, when an owner and prospective buyer have a binding contract for the sale of farmland, the state or municipality can purchase, usually on the same terms the buyer had arranged. The land can then be conveyed to a farmer who needs additional land. In Germany, Land Settlement Corporations can use the pre-emptive right, if authority for a land transfer has been denied; pre-empted lands can be assigned to farmers when necessary to improve agricultural structure. In France, SAFERs (non-profit public corporations controlled by the government) have the legal option to buy agricultural land coming on the market; these organizations tend to control the farmland market. Even neighbours active in farming may have the right to pre-empt and purchase land offered for sale (in Italy). In some countries (e.g. Netherlands, Belgium) the lessor who wants to sell his leased land has to offer it first to the lessee.

Expropriation (eminent domain), too, is often a power of government. Although governments may own substantial quantities of land (e.g. federal lands in the US and Crown lands in New Zealand), other land may be needed for specific public purposes. Normally, compensation must be paid to the landowner when land is expropriated for an authorized public purpose (e.g. United States, Canada, Netherlands, certain forest land in Denmark). Sometimes government actions merely regulate, rather than actually take, privately-owned land. Frequently there is a question of whether the government action is a 'taking' for which compensation must be paid, or merely a regulation, which must be endured without compensation. Constitutional distinctions are often important in this context (e.g. Germany, United States).

Countries differ on the issue of whether restrictions in the interest of nature conservation will require compensation. In Denmark, normal restrictions under the Nature Conservation Act are not expropriation; certain types of involuntary conservation easements, however, involve serious restrictions on land-use and require compensation. Limits on property use to protect landscapes in certain classified areas can be compensated in Belgium, whereas in Norway a farmer will only rarely receive payment for nature conservation restrictions. (In Norway, also, the government can expropriate farmland for misuse of the land.) In Germany, a distinction between restrictions on prospective uses (no compensation) and already existing uses (compensation) may be fading, at least in the sense that environmental protection restrictions must often be tolerated without compensation.

## D. Setaside and laying fallow

In a sense, the European setaside regulations also can be considered part of a system that protects agricultural land. These regulations are intended to stimulate farmers (in a situation of surplus production) to take arable land out of production, but at the same time to maintain the agricultural productivity of that land. The Member States of the European Community have an obligation to introduce an aid scheme to encourage the setaside of agricultural land. According to the EC regulation on this subject, Member States have a choice of several possible measures, of which laying fallow (with or without crop rotation) and afforesting are the most important. This regulation is implemented, with slight differences, in the European Member States. In some countries, other programmes for extensified farmland use are motivated by ecological considerations (e.g. Germany, the Netherlands).

The issue of fallow land is, of course, relevant outside the context of the relatively recent EC regulations. In some countries, laying fallow and afforesting are considered a threat, rather than protection, for agricultural land. In France, an EC Member State, special agricultural districts can be defined, in which any tree or timber plantation is prohibited. In Norway, a country outside the EC, the Land Act obliges landowners to preserve the cultivated land, keep it in proper condition, and actually use it for farming purposes; if the land is found in improper condition or laying fallow, the County Agricultural Board may instruct the owner as to the steps to be taken. In certain situations, the land can even be expropriated by the king (i.e. the government) to transfer to other farmers who agree to run it in a proper manner. These are far-reaching measures, perhaps necessitated by the scarcity of agricultural land in Norway.

## E. Afforestation

Forests seem to be viewed either as an important component of agriculture or as a threat to agricultural production. In French law, for example, forestry is viewed as a threat to farmland, and the trend in French law is to prefer farmland over timberland. Nonetheless, both forestry and zoning laws recognize the importance of trees for protecting fragile soil. Belgium, too, makes a clear distinction between farming and forests. In farm leases, both landlord and tenant are prohibited from planting trees unless certain conditions are met. The Belgian forestry code focuses primarily on the management of public woods. New Zealand law indicates concern about the impact of forestry on landscape, soil erosion, and agricultural structure.

In contrast, other countries have adopted laws specifically to protect forests and other woodlands. German forestry law protects forestry for wood production, ecology, and recreation. Prior authorization is required for conversion of forest land or for afforestation. In Denmark, owners must preserve forests, and licences are required to use forest land for other purposes; special afforestation areas exist, and financial grants help landowners plant trees. Laws have been rather successful in protecting forests. Norway views both forestry and farming as agricultural activities. Laws are intended to increase productivity of forests and to promote afforestation, although in the light of environmental and recreational considerations. In the Dutch forest legislation, the object is to maintain a forest acreage of reasonable dimension and quality.

The European Community, too, has a provision to aid farmers in the afforestation of their agricultural land. To farmers whose chief occupation is farming, the Member States may grant aid (paid by the EC) for investments in certain types of woodland improvements and for forest roads.

This aid may be combined with the aid schemes for setaside, extensification, conversion to non-surplus products, or cessation of production.

## F. Nature conservation measures

Nature conservation is not a subject, as such, in a book about agrarian land law. Nevertheless, in several chapters nature conservation is relevant, primarily because in most countries agriculture and nature and landscape are in fact very much interwoven and so influence each other, even in a legal way. In several countries, this has led to legislation to protect nature and landscape by putting limitations on the use of agrarian land. This is the case in Denmark and Belgium, for instance. In the United Kingdom, restrictions can be put on agricultural operations in Sites of Special Scientific Interest, National Parks, and Nature Reserves.

In the Netherlands, as in several other countries, the interrelation between agriculture and nature and landscape conservation has influenced the development of a special legal provision, the management agreement. This is a voluntary contract between an individual farmer and the government, under which the farmer will adapt farming practices to the requirements of nature and landscape preservation in exchange for financial compensation. In the United Kingdom too, management agreements play an important role, because the conservation policy in that country has long been to encourage the voluntary participation by landowners and farmers in conservation measures. Management agreements can be applied in areas designated as Environmentally Sensitive Areas, Nature Reserves, or Nitrate Sensitive Areas.

In the countries of the European Community, the types of measures mentioned here are encouraged by EC aid schemes on farming in less-favoured areas and in Environmentally Sensitive Areas. Less-favoured areas (regions that suffer from permanent natural handicaps) are typically dependent on agriculture, but they are threatened by a tendency towards depopulation and decline in agricultural activity. For purposes of the EC policy, they include mountain areas in which farming is necessary to protect the countryside and other areas in which the conservation of the countryside is not ensured. In Environmentally Sensitive Areas, EC aid is intended to encourage farming practices that are compatible with the requirements of the environment and of natural resources or with the requirements of the maintenance of the landscape and the countryside.

## G. Public access to agrarian land

In recent years the public demand for recreational land has increased, and much of this demand has focused on privately owned land in the countryside. Some legal systems focus on individual right of ownership to the exclusion of the public at large, while others provide public access even to privately owned land. In New Zealand, for example, access to agrarian land is controlled by the owner or occupier, and no public right of access exists, apart from use of some public roads and walkways. Similarly, in the United States, the law does not permit public access to private land; permission of the owner or occupier is required. In many states, however, recreational use of private land is encouraged by laws that restrict the landowner's liability for injuries to persons entering on the land.

Other nations have less exclusive views of the rights of private landowners, although public access is normally restricted to protect agriculture. Forests, particularly, are viewed as open to free access for recreation and other outdoor activities in Norway, Denmark (in private Danish forests, during the daytime by foot), and Germany (for recreation). In some countries, too, uncultivated farmland is available for public access. In Norway, people can enter frozen or snow-covered cultivated land, but never between 30 April and 14 October. In Germany, everyone has the right to walk on open, unused farmland, although this right can be restricted in the *Länder* for special reasons like nature protection or farming.

## H. The environment

More and more environmental issues are influencing agrarian land and becoming part of agrarian land law. Since agriculture depends to a large extent on clean soil, clean water and clean air, environmental regulation in these areas is important for agrarian land. The different chapters in this book show that most countries have, or are preparing, legislation to protect soil, groundwater, and surface water against pollution. In this regard, agriculture, like some other activities, is protected by environmental legislation and so plays the role of 'consumer' of environmental law.

However agriculture also plays the role of polluter, and in some countries has become its own victim. The use of too much pesticide and herbicide can be a threat to the environment, and so is regulated in several countries (e.g. Germany, Italy, Denmark). In some countries a manure surplus, or the misapplication of manure, endangers the environment and agriculture. This situation has given rise to (sometimes elaborate) legislation in the Netherlands, Denmark, France, Norway, and several *Länder* in Germany.

Not all countries regulate strictly, however. In Belgium, for example, environmental policy relies on levies and indirect incentives; no environmental laws directly regulate the use of agrarian land. Even here, however, direct regulation can be anticipated for the future.

In some nations, regulatory programmes are directed at protection of the soil in 'damaged districts' (e.g. France) and soil conservation from erosion, floods, and other damage (e.g. United States, New Zealand, Italy). The British Nitrate Sensitive Areas and Water Protection Zones fall into the same category. In Australia, where European-style cultivation of fragile agrarian land has caused serious land degradation, environmental law has not been particularly effective in preventing soil erosion and other damage. Present federal efforts in the direction of ecologically sustainable development may be able to ameliorate the problems, if not rehabilitate the land to its former productive capacity.

The increasingly alarming degradation of the environment is likely to affect agrarian land legislation more and more. Regulations to combat and undo existing environmental problems are no longer sufficient. The laws and regulations that must eventually be imposed from an environmental point of view are likely to take the form of limiting cnditions that will affect every use of land. The issue is no longer certain inconvenient rules that agriculture must endure. Threats to the continued existence of agriculture itself, from polluted land, loss of soil fertility and other damage, mean that a more stringent regulation of agricultural practices must be imposed. More intrusive regulation of agricultural land use will require a total change of mentality in the agricultural world, a change that will be difficult to achieve. In the western world, the freedom of farmers to do with their land what they like is still the predominant attitude. The different chapters in this book have indicated that this freedom can lead to serious environmental problems, for instance, land degradation in Australia and the manure surplus in some countries of western Europe.

Therefore, it is likely that in the near future, environmental policy and legislation will affect agrarian land more directly. In some situations, mandatory land-use regulations in pursuit of environmental goals may have the same legally binding effect that physical planning now already has in certain countries.

## III. Farm Tenancy Law

In many of the nations represented in this book, agricultural leases are an important component of agricultural structure. Although many landlords are individual landowners, in some instances farmland may be leased from the government (Australia). Landlords surrender possession to farm tenants, who produce agricultural products and care for the land. In some nations, farm leases are a matter of contract, with a minimum of legislative intervention (e.g. United States, Denmark). In others, however, a complex system of regulation governs.

To encourage best use of the farmland through improvement of the farm business and capital expansion, it is often desirable to provide security of tenure for the tenant. A number of laws reflect the importance of security of tenure, although in some countries short-term leases are common (e.g. the United States, where many tenants have 1-year leases). In the United Kingdom, most tenancies of farmland are annual tenancies, but the Agricultural Holdings Act gives many tenants extensive rights to security of tenure, in part by limiting the reasons for which a landlord can terminate a lease with a tenant who is farming properly. In a number of countries, statutory minimum lease terms are used to ensure security of tenure. In the Netherlands, 6 years is the minimum lease term (12, if the lease also involves the farm buildings); in Belgium and France, 9 years, with automatic renewal, absent notice to quit; in Italy, 15 years. Although no statutory minimum lease term exists in Germany, the agricultural tribunal may sometimes extend a tenancy contract to a maximum term of 12 years for plots of land or 18 years for a whole farm. In Denmark, the statutory maximum lease term for a whole farm is 30 years. Moreover, it is often difficult to terminate successfully a tenancy relationship, even at the end of a lease term, unless the landlord plans to farm the land himself or the tenant's work demonstrates poor husbandry.

The amount of rent the landlord can lawfully charge may also be set by law or regulation (e.g. in the Netherlands, France, and Italy), although in some nations, market price governs (e.g. Denmark and United States). In the United Kingdom, the parties can agree on the initial rent, but later reviews by arbitration are governed by a formula. When an arbitrator is called to fix rent in a particular case, he must consider the 'productive capacity' and 'related earning capacity' of the holding.

To protect the landlord's investment in the real property, the tenant is normally obliged to farm properly. The tenant may have significant freedom of husbandry, that is, the right to farm without interference from the landlord (e.g. Belgium and France), so long as the tenant actually farms. In Germany, the State renting state-owned farms to a farmer may set limits for ecological reasons; private landlords rarely do so. There may be limits on land-use changes like tree planting (Belgium). Poor husbandry will normally justify termination of the lease, although the definition of poor husbandry is not always clear. In France, poor husbandry would seem to involve reduction of production and income from the farm, rather than farming that damages the land. Recent enhanced awareness of environmental concerns on agricultural land may challenge current definitions of poor husbandry.

Farming the land often gives the tenant the right to make capital improvements. Sometimes the tenant must get the landlord's approval for new structures; failing landlord approval, a court or agricultural tribunal may authorize improvements (e.g. in Germany, Belgium). At the end of the lease, the tenant may also have the right to receive compensation for the improvements, at least to the extent that they are not amortized.

In some countries agricultural policy reflects the importance of owner-operated farms. Thus, agricultural tenancy laws often provide that if the landlord decides to sell the property, the tenant has the first right to buy the land. This right of pre-emption may be limited if, for example, the landlord's relatives or co-owners plan to buy the land (e.g. Belgium, Netherlands).

The tenancy system may be supervised by a specialized government agency or a special tenancy court, or both. In some countries, farm leases must be submitted for approval (e.g. Netherlands, Germany, Norway, New Zealand), although enforcement of this requirement is not uniformly stringent.

## IV. Administrative and Political Context

Despite all the differences between the various countries shown in this book, the administrative and political context for decisions about agrarian land policy seems to be quite similar. Decisions about the agrarian land policy of a country, the measures to be taken to keep agrarian land agricultural, and freedom or restrictions in the use of agrarian land are all made by the institutions with general legislative and administrative power (that is, government and parliament) in each country. These decisions occur at the national level or (in the federal countries) at the state or provincial level. This allocation of decision-making power is not surprising: decisions affecting agrarian land usually are linked closely with decisions by the same institutions in other policy fields and so involve the weighing of often-conflicting interests. In addition, the decisions will often involve legislation or other forms of regulation, which is the competence of government and parliament. Decisions about agrarian land policy are influenced by (sometimes powerful) pressure groups and lobbies, a situation that is normal in a democratic system.

The implementation of agrarian land policy and legislation involves more variety. Decisions, in the framework of physical planning or zoning, about the identification of land to be kept agricultural and the protection and limitations connected with that identification can be made at the national or state level, but are more often the responsibility of the lower (regional or even local) authorities. In that situation it is relevant whether (and how) the national or state government has the ability to influence or undo the decisions of the lower authorities in case these decisions conflict with national or state agricultural policy. For decisions on a still smaller scale, like building permits or approval of development or subdivision, the competence of the lower level of government (mostly local) is the rule. The division of responsibility among the different levels of government may reflect the confidence each country has in the way lower governments can deal with decisions about agrarian land. In rural areas, local governments are normally connected closely with the agrarian population and so will have a keen eye for (local) agrarian interests. This can mean that in decisions about agrarian land on a local level, non-agricultural interests, rather than agricultural, must be protected. (Thus, it may seem unusual that in Denmark the implementation of the manure legislation is deliberately given to local governments.)

The implementation of agrarian land policy shows another type of variety: the existence in some countries of special agrarian organizations that play a role in decision-making. These organizations include special commissions, boards, or courts. These are not the offices and services that are part of the normal government agencies staffed by civil servants. Instead, these special organizations can have an advisory function for decision-makers with general legislative and administrative power. An example of one such organization is the Dutch Central Land Development Committee, which acts as an advisory board for the Minister of Agriculture and prepares their decisions in the field of land development. Other examples are the Nature Conservancy Council for England and the Countryside Council for Wales, which can designate land as Sites of Special Scientific Interest or as Nature Reserves, with limitations on agricultural use. In most situations, the influence of organizations like these depends on their expertise in the field of agrarian land law. Nonetheless, responsibility for the decisions made stays with the government rather than these special-purpose organizations.

Another type of organization active in the field of agrarian land law is the special board with decision-making powers. In Norway, for example, County Agricultural Boards have far-reaching powers under the Land Act: for instance, to instruct a landowner about the measures required to improve the condition of his land or to lease the land to another (better) farmer. In British Columbia, Canada, the Provincial Agricultural Land Commission acts as an agricultural land zoning authority and has the power to make decisions to keep agrarian land agricultural, for example by refusing permits to convert farmland to non-agricultural uses. In New Zealand, the Land Valuation Tribunal must consent to any contract for the purchase or lease of more than 2 ha of agricultural land. In a way the French SAFERs fit in this category, too; as non-profit public corporations controlled by government and owned by farmers' unions and other agricultural entities, they can buy, sell, and lease agricultural land and even have a legal option to purchase.

In a democratic system, special boards with such powers always evoke the question who is responsible for their decisions, and if appeal against those decisions is possible. The more public power these boards have, the more some form of public control and accountability will be necessary.

Special agricultural courts or tribunals are another kind of organization vested with jurisdiction in certain fields of agricultural land law. These special courts offer expertise in typical agricultural matters, and their authority is often exercised by a combination of professional judges and agricultural experts. As already noted, Germany, France, and the Netherlands have special agricultural courts that decide in appeal about tenancy cases. The Land and Environment Court in New South Wales employs specialist judges and assessors who have final decision-making power in matters relating to planning and land use; in other Australian states, too, a variety of tribunals and courts for land-use matters are active.

## Conclusion

The discussions in this chapter and in the individual chapters in this book indicate that the countries of the western world take a variety of approaches to the legal regulation of agrarian land. Every country faces a number of analogous issues in agrarian land law, for example, issues connected with landownership, development on agricultural land, and farm tenancy. These analogous issues, however, have elicited a variety of approaches to law and regulations in different countries.

Some agrarian land issues are uniquely related to political, social, or geographical features in a particular country. As expected, these issues have been addressed by policies, laws, and regulations especially tailored to the unique situation. However, even in instances where the basic structure of law is intended to be similar, variety exists. For example, Member State implementation of European Community programmes also shows disparities in implementation.

Indeed, it seems to the editors, as it may to the readers, that more differences than similarities exist in the agrarian land legislation in the countries represented in this volume. Awareness of those differences, along with the similarities, will enhance the understanding of agrarian land law in the western world. And perhaps, in some small way, this understanding will encourage law and policy-makers in all countries to ensure both that agrarian land will be used productively and wisely now and that its productivity and special natural features will be protected for succeeding generations.

# INDEX

*EC = European Community; B = Belgium; D = Denmark; F = France; G = Germany; I = Italy; NL = the Netherlands; N = Norway; UK = United Kingdom; US = United States of America; C = Canada; A = Australia; NZ = New Zealand; WW = Western World (concluding chapter)*